The Fun Seeker's Miami

THE ULTIMATE GUIDE TO ONE OF THE WORLD'S HOTTEST CITIES

THE FUN ALSO RISES TRAVEL SERIES

Credits

Executive Editor	Alan S. Davis
Series Editor	Christina Henry de Tessan
Copy Editor	Gail Nelson Bonebrake
Book Design	DeVa Communications
Maps	Chris Gillis
Production	Samia Afra

Back Cover Photo Credits: Outdoor Dining Photo (left) courtesy of Greater Miami Convention & Visitors Bureau; Mynt Lounge (center) courtesy of Mynt Lounge and Tara Ink; Beach Photo (right) courtesy of Greater Miami Convention & Visitors Bureau.

Special Sales

For information about bulk purchases of Greenline books (ten copies or more), email us at bookorders@greenlinepub.com. Special bulk rates are available for charities, corporations, institutions, and online and mail-order catalogs, and our books can be customized to suit your company's needs.

GREENLINE PUBLICATIONS
Extraordinary Guides for Extraordinary Travelers
P.O. Box 590780
San Francisco, CA 94159-0780

The Fun Seeker's Miami

The Ultimate Guide to One of the World's Hottest Cities

Gretchen Schmidt

GREENLINE PUBLICATIONS

To Our Readers:

In 1998 I wrote and published *The Fun Also Rises Travel Guide North America*, followed in 1999 by *The Fun Also Rises International Travel Guide*. Together, these books covered the world's most fun places to be at the right time—from the Opera Ball in Vienna to the Calgary Stampede.

The success of these guides persuaded me of the need for a different approach to travel book publishing—*extraordinary guides for extraordinary travelers*. Greenline Publications was launched as a full-scale travel book publisher in December 2002, with *The 25 Best World War II Sites: Pacific Theater*, the first book in the Greenline Historic Travel Series.

The Fun Also Rises Travel Series was introduced in 2003 with an updated version of the first book—now called *The Fun Seeker's North America*. Like Ernest Hemingway's The Sun Also Rises, which helped popularize what has become perhaps the most thrilling party on earth (Pamplona's Fiesta de San Fermín, also known as the Running of the Bulls), The Fun Also Rises travel guides take readers to the world's most fun places.

For the series, we have identified 21 cities worthy of five-star ratings for fun. Greenline is releasing original, single-destination guides for each of these cities, including Las Vegas, Los Angeles, New York, San Francisco, Athens, and London.

Greenline's guiding principle is simple: *never settle for the ordinary*. We hope that a willingness to explore new approaches to guidebooks, combined with meticulous research, provides readers with unique and significant travel experiences.

Please let us know if our guides fail to meet your expectations in any way. To reach us, or for updated information on all Greenline books, please visit our website at www.greenlinepub.com.

Wishing you extraordinary travels,

Alan S. Davis
Publisher

This book is dedicated to the memory of my uncle
Morton (Morty) Kesten, whose infectious spirit of fun
has brightened my life.

—Alan S. Davis

ACKNOWLEDGMENTS

Thanks to Michelle Revuelta and Jeanne Sullivan of the Greater Miami
Convention & Visitors Bureau. Special thanks to Pat and Harold Gelber,
Gregg Nathan, Miami's fine concierges, and the locals who revealed their
secrets. My thanks to Robert, Katie, Andrew, Ricky, Kristina, Jamie, Kim,
Shelly, Wei Lun, Scott, and Joe, all of whom helped me explore countless
South Florida sites. And my most heartfelt gratitude is reserved for my sister
Ann, who has showed so many how to travel, and travel well.

Gretchen Schmidt

ABOUT THE AUTHOR

Longtime Miami resident Gretchen Schmidt is a writer and editor whose
work has appeared in *Time Out*, *Fodor's*, and other travel trade, consumer,
and culinary publications. She is a past winner in the romance category of
the Bulwer-Lytton contest for bad fiction. If she's not goofing off in Bali or
Red Lodge, Montana, she's probably in her garden following the seductive
perfume from the *Brunfelsia lactea*, and never, ever tiring of it.

Behind These Pages

Seeking Fun

Travel should include all of a destination's peak experiences: an amazing museum, a unique spa, a spectacular view. But travel also should be fun—specifically, urban grown-up fun, the kind that thrives by night as well as by day. Fun is a hip nightclub or a trendy restaurant. It is finding a great beach with lots of other fun people, not escaping from them. It is not lonely planet; it is LIVELY planet.

Choosing the Right Place, Right Time

At the restaurants we recommend, food is important, but so is the scene. The hotel selections, which tend to be 4- or 5-star properties, make their guests feel special. At our wide range of nightlife choices you won't find kids with fake IDs. And the attractions must be remarkable. But experienced travelers know these criteria do not on their own guarantee fun. Going to a restaurant can be a totally different (and less fun) experience at 7 p.m. than at 9 p.m.; a champagne boat cruise might be ordinary in the afternoon but spectacular at sunset. With these considerations in mind, we construct our itineraries.

Striving for Perfection

Your time is precious. That is why our executive editor, editors, and writers (locals who are in touch with what is great—and what is not) have spent more than a thousand hours researching, writing, and debating selections for each guide. In *The Perfect Miami* we have chosen the best of the best in 33 categories that highlight what is great about the city. Because fun comes in many colors, we've divided *The Miami Experience* into four distinct thematic approaches to exploring greater Miami, each with its own three-day itinerary to provide an unbeatable fun time.

Of course, all the information you need is at your fingertips to fashion your own perfect visit. *The Miami Black Book* lists all the hotels, restaurants, nightlife (we include here drinking and entertainment even if it is not at night), and attractions that appear in *The Perfect Miami* and *The Miami Experience* chapters, with contact information and page references. Our bottom line: if you find the information easy to use and have an extraordinary trip, we have succeeded.

We review and value all feedback from our readers. **Please contact us at feedback@greenlinepub.com.**

Table of Contents

Key to Pricing Symbols

Hotel symbols
indicate each hotel's best
non-suite double room
price per night.

Restaurant symbols
indicate average cost of one entrée.
Nightclub and **attraction** symbols
indicate cover or entry fee.

$ =	up to $10
$$ = up to $200	$$ = $11 to $20
$$$ = $201 to $300	$$$ = $21 to $30
$$$$ = $301 to $400	$$$$ = $31 to $40
$$$$+ = more than $400	$$$$+ = more than $40

Introduction

Miami: What It Was, What It Is

Welcome to Miami—fun and sun capital of the world. The American Riviera. The Magic City. Gateway to the Americas. In 1897, this was America's sunporch. In 2004, J-Lo proclaimed it the steamiest, sexiest city on the planet. Whatever you call this subtropical metropolis on Florida's southeastern coast—wild party town or relaxing resort—Miami is delighted to extend a warm hand and a friendly *abrazo*.

The area's history begins with the Paleo-Indians who settled south of the present-day city 10,000 years ago. Recent archaeological discoveries show evidence of Tequesta Indian settlements at the mouth of the Miami River and Key Biscayne 2,000 years ago. Their reasons for settling here—mild weather, clean water, and abundant seafood—sound pretty familiar today. In the early 1500s, Juan Ponce de León landed in Florida and claimed the land for Spain, and over the next 200 years, warfare and disease wiped out the Tequestans and numerous other tribes. In 1819, Spain sold Florida to the United States, and in 1821, Florida became a U.S. territory. But it was only sparsely populated, by Creek tribes from Alabama and Georgia, now known as Seminoles; Bahamian farmers along the Miami River; some pioneers who set up plantations; and others who came to salvage cargo from shipwrecks off the coast. A series of wars with the Seminoles and the area's remoteness discouraged settlers, and it remained a relative wilderness. In 1895, Standard Oil cofounder Henry Flagler was convinced to extend his railroad to Miami by landowner Julia Tuttle with a land offer and some fresh orange blossoms that proved Miami was frost-free. A year later, Miami had not only a railroad but a hotel as well.

The floodgates opened. Northerners flocked to Flagler's 350-room clapboard Royal Palm Hotel in downtown Miami, lured by its bay-water swimming pool, twinkling electric lights, and clock-golf course. Off-season, newcomers came for cheap land. As the new century began, Miami went from frontier town to boom town. Canals were dredged to drain water from the Everglades—only three miles west of Biscayne Bay—thus creating more land for development. Miami Beach, a mangrove-covered jungle, was opened to the mainland by a bridge, and millionaire Carl Fisher set out to remake the landscape and develop the beach. By the 1920s, the great Florida land boom was in full swing. Among the biggest projects was Coral Gables, one of the country's first planned communities. Landmarks from that era, such as the Biltmore Hotel and the Venetian Pool, remain today. During the carefree Roaring

Twenties, Miami was the perfect place to be: bootleg liquor flowed freely and top names entertained leading socialites who came down from the Northeast. Then came the disastrous 1926 hurricane, followed by the Depression. The boom went bust, but the flow of visitors wasn't completely stemmed. Early versions of Miami vice flourished, as rumrunners made good use of Coral Gables canals, Al Capone moved into a mansion on Palm Island, and legislators legalized horse and dog tracks and jai-alai frontons.

The 1930s saw a new architectural style called Art Deco, and it was then applied to most of the hotels built in South Beach. During World War II, many of those hotels and beaches were used as barracks and training grounds, and after the war many veterans returned as permanent residents. In 1954, the grand Morris Lapidus creation The Fontainebleau opened, bringing with it the era's glamorous stars: Rat Packers Frank Sinatra, Sammy Davis, and Dean Martin; Joan Crawford; and Marlene Dietrich. In the 1960s, the city's makeup changed forever when Fidel Castro took over Cuba, leading to an exodus of Cubans who left everything to start afresh in Miami. By the 1980s, the Cuban and Haitian refugee population had soared. At the same time, the illicit drug economy flourished and so did major crimes, dramatized for the whole world in the television show *Miami Vice* and the Al Pacino movie *Scarface*.

As the federal government worked to bring the drug situation under control, South Beach began transforming from a blighted, crime-infested neighborhood into a National Historic District discovered one day by European fashion photographers. Overnight, chic cafes and hot nightspots sprang up to serve the invasion of leggy models. Madonna and Sylvester Stallone moved in, attracting more paparazzi and star-searching tourists. Not even Hurricane Andrew, which hit hard south of Miami in 1992, could stanch the tide of fabulousness flowing into Miami.

Today's greater Miami is an overflowing cultural melting pot of more than 2 million people. More than half claim Spanish as their native language, and you are likely to hear Creole, Portuguese, French, Italian, Russian, Yiddish, Hebrew, and many Caribbean dialects of English. Don't assume all those

> **The Native Americans' reasons for settling in this subtropical area thousands of years ago—mild weather, clean water, and abundant seafood—sound pretty familiar to us today.**

who speak Spanish are Cuban—large numbers of Nicaraguans, Colombians, Venezuelans, Puerto Ricans, and Mexicans also live here. The Latino influence goes far beyond the ubiquitous Cuban cafe counters and fast-food Pollo Tropical outlets and extends into every aspect of the business world. The Latin Grammys, MTV's Latin Music Awards, and the Billboard Latin Music Awards are all hosted here. Spanish-language soap operas *Rebeca* and *Amor Descargado,* among several others, are produced locally. Some of the heaviest hitters of the Latin-American music industry are here year-round. (Superstars Gloria Estefan and her husband Emilio, Ricky Martin, Enrique Iglesias, Jon Secada, Shakira, Thalia, and Marc Anthony either have homes here or spend time recording in Miami.) Miami's African-American and Caribbean communities are also key ingredients in this cultural stew. Urban Beach Week on Memorial Day transforms the Art Deco district into a hip-hop wonderland. Greater Miami also hosts The Source Hip-Hop Music Awards, the American Black Film Festival, and the Miami/Bahamas Goombay Festival every June.

This picturesque city, where *Goldfinger* and *The Bellboy* were filmed, serves as a backdrop for major film and television productions, including *CSI: Miami, Karen Sisco,* and *Nip/Tuck.* Some movies are big blow-'em-up spectacles, like *True Lies, Bad Boys* and *Bad Boys II, 2 Fast 2 Furious;* others are classic comedies like *The Birdcage, There's Something About Mary,* and *Stuck on You;* and still others are just plain silly: *From Justin to Kelly, Wild Things,* and *Jackass: The Movie.* Every movie filmed here ratchets up the celeb awareness factor, as gossip columns and local tabloid television duly report sightings of Cameron Diaz and Will Smith.

This brings us to another element central to Miami's character—its beautiful people. In addition to all the fashion models and celebrities and their high-style entourages, Miami is a magnet for surgically enhanced boobalicious babes and tanned buff males, straight and gay. Botox, collagen, lipo, tooth whitening, butt implants, and other forms of strictly cosmetic surgery are routine procedures for people under 25. Are Miami's good looks only skin deep? Sometimes, sure—they didn't name it the South Beach Diet for nothing. Going to the gym is as much a social occasion as a physical necessity. South Beach is also a major gay-party mecca, a place that venerates its drag queens, like Adora and Elaine Lancaster, who host popular parties in South Beach. This is a town where it's all about looking good and flaunting it, where glamour and sexiness reign supreme.

Note that there is also a more serious cultural side to Miami, if you choose to explore that route. When Art Basel's international art show first came to Miami Beach in 2002, the arts scene's cachet skyrocketed, spawning a tizzy of exhibitions, events, and parties attracting connoisseurs from all over the world. A massive—if long delayed—performing arts center on Biscayne Boulevard will be the dazzling new home of the New World Symphony, the Florida Grand Opera, the Miami City Ballet, and the Concert Series of South Florida in the next year or so. It's intended to be the focal point of the growing downtown Arts, Media, and Entertainment District, and, coupled with the hip Design District and Wynwood neighborhoods, makes an impressive case for Miami's role as an arts hub. And some first-rate writing comes out of South Florida, a bottomless source of juicy fodder for authors of fiction and nonfiction, including former and current *Miami Herald* columnists Dave Barry, Carl Hiaasen, and Edna Buchanan, as well as writers Elmore Leonard, Les Standiford, Paul Levine, and John Katzenbach.

> **Today's greater Miami is an overflowing cultural melting pot of more than 2 million people. More than half claim Spanish as their native language, and you are likely to hear more than a dozen languages and dialects.**

Miami's seductive natural beauty is also a potent draw. Aside from palmy beaches, you'll find lush subtropical gardens, brilliant underwater coral reefs, and wildlife like vivid hyacinth macaws and two-foot iguanas, and tropical flowering trees blaze in vibrant shades of orange, fuchsia, yellow, and deep purple. Night-blooming jasmine, gardenias, and frangipani release perfumes that make you swoon.

But don't get too bogged down in heady stuff. You're here to have fun, and you will have no problem finding it, wherever you choose to search. This is a town that does not take itself too seriously. After all, if homegirl and former US Attorney General Janet Reno can proudly step out as the grand marshal of Coconut Grove's campy King Mango Strut, it's a sure bet that you've come to one of the most fun places under the sun.

Welcome to fabulous Miami...

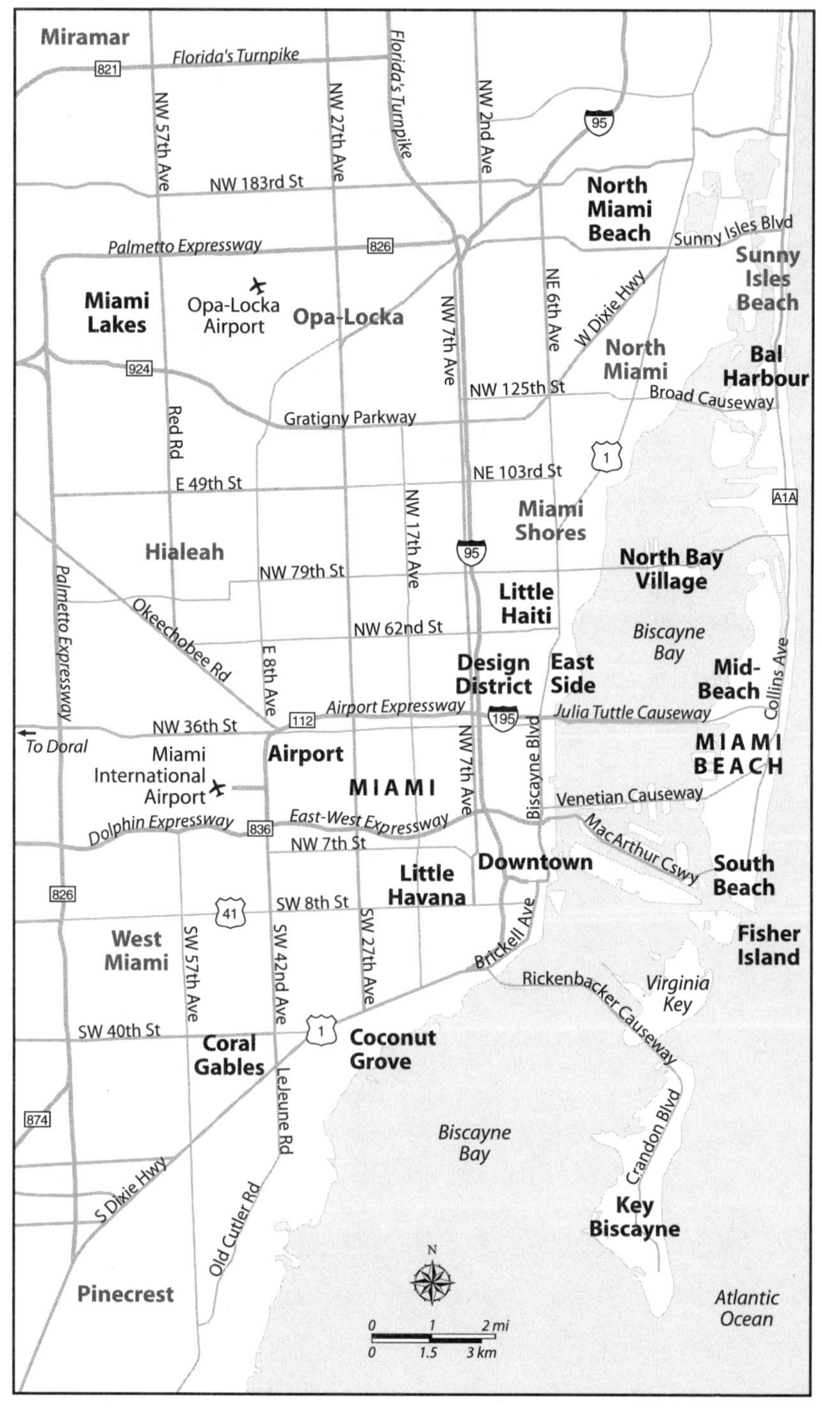
Miramar
821
Florida's Turnpike
NW 57th Ave
NW 27th Ave
Florida's Turnpike
NW 2nd Ave
95
North Miami Beach
Sunny Isles Blvd
Sunny Isles Beach
826
Palmetto Expressway
Opa-Locka Airport
Opa-Locka
NW 7th Ave
NE 6th Ave
W Dixie Hwy
North Miami
Bal Harbour
Miami Lakes
924
NW 125th St
Broad Causeway
Red Rd
Gratigny Parkway
E 49th St
NE 103rd St
1
Miami Shores
A1A
Hialeah
NW 17th Ave
95
North Bay Village
NW 79th St
Little Haiti
NW 62nd St
Biscayne Bay
Okeechobee Rd
E 8th Ave
Design District
East Side
Mid-Beach
Collins Ave
Airport Expressway
195
Julia Tuttle Causeway
Palmetto Expressway
NW 36th St
112
MIAMI BEACH
To Doral
Miami International Airport
Airport
MIAMI
NW 7th Ave
Biscayne Blvd
Venetian Causeway
Dolphin Expressway
836
East-West Expressway
MacArthur Cswy
South Beach
NW 7th St
826
Little Havana
Downtown
41
SW 8th St
Fisher Island
West Miami
SW 57th Ave
SW 42nd Ave
SW 27th Ave
Brickell Ave
Rickenbacker Causeway
Virginia Key
SW 40th St
1
Coral Gables
Coconut Grove
874
LeJeune Rd
Biscayne Bay
Crandon Blvd
S Dixie Hwy
Old Cutler Rd
N
Key Biscayne
Pinecrest
0   1   2 mi
0   1.5   3 km
Atlantic Ocean

Hit the Ground Running

See and do Miami just like a native. Here's everything you'll need to know as you plan your trip—from what to wear and how to get around, to when to go and what resources are available once you are there. You'll also find tips for making business trips a pleasure as well as how to impress a local with your knowledge of a few surprising facts!

City Essentials

Getting to Miami

By Air: Miami International Airport (MIA), 4200 NW 21st St., Miami, 305-876-7000, www.miami-airport.com

As gateway to the Americas, Miami International is one of the country's busiest airports. It's a bustling hub for travelers from Central and South America and the Caribbean, and a source for nonstop flights to the Northeast and Europe, serving more than 100 airlines and about 150 destinations around the globe. MIA is the number one airport in the U.S. for international freight—more than 140,000 tons of fresh-cut flowers come through here every year. Add to that the chronic expansion in and around the terminal, and a major intermodal center car rental facility under construction outside the airport, and it's no surprise that crowds and chaos are the norm, particularly around peak holiday travel times.

On the plus side, MIA has added many user-friendly features in recent years, including vastly improved restaurants and shops, sleekly designed concourses, and a colorful new parking garage plaza. The airport's layout is simple: the U-shaped terminal has eight concourses, which you can quickly traverse using the third-level moving walkway. Departures with curbside baggage check-in are on the second level, while baggage claim is on the ground level, with taxi and shuttle service only steps away. You can hire skycaps or rent luggage carts. The main Tourist Information Center is located on Level 2, Concourse E. In the main concourse, you'll find ATMs, currency exchange booths, drugstores, a barbershop, a bank, and a post office. Restaurants include branches of Cuban cafes Versailles and La Carreta, a Sam Adams Brewhouse, and several fast-food joints; the Miami International Airport Hotel has a sushi bar and the Top of the Port Restaurant on the seventh floor.

Flying to Miami

From	Time (hr.)
Chicago	3.0
Las Vegas	4.5
London	9.0
Los Angeles	5.0
Mexico City	3.0
Montreal	3.5
New York	3.0
San Francisco	5.0
Seattle	5.5
Toronto	3.0
Washington, D.C.	2.5

If you find yourself stuck at MIA, ditch that Dan Brown novel and take some time instead to explore some of the airport's interesting Art in Public Places projects, such as Michele Oka Doner's *A Walk on the Beach*, terrazzo floors with bronze and mother-of-pearl inlays in Concourse A; Christopher Janney's melodic *Harmonic Runway* in Concourse A; or Robert Calvo's *Flight Patterns* in Concourse H. You can also visit the Mia Gallery, an enclosed space with changing exhibits in Concourse E.

Miami International is about 20 minutes from Downtown Miami by car, and about 30 minutes from South Beach, longer during rush-hour traffic.

Major Airlines Serving Miami International Airport

Airlines	Website	800 Number	Concourse
Aeromexico	www.aeromexico.com	800-237-6639	B
Aerolineas Argentinas	www.aerolineas.com.ar	800-333-0276	F
Air Canada	www.aircanada.ca	888-247-2262	G
Air France	www.airfrance.us	800-237-2747	A
Air Jamaica	www.airjamaica.com	800-523-5585	E
Alitalia	www.alitaliausa.com	800-223-5730	E
America West	www.americawest.com	800-235-9292	G
American Airlines	www.aa.com	800-433-7300	C/D
ATA Airlines	www.ata.com	800-435-9282	E
Avianca	www.avianca.us	800-284-2622	F
Bahamas Air	www.bahamasair.com	800-222-4262	H
British Airways	www.britishairways.com	800-247-9297	A
Continental Airlines	www.continental.com	800-525-0280	G
Delta Airlines	www.delta.com	800-221-1212	H
El Al	www.elal.co.il	800-223-6700	G
Iberia	www.iberia.com	800-772-4642	F
KLM Royal Dutch Airlines	www.klm.com	800-225-2525	G
Lufthansa	www.lufthansa.com	800-645-3880	F
Mexicana	www.mexicana.com	800-531-7921	F
Northwest Airlines	www.nwa.com	800-225-2525	G
United Airlines	www.united.com	800-241-6522	F
US Airways	www.usairways.com	800-428-4322	H
Virgin Atlantic	www.virgin-atlantic.com	800-862-8621	B

Airport Shuttle Service: SuperShuttle (305-871-2000 or
800-874-8885) vans are available on the Arrival (ground) level at Miami
International Airport outside the baggage claim areas. Fares are cheaper than
taxis, with the typical fare to South Beach about $13 per passenger.

Rental Cars

All of the following major rental car companies have counters inside
the airport. Courtesy shuttle vans can be flagged down outside the
baggage claim area to take you to their offices for vehicle pickup.

Agency	Website	800 Number	Local Number
Alamo	www.alamo.com	800-327-9633	305-633-6076
Avis	www.avis.com	800-331-1212	305-341-0936
Budget	www.budget.com	800-527-0700	305-871-2722
Dollar	www.dollar.com	800-800-4000	305-887-6000
Enterprise	www.enterprise.com	800-325-8007	305-633-0377
Hertz	www.hertz.com	800-654-3131	305-871-0300
National	www.nationalcar.com	800-227-7368	305-638-1026
Royal Rent A Car	www.royalrac.com	800-314-8616	305-871-3000
Thrifty Car Rental	www.thrifty.com	800-367-2277	305-871-5050

Luxury

B&B Exclusive Auto Rentals	www.cococar.com	800-324-3489	305-672-9449

Limos

Absolute Limousines	www.absolute-limousines.com	954-227-6666

Additional Airport in the Miami Area: Fort Lauderdale-Hollywood
International Airport (FLL), 320 Terminal Dr., Fort Lauderdale,
954-359-1200, www.fll.net.

Although it's about 45 minutes from Miami Beach, Fort Lauderdale-
Hollywood International Airport is popular with Miami-bound travelers
because it's less crowded, very user-friendly, and, most important, home to
low-fare carriers, including JetBlue, AirTran, Southwest, Spirit, Song, and
TED, as well as major airlines Continental, Delta, Northwest, United, and US
Airways. Twelve rental car companies are located here. Other services
include door-to-door shared-ride limousines, taxis, and shuttle service.

By Car: You can get to Miami on a number of major highways. From the
north, I-95 runs from Maine south along the eastern coast ending in Coconut

Grove. Florida's Turnpike starts in the north off I-75 at Wildwood, south of Ocala; it's quick, flat, boring, and will set you back around $15. If time is not a concern, the lengthier A1A/U.S. 1 route that hugs the coastline from Jacksonville south to Key West is far more scenic. If you're coming from Florida's west coast, I-75 will take you south through Tampa, Sarasota, and Naples, where it then becomes Alligator Alley and heads east across the Everglades to Fort Lauderdale. Another east-west route from Naples is U.S. 41. Also known as the Tamiami Trail, it's a picturesque route through the Everglades and Big Cypress National Preserve.

Driving to Miami

From	Distance (mi.)	Time (hr.)
Atlanta	695	11
Chicago	1,400	23
Houston	1218	20
Jacksonville	350	6
New Orleans	895	15
New York	1,330	22
St. Louis	1250	21
Tampa	280	5
Washington, D.C.	1,060	17

By Train: Amtrak (800-872-7245, www.amtrak.com) offers service between New York City and Miami on its Palmetto and Silver Service trains. In the north, these trains serve New York City, Philadelphia, Baltimore, Washington, Richmond, stopping in Jacksonville, Daytona Beach, Orlando, Tampa, West Palm Beach, Fort Lauderdale, Hollywood, and Miami.

Tri-Rail (800-874-7245, www.tri-rail.com) is South Florida's commuter transportation system and serves Miami-Dade, Broward, and Palm Beach counties along its 72-mile corridor. It runs from Miami International Airport

Street Numbers in Miami

It's easy to find your way around in most of Miami because of its simple address numbering system. Addresses are located within four quadrants: NW, NE, SW, and SE, with the intersection of Flagler St. and Miami Ave. in Downtown Miami as the starting point. Confusion sets in when you get to municipalities like Coral Gables, Coconut Grove, and Key Biscayne, where streets have names instead of numbers; and Hialeah, which has its own numbering system. (Be sure to bring along a detailed map if you plan to explore those areas.) South Beach has both names and numbers, but fortunately is compact enough so that it's hard to get lost.

north to West Palm Beach; fares range from $9.25 for a round-trip weekday fare from Miami to West Palm Beach, to $4 for an all-day weekend fare.

Getting Around Miami

About Miami: Greater Miami is a sprawling metropolis that includes a mainland—home to Downtown, Coconut Grove, Coral Gables, the Design District, and other cities and neighborhoods—and various islands. Miami Beach, Key Biscayne, Brickell Key, Virginia Key, and a host of smaller man-made islands like Palm, Star, and the Sunset islands are connected by causeways, some free and some toll. Fisher Island is only accessible by private boat or ferry. Miami Beach is a municipality that stretches from the southern tip of the island known as South Pointe Park north to Surfside; South Beach, not a proper city, refers to the southern tip of the beach south of 23rd Street.

By Car: Greater Miami is a city where you absolutely need a car to get around. The exception is if you plan to spend your entire stay on South

Park It

Street parking is hard to come by in South Beach. Bring lots of quarters, and make sure you're not parking in a residential zone (look for street signs), or your car will be towed. Coconut Grove has instituted a new Pay & Display plan, which allows you to purchase any time allotment of parking from a machine on the street, and display a time-stamped receipt on your dashboard. In Coral Gables, parking meters take coins or cash keys, available at some supermarkets and stores. The fine for expired meters is $18, which jumps to $45 if it's not paid within 30 days.

Public lots and garages are less pricey than valet parking, and a lot easier to find than a free space on the street. Here are some of the bigger facilities where you'll pay either a flat fee or an hourly rate:

South Beach

    7th Street Garage at Washington and Collins
    12th Street Garage—Half-block west of Washington
    13th Street Garage—Half-block east of Collins on 13th St.
    Parking lot at Washington and 17th St.

Coconut Grove

    3310 Mary St.

Coral Gables

    Andalusia Ave. and Salzedo St., one block south of Miracle Mile

Beach, in which case you can get around via taxis or on foot, and save yourself hefty parking and valet fees. That said, rental cars are cheap and plentiful—cool convertibles in particular—so your best bet is to get a car, put the top down, and enjoy the whole wind-in-your-face experience. All major rental car firms will make sure you receive a map with detailed directions into the city. It should take 15 minutes to drive to Coral Gables and Coconut Grove; 20 minutes to Downtown; and about 25 or 30 minutes to South Beach.

Traffic is dreadful most of the day, with rush hours between 7 and 9:30 a.m. (south and eastbound into downtown Miami) and 3:30 and 7 p.m. (north and westbound out of downtown). Carpool lanes (which you can use if there are two or more people in the car) and their hours are clearly marked, and you will be fined $115 if you're caught driving alone when you shouldn't be.

By Train and Bus: Metrorail, Metromover, Metrobus (305-770-3131, www.co.miami-dade.fl.us/transit)

Miami-Dade County's 22-mile elevated rapid transit system is more useful to residents than to visitors, which is not saying much. It starts in the suburbs, running from Kendall through South Miami, Coral Gables, and Downtown Miami; to the Civic Center/Jackson Memorial Hospital area; and to Brownsville, Liberty City, Hialeah, and Medley in northwest Miami-Dade, with connections to Broward and Palm Beach counties at the Tri-Rail/Metrorail transfer station. (There's no service in Miami Beach). Metrorail links downtown with Metromover, a handy way to get around Downtown Miami. This free automated people-mover system makes an inner and outer loop connecting Downtown major office buildings, hotels, and retail centers, the Cultural Plaza, and the Brickell business district. The trains connect with Metrobus, which offers countywide service using 900 buses on 94 routes. Stops and destinations are clearly marked, and buses are clean and modern, but use them only as a last resort unless you have lots of time on your hands. Bus and Metrorail fares are $1.25–$1.50; Metromover is free.

By Taxi: You'll find taxis at the airport, in front of major hotels, and in South Beach. Elsewhere, have restaurants or hotels call for a cab. Flat rates apply from the airport to various zones; typical fares are $19 to Coconut Grove and Downtown Miami and $28 to South Beach. Otherwise, meters start at $1.70 and charge $2.20 per mile. Many drivers speak little English.

Central Cab 305-532-5555
Metro Taxi 305-888-8888
Super Yellow Cab 305-888-7777
Yellow Cab Company 305-633-0503

By Trolley: Can't walk another step? In South Beach, ride the multihued Electrowave, an all-electric transit system that makes 37 stops along Washington Ave. between 17th St. and South Pointe Drive till 1 a.m. Fare is 25 cents. In Coral Gables, quaint-looking hybrid-electric trolleys have two routes: one running north-south on Ponce de Leon Blvd., and another running east-west from the Venetian Pool to Douglas Road along Miracle Mile. The trolleys operate Mon.–Fri. and are free.

Other Practical Information

Weather: The sun shines year-round in humid subtropical Miami, where the average daily temperature is a balmy 76 degrees. There are two seasons here: the seven-month dry season, from November through May; and the five-month rainy season, from June through October. It's no surprise that Miami's gorgeous weather in the winter months is high season, when freezing temperatures kick in up north. From December through April, snowbirds flock here in droves to escape the blizzards and grayness. But a few of those cold fronts manage to push their way south, and nighttime temperatures occasionally could dip as low as the 40s. Otherwise, winter is a time of year when the humidity is low, skies are clear and blue, flowering trees are in bloom, and Miami is downright glorious. The rainy season has its own appeal for those who don't mind its steamy lushness—and, of course, more affordable hotel prices and smaller crowds. Summer temps rarely go higher than the low 90s, and you can easily plan your days around the regular summer afternoon thunderstorms.

Average Monthly Temperatures

Month	Fahrenheit High/Low	Celsius High/Low	Rainfall in.	Rainfall cm.
January	75–59	24–15	2	5
February	76–60	24–16	2	5
March	79–64	26–18	2	6
April	83–68	28–20	3	8
May	85–72	29–22	6	16
June	88–75	31–24	9	24
July	89–77	32–25	6	14
August	89–77	32–25	8	19
September	88–76	31–24	8	19
October	85–72	29–22	6	14
November	80–67	27–19	3	7
December	77–62	25–17	2	5

Hurricane season runs from June through November, with August and September the most active months. Like any natural phenomena, storms come and go where and when they please—years pass without any tempests of consequence, and then an unprecedented four storms make landfall in Florida within a few weeks. Unlike earthquakes or tornados, hurricanes come with plenty of advance warning. Depending on the severity of the storm, warnings are issued that give you ample time to evacuate islands and other low-lying areas and head for shelter.

Attire: Between Greater Miami's warm and sunny climate and hotels, restaurants, and other buildings that are heavily air-conditioned, it's more challenging to find the right weight of clothing than the right look. Bring a light sweater, jacket, or wrap to restaurants, theaters, or museums, which tend to be chilly inside. Dress is generally casual, hip, and relaxed—this is a resort town, after all. Sandals, body-baring tops, short skirts, and lightweight natural fabrics—dubbed South Beach Chic or Casual Chic—are the norm. Be advised that some clubs have strictly enforced dress codes. This means no sneakers, shorts, T-shirts, or sports attire. During the coldest months, January and February, be prepared to dress for temperatures that can dip into the 40s at night. In the summer season, umbrellas come in handy for summer rainstorms. Sunglasses are an absolute must, and hats always a good idea.

Emergency: Call 911 for the police, fire department, ambulance, and paramedics. Along the expressways, you'll find call boxes for emergency use. You can also dial *FHP on a cell phone to report crashes, stranded or disabled motorists, drunk drivers, or suspicious incidents on the roadways. The Visitors Medical Hotline (305-674-2273) is a 24-hour medical referral service provided by Mount Sinai Medical Center. The Dental Referral Service (800-577-7322) is open 24 hours a day, seven days a week, for dental referrals. Emergency rooms include Mount Sinai Medical Center & Miami Heart Institute (4300 Alton Rd., Miami Beach, 305-674-2064), and Jackson Memorial Hospital (1611 NW 12th Ave., Miami, 305-585-1111). Your concierge should know the nearest pharmacy; 24-hour pharmacies are Walgreens in South Beach (1845 Alton Rd., Miami Beach, 305-531-9922), and Downtown Miami (1201 SW 1st St., Miami, 305-324-6151).

Hotlines: Crisis and Suicide Counseling (called Switchboard of Miami) 305-358-4357; Florida Poison Information Center 800-282-3171; Rape Hotline 305-585-7273.

Safety: Miami has its share of urban crime, coupled with a reputation that's reinforced with every rerun of *Miami Vice*. Those cocaine cowboy days are in the past—today, major tourist areas are well protected and most of the city is safe to visit. But keep your wits about you. Lock valuables in hotel safes; don't leave luggage in parked cars; keep your wallets and handbags close to your side; ask for directions before venturing into unfamiliar areas.

There are also a few natural hazards to be aware of in South Florida. One of the most dangerous forces at the beach is a rip current, a seaward stream that can carry you offshore with possibly deadly consequences. Another somewhat less serious hazard is men o' war, purplish balloon-like sea creatures with stinging tentacles that wash up on the beach and can cause intense (if not lethal) pain if you are unfortunate enough to step on one. Lifeguard stands post warnings about both of these hazards. Finally, if you're touring outdoors, or in the Everglades, particularly during the summer months, use plenty of mosquito repellent.

Gay Travel: Sun-and-fun capital of the world Miami doesn't play favorites. Ages ago, it rolled out the rainbow welcome mat, with so many gay-friendly and gay-specific lodgings, restaurants, and nightclubs that it's known today as the Gay Riviera. Some key circuit events are hosted here, including November's White Party, March's Winter Party, and Aqua Girl Weekend in May. For current information on the local scene, be sure to pick up *TWN*, *Hot Spots, Scoop,* and *Wire.* You can also visit the Greater Miami Convention & Visitors Bureau website, www.miamiandbeaches.com, for resource materials for the gay and lesbian market.

General Information for Visitors

Art Deco Welcome Center
1001 Ocean Dr., South Beach, 305-531-3484, www.mdpl.org.
Pick up brochures, maps, tour information, and Art Deco memorabilia.
Open daily 10 a.m.–4 p.m.

Greater Miami Convention & Visitors Bureau
701 Brickell Ave., Ste. 2700, Miami, 305-539-3063 /
800-933-8448, www.miamiandbeaches.com.
This dynamic agency has city maps, calendars of events, specialized brochures, and current information about what's going on in town.
Open Mon.–Fri. 8:30 a.m.–6 p.m.

Coconut Grove Chamber of Commerce
2820 McFarlane Rd., Coconut Grove, 305-444-7270,
www.coconutgrove.com.

Miami Beach Chamber of Commerce
1920 Meridian Ave., Miami Beach, 305-672-1270,
www.miamibeachchamber.com.

Tropical Everglades Visitor Association
160 U.S. Hwy. 1 Florida City, 305-245-9180,
www.tropicaleverglades.com.

Media: The *Miami Herald*, one of the nation's top dailies, covers entertainment in depth in the Friday pull-out *Weekend* section. In addition to checking out the detailed nightclub listings, check out *Velvet Underground*, a column that appears in Friday's *Miami Herald*, for the latest scoop on what's hot in town. *Street* is the *Herald's* slightly edgier free tabloid and a worthwhile source of nightlife and restaurant information. The outstanding free alternative weekly, *New Times,* is available at newsstands throughout the county, and provides in-depth information on events, nightclubs, restaurants, and local issues. Hefty *Ocean Drive* magazine fawns over celebs and local party people in living color; its slim knockoffs are, predictably, *Collins Avenue* and *Lincoln Road.*

Legal Drinking Age: The legal drinking age is 21, but some nightclubs where food is served also allow entrance to guests under 21. Most South Beach nightclubs and many lounges stay open until 5 a.m.; some clubs in Downtown Miami stay open past daybreak.

Radio Stations (a selection)

FM Stations

88.9	WDNA	Jazz
91.3	WLRN	NPR
93.1	WPYM	Dance, Techno
93.9	WLVE	Soft Rock
94.9	WZTA	Alternative Rock
95.7	WXDJ	Spanish Pop
96.5	WPOW	Top 40
99.9	WKIS	Country
100.7	WHYI	Top 40
101.5	WLYF	Adult Contemporary
102.7	WMXJ	Oldies
105.1	WHQT	Urban
105.9	WBGG	Classic Rock

AM Stations

560	WQAM	Sports/Talk
610	WIOD	News Talk Radio
790	WAXY	Sports/Talk
1140	WQBA	Spanish News/Talk

Conventioneers & Business Travelers
Making Business a Pleasure

If you're in town for a meeting, convention, trade show, or business retreat, Greater Miami is an excellent place to mix pleasure with business—and we don't mean settling for a beer in a lonely lobby bar or checking the in-room movies. If your event is at the Miami Beach Convention Center, you're within walking distance of Lincoln Road and South Beach's clubs, restaurants, and hotels. The Miami Convention Center is near the Brickell Financial District's restaurants and nightspots, and you're a quick taxi ride from the lively pedestrian-friendly downtowns of Coconut Grove and Coral Gables.

Addresses to Know

Convention Centers

City of Miami Convention Center
The James L. Knight Center
400 SE 2nd Ave., Miami, FL 33131
305-372-4633 • www.jlkc.com

Miami Beach Convention Center
1901 Convention Center Dr., Miami Beach, FL 33139
305-673-7312 • www.miamibeachconvention.com

City Information

City of Miami Beach
1700 Convention Center Dr., Miami Beach, FL 33139
305-673-7577 • www.miamibeachfl.gov

Greater Miami Convention & Visitors Bureau
701 Brickell Ave., Ste. 2700, Miami, FL 33131
305-539-3000 / 800-933-8448 • www.gmcvb.com

Business and Convention Hotels

These top business hotels are in addition to those recommended in the Black Book (see p. 208).

Miami Beach

Loews Miami Beach 1601 Collins Ave. (16th St.), 305-604-1601
Buzzy beachfront hotel with historic St. Moritz Hotel, Emeril's restaurant. $$$

South Beach Marriott 161 Ocean Dr. (1st St.), 305-536-7700
Beachfront hotel in trendy SoFi district, close to clubs and restaurants. $$

Royal Palm Crowne Plaza Resort 1545 Collins Ave. (16th St.), 305-604-5700
Beachfront hotel near Miami Beach Convention Center, shops, restaurants. $$

Downtown

Conrad Miami 1395 Brickell Ave. (SE 14th St.), 305-503-6500
Dramatic new concave glass-and-steel luxury hotel with bay and city views. $$$

Hyatt Regency 400 SE 2nd Ave. (Brickell Ave.), 305-358-1234
Riverfront atrium hotel adjoins the Miami Convention Center, Metromover. $$

InterContinental Miami 100 Chopin Plaza (Biscayne Blvd.), 305-577-1000
Sleek highrise over Biscayne Bay, near Bayfront Park and Bayside Marketplace. $$$

JW Marriott 1109 Brickell Ave. (SE 11th St.), 305-329-3500
Elegant Financial District hotel, Isabela's features Mediterranean cuisine. $$$

Business Entertaining

Need to impress a client or network over drinks? These places will help seal the deal.

Acqua, Four Seasons Hotel Miami, 1435 Brickell Ave. (SE 14th St.), 305-381-5590
Northern Italian cuisine, art-filled interior. $$$$

Azul (p. 139), Mandarin Oriental, Miami, 500 Brickell Key Dr. (Brickell Ave.),
305-913-8254
Innovative international cuisine, impeccable service, gorgeous skyline views. $$$$

Fallabella Bar (p. 120), The Albion, 1650 James Ave. (Lincoln Rd.), 305-913-1000
Smart hotel lobby bar catering to fashionistas.

Flute Champagne Lounge (p. 90), 500 S. Pointe Dr. (Collins Ave.), 305-674-8680
Miami edition of Manhattan champagne bar, caviar, live jazz.

Mark's South Beach (p. 84), Hotel Nash, 1120 Collins Ave. (11th St.), 305-604-9050
Top Florida chef Mark Militello's New World cuisine. $$$$

Tropical Cigars (p. 178), 740 Lincoln Rd. (Meridian Ave.), 305-673-3194
Sidewalk cigar cafe with great mojitos, live Latin music. $

Also see: **Best Classic Hotel Bars** (p. 39)
Best Fine Dining (p. 43)
Best Power Lunches (p. 55)

Ducking Out for a Half Day

All work and no play can't be good for you, so try one of these liberating pursuits.

Beach Scooter Rental (p. 125), 1341 Washington Ave. (13th St.), 305-538-7878
Scooter and bicycle rentals. $$$–$$$$

Fairchild Tropical Botanic Garden (p. 153), 10901 Old Cutler Rd., 305-667-1651
83-acre subtropical botanic garden with narrated tram rides, gift shop. $

Lincoln Road Mall (p. 127), Lincoln Rd. (Alton Rd. and Washington Ave.)
Sidewalk cafes, art galleries, people watching, quirky shops, cultural venues, clubs.

The Wolfsonian—FIU (p. 129), 1001 Washington Ave. (10th St.), 305-531-1001
Unusual collection of modern art, design objects, cool gift shop. $

Also see: **Best Golf Courses** (p. 45)
Best Spas (p. 59)

Gifts to Bring Home

Don't settle for that tacky alligator T-shirt at the airport—find some bona fide Miami
memorabilia at some of these places.

Art Deco Welcome Center (p. 179), 1001 Ocean Dr. (10th St.), 305-531-3484
Beachfront Deco headquarters gift shop has posters, souvenirs, and collectibles.

Britto Central (p. 125), 818 Lincoln Rd. (Meridian Ave.), 305-531-8821
Full variety of the colorful works of Brazilian pop artist Romero Britto.

Little Havana To Go (p. 182), 1442 SW 8th St. (SW 14th Ave.), 305-857-9720
T-shirts, Cuban CDs, dominoes, cigars, guayaberas, gifts, posters, and collectibles.

Party Conversation—a Few Surprising Facts

• Roll on up for some quick cash at the first automated teller machine—it was installed especially for rollerbladers (it's at the Citibank branch at Washington Ave. and 17th St.).

• Miami is a well-known recording haven for Latin American superstars Gloria Estefan, Ricky Martin, Enrique Iglesias, and Jon Secada, but they're just part of the big picture. Artists like Aerosmith, the Allman Brothers, Lenny Kravitz, Celine Dion, Dr. Dre, Eric Clapton, the Bee Gees, David Bowie, Prince, U2, the Eagles, the Rolling Stones, and Aretha Franklin have all cut records or laid down tracks here.

• Greater Miami is the only metropolitan area in the U.S. whose borders encompass two national parks. Hike through pristine Everglades National Park or ride on glass-bottom boats across Biscayne National Park.

• *Miami Vice?* Please, that's so 1980s. Current Miami television productions include *CSI: Miami, Nip/Tuck,* and *The Simple Life 2* starring Paris Hilton and Nicole Richie.

• Miami Beach pharmacist Benjamin Green invented the first suntan cream in 1944 by cooking cocoa butter on his kitchen stove.

• In 1937, Amelia Earhart took off from Miami for an around-the-world flight and was never seen again. There's a park named in her honor in the city of Opa Locka.

• The world's largest conga was held in 1988 at the Calle Ocho Festival in Little Havana, the huge annual street party that claims to draw more than 1 million revelers every year.

• Forget Starbucks. Miamians are hooked on *café cubano*—sweet, hot, and potent—sold at lunch corners as handy shots (*un cafecito*), or as *café con leche* (with milk).

• Just what was the Miami Circle used for? The 38-foot-diameter stone structure was unearthed in 1998 during a routine archaeological survey on the south bank of the Miami River at Biscayne Bay. It's believed to have been built by the Tequesta people who lived there more than 2,000 years ago, but its purpose remains a mystery.

The Cheat Sheet
The Very Least You Ought to Know About Miami

It's always a good idea to know a bit about the place you're going. Here's a countdown of the ten most essential facts and factoids you need to keep from looking like a *turista*.

Ten Neighborhoods

Aventura, one of Greater Miami's newest municipalities, is an affluent condo community located on the Intracoastal Waterway in the northeastern corner of the county. It's home to the mega-shopping center Aventura Mall and the 300-acre Fairmont Turnberry Isle Resort with its two highly rated golf courses.

Brickell Village is a new name for a historic area of downtown Miami that's undergoing dizzying growth. Named for the pioneers who bought this land along the Miami River in the 1870s, this pretty urban neighborhood in the big-money Financial District is becoming a new hot spot, with new restaurants, nightlife, and retail geared toward upscale condo owners, business travelers, and downtown workers.

Coconut Grove—a verdant bayfront village known for its bohemian, artsy character—is becoming heavily commercialized, with garish McMansions and mainstream chain stores crowding Main Highway. This pedestrian-friendly district has a lively nightlife and arts scene, plus some outstanding historical sites like The Barnacle, the Coconut Grove Playhouse, and The Kampong.

Coral Gables, created in 1925 as one of the nation's first fully planned communities, is a wealthy, beautifully landscaped, and well-preserved city with outstanding examples of Mediterranean Revival architecture. The magnificent Biltmore Hotel is located here, along with the Venetian Pool, Fairchild Tropical Botanic Garden, and a revitalized downtown shopping, dining, and entertainment district.

Downtown Miami is a vibrant conglomeration of government buildings, geometric skyscrapers, and discount stores, where everyone from Brazilian tourists to banker and lawyer types to colorful urban characters file along its diverse streets. Along palm-lined Biscayne Boulevard is the 1925 Freedom Tower, patterned after Spain's Giralda tower; the modern AmericanAirlines Arena; and the dramatic Cesar Pelli–designed Performing Arts Center, still under construction.

Little Havana's residents aren't necessarily from Cuba—they're immigrants from many South and Central American countries, working and living in this poor but energetic neighborhood. It's alive with Hispanic sights and sounds: cigar factories, Latin music stores, *botanicas* selling herbs and potions, and all kinds of places to eat, from lunch counters to fine Spanish restaurants.

SoFi is the cutesy acronym for South of Fifth, or the southernmost tip of South Beach, where venerable places like Joe's Stone Crab sit in the shadows of huge high-rises, sizzling nightclubs, and hip new restaurants.

South Beach—not a proper city—refers to the southern third of the island of Miami Beach, 21 blocks of Art Deco hotels and hundreds of stylish restaurants and nightclubs flanked on the east by gorgeous Atlantic beaches. The hot thoroughfares are the pedestrian-only Lincoln Road, waterfront Ocean Drive, bustling Collins Avenue, and colorful Washington Avenue.

Sunny Isles Beach is old Florida, rapidly changing. In this new city in the north end of the county, tacky mom-and-pop motels and souvenir stands are being bulldozed to make way for luxury high-rises, including Ocean Point and the Trump International Sonesta Resort, along its handsome beaches.

Upper East Side Miami, a trendy moniker for the part of town along Biscayne Boulevard from 71st Street south to downtown, was formerly known for no-tell motels and hookers. Now, hipsters are moving into renovated bungalows, hanging out in restaurants like Soyka and Dogma Grill, and doing the burgeoning nightlife scene in the nearby Design District.

Nine Shopping Centers

Aventura Mall One of South Florida's biggest malls, with Macy's, Bloomingdale's, Bailey Banks & Biddle, movies, and restaurants.
19501 Biscayne Blvd., Aventura, 305-935-1110,
www.shopaventuramall.com

Bal Harbour Shops Exclusive shopping center with Neiman-Marcus, Saks Fifth Avenue, and Versace, Bulgari, Giorgio Armani, and Chanel.
9700 Collins Ave., Bal Harbour, 305-866-0311, www.balharbourshops.com

Bayside Marketplace Bayfront shopping and entertainment with Hard Rock Cafe, kiosks, shops, restaurants.
401 Biscayne Blvd., Miami, 305-577-3344, www.baysidemarketplace.com

CocoWalk Open-air mall with boutiques, movie theaters, restaurants, and watering holes like Fat Tuesdays.
3015 Grand Ave., Coconut Grove, 305-444-0777, www.galleryatcocowalk.com

Dadeland Mall Longtime megamall anchored by new Nordstrom, Macy's, the country's largest The Limited/Express, and 185 specialty stores.
7535 N. Kendall Dr., Miami, 305-665-6226, www.simon.com

Dolphin Mall West of Miami International Airport, this enormous outlet center includes Neiman-Marcus Last Call Clearance Center, Off 5th Saks Fifth Avenue Outlet Center, plus restaurants and entertainment.
11401 NW 12th St., Miami, 305-365-7446, www.shopdolphinmall.com

The Falls Lush, tropically landscaped suburban mall anchored by Bloomingdale's and Macy's.
U.S. 1 at SW 136th St., Miami, 305-255-4570, www.shopthefalls.com

The Shops at Sunset Place Lively open-air shopping and entertainment center, with Virgin Megastore, movies, boutiques, and kiosks.
5701 Sunset Dr., South Miami, 305-663-0482, www.simon.com

Village of Merrick Park New upscale shopping and dining center with Nordstrom, Neiman Marcus, Donald Pliner Couture, Carolina Herrera.
358 San Lorenzo Ave., Coral Gables, 305-529-0200,
www.villageofmerrickpark.com

Eight Performing Arts Venues

Actors Playhouse Professional theater performances year-round in the splendidly restored Miracle Theatre in downtown Coral Gables.
280 Miracle Mile, Coral Gables, 305-444-9293, www.actorsplayhouse.org

AmericanAirlines Arena Home to the NBA's Miami Heat, this futuristic arena on Biscayne Bay in Downtown Miami is the main venue for major concerts, family shows, and special events like the MTV Video Music Awards.
601 Biscayne Blvd., Miami, 786-777-1000, www.aaarena.com

Coconut Grove Playhouse Originally built as a movie house in 1926, this building was the site of the U.S. premiere of Beckett's *Waiting for Godot* in 1956, and has been home to many of theater's top names ever since.
3500 Main Hwy., Coconut Grove, 305-442-4000, www.cgplayhouse.com

Jackie Gleason Theater For more than 50 years, this performing arts facility has hosted a variety of television productions and theater, including The *Ed Sullivan Show, The Jackie Gleason Show,* and Miss Universe and Miss USA pageants; and countless concerts and arts productions, including the Miami Beach Broadway Series and the Miami City Ballet.
1700 Washington Ave., Miami Beach, 305-673-7300,
www.gleasontheater.com

James L. Knight International Center Located at the Downtown Hyatt Regency, this venue is used for concerts and public assemblies.
400 SE 2nd Ave., Miami, 305-372-4634, www.jlknightcenter.com

Lincoln Theatre This magnificent original 1935 Streamline Moderne building is home to the New World Symphony and presents performances from national, international, and local performing groups.
541 Lincoln Rd., South Beach, 305-673-3330, www.nws.org

Olympia Theater at the Gusman Center for the Performing Arts First opened in 1926 as a silent movie palace, this Downtown theater—listed on the National Register of Historic Places—is renowned for its ornate Moorish architecture and simulated night sky with twinkling stars. Elvis Presley, Sarah Vaughan, and Luciano Pavarotti have performed here; now, it's used for dance and musical performances, and as a venue for the Miami International Film Festival.
174 E. Flagler St., Miami, 305-374-2444, gusmancenter.org

Performing Arts Center of Greater Miami Slated to open in 2005 or thereabouts, this Cesar Pelli–designed center will be one of four major centers in the country with three performance facilities for ballet, opera, theater, and symphonic music.
1444 Biscayne Blvd., Downtown Miami, 305-372-7611, www.pacfmiami.org

Seven Causeways

79th St./JFK Causeway goes through the three islands that make up North Bay Village, connecting with Miami Beach.

Broad Causeway, a toll road, links the mainland with Bay Harbor Islands and meets the beach at Bal Harbour.

Julia Tuttle Causeway (I-195) branches off I-95 to connect the mainland with Miami Beach at 41st St., where neon-ringed palm trees welcome visitors to Miami Beach.

MacArthur Causeway (I-395) joins Downtown Miami and South Beach, with access to Watson, Star, Palm, and Hibiscus Islands, and the Fisher Island ferry point.

Rickenbacker Causeway, a toll road, has a dramatic bridge and beaches on both sides as it links the mainland with Virginia Key and Key Biscayne.

Venetian Causeway, a toll road and the oldest remaining causeway in South Florida, runs from the Downtown mainland to South Beach through a series of small residential islands.

William Lehman Causeway in the north end of the county crosses through the condos of Aventura before reaching Sunny Isles Beach.

Six Expressways

State Road 112/Airport Expressway runs east from north of Miami International Airport to I-95.

State Road 836/East-West/Dolphin Expressway runs east from Florida's Turnpike through SR 826 and I-95.

Florida's Turnpike starts in Wildwood in the north central part of the state, connects with other main highways at the Golden Glades Interchange, and continues south to Florida City, the gateway to the Florida Keys.

I-75 connects with the Palmetto Expressway in northwest Miami-Dade County, and continues as Alligator Alley across the Everglades to Florida's southwest coast.

I-95 starts in Coconut Grove and runs north along the coast of Florida and the Southeast United States to Maine.

SR 826/Palmetto Expressway starts in Kendall in South Miami, running north until it turns east in Miami Lakes and merges with I-95 and other highways at the Golden Glades Interchange.

Five Sports Stadiums

AmericanAirlines Arena (basketball), 601 Biscayne Blvd., Miami, 786-777-1000, www.aaarena.com

Homestead-Miami Speedway (auto racing), One Speedway Blvd., Homestead, 305-230-5000, www.homesteadmiamispeedway.com

Office Depot Center (hockey), One Panther Parkway, Sunrise, 954-835-8000, www.officedepotcenter.com

Orange Bowl Stadium (University of Miami Hurricanes), 1501 NW 3rd St., Miami, 305-643-7100, www.orangebowlstadium.com

Pro Player Stadium (football, baseball), 2269 NW 199th St., Miami, 305-623-6100, www.proplayerstadium.com

Four Sports Teams

Florida Marlins, Major League Baseball, 877-627-5467,
www.flamarlins.com

Florida Panthers, NHL Hockey, 954-835-7825, www.flpanthers.com

Miami Dolphins, NFL Football, 305-573-8326, www.miamidolphins.com

Miami Heat, NBA Basketball, 800-462-2849, www.nba.com/heat

Three Streets

Biscayne Boulevard—Downtown Miami's royal palm–lined Champs
Elysées—runs north-south through downtown Miami to the northern end of
the county.

Collins Avenue is Miami Beach's main hotel drag. It starts at the southern
tip of South Beach and goes to the northern end of the county.

Ocean Drive, Miami's famous oceanfront promenade, begins at the
southern tip of South Beach and runs along the oceanfront to Espanola Way.

Two Area Codes

305 and **786.** Note that 10-digit dialing is required at all times, even when
you're dialing within the same area code.

One Time Zone

Miami runs on **Eastern Time**, the same as New York (unofficially, it's on
Cuban time, at least one hour late for parties and functions).

A note on Daylight Savings Time: clocks are set ahead one hour at 2 a.m. on
the first Sunday in April and set back one hour at 2 a.m. on the last Sunday
in October.

The Perfect Miami

When you're on a trip, you don't want a city with all its flaws and inconsistencies. You want the perfect city. With 33 categories that represent all of Miami's most outstanding features, you'll have the hottest, hippest places right at your fingertips. Here are the very best places to eat, drink, dance, lounge, see and be seen, work on your tan, and make the most of a city that's all about fun. Listings that also appear in The Miami Experience chapter are noted, so that you can easily combine your choices with other activities.

Always-Trendy Tables

In a town where hot restaurants come and go as quickly as J-Lo's marriages, these places are still going strong. Why? The food is outstanding, the space is dazzlingly cool, and the folks behind them aren't the usual fly-by-nighters.

Blue Door

Delano, 1685 Collins Ave., South Beach, 305-674-6400 • Hot & Cool

The Draw: The A-list clientele is only a side dish—Claude Troisgros' fabulous refined cuisine is the real reason you should book your table here *toute de suite*.

The Scene: Billowing curtains, white leather curved banquettes and sofas, candelabra strung with strands of Swarovski pearls, and custom floor lamps are all part of the fantasy ice palace décor.
Open for breakfast daily 7–11:30 a.m.; brunch Sun. 10:30 a.m.–2:30 p.m.; lunch 11:30 a.m.–4 p.m.; dinner 7–11:30 p.m. $$$$

Hot Tip: An indoor table may give you a better look at who's coming and going, but the best tables are on the terrace overlooking the garden.

China Grill

404 Washington Ave., South Beach, 305-534-2211 • Arty Party

The Draw: Back in the day, it packed in the likes of Oprah, Madonna, Cher, Prince, and even some people with surnames. It hasn't stopped being a must-visit—just look at the fashion-forward locals and star-gazing tourists waiting to get in.

The Scene: Underneath the landmark neon-colored tower, this glass, onyx, and lime-stone complex has a vast main dining room and bar, plus the intimate new Dragon Room for sushi and saketinis.
Open for lunch Mon.–Fri. 11 a.m.–6 p.m.; dinner Mon.–Fri. 6 p.m.–midnight, Sat.–Sun. 6 p.m.–1 a.m. $$$

Hot Tip: Portions are huge and meant for sharing, except for the crispy spinach, which you should keep all for yourself.

The Forge

432 41st St., Mid-Beach, 305-538-8533 • Clásico

The Draw: This lavish steakhouse and bar that once hosted luminaries from Judy Garland to Richard Nixon to Jackie Gleason now gets younger glitterati.

The Scene: Over-the-top opulence, with 20-foot ceilings, a massive crystal chandelier, gilded framed paintings, engraved stained glass, and tropical murals—and that's just in the main salon. The wine cellar has more than 300,000 vintages.
Open Mon., Tues., Thurs., Sun. 6–11 p.m.; Wed., Fri., Sat. 6 p.m.–midnight. $$$$

Hot Tip: Reserve your seat in Lovers Lane, a series of banquettes just off the main dining room, perfect for romantic dinners for two and for watching the energetic crowd.

Art Spaces

Miami's art scene has exploded only recently, due in large part to the arrival of the annual Art Basel, and to world-class private collections now open to the public. Miami is also a major showcase for Latin American artists. You'll see some of the best art in town at these institutions.

Bass Museum of Art

2121 Park Ave., South Beach, 305-673-7530 • Hot & Cool

The Draw: Sweeping collection of works on display, ranging from paintings by masters Sandro Botticelli and Peter Paul Rubens to beaded handbags by Argentine artist Victoria Gittman.

The Scene: A long-awaited expansion added a geometric two-story structure by architect Arata Isozaki. This more than doubled the size of the 1930 Tropical Art Deco building, which was originally a library.
Open Tues., Wed., Fri., Sat. 10 a.m.–5 p.m.; Sun. 11 a.m.–5 p.m.; every Thursday 10 a.m.–9 p.m. Closed holidays. $

Hot Tip: Check out the museum shop, open during business hours, for its eclectic selection of art books, folk art, jewelry, toys, and original artwork for under $1,000.

Museum of Contemporary Art—MoCA

770 NE 125th St., North Miami Beach, 305-893-6211 • Arty Party

The Draw: Count on seeing fresh discoveries here, thanks to dynamic director Bonnie Clearwater's commitment to emerging new artists.

The Scene: Within the stunning 23,000-square-foot structure designed by acclaimed architect Charles Gwathmey are works from contemporary artists, including Louise Nevelson, John Baldessari, Julian Schnabel, and Dennis Oppenheim.
Open Tues.–Sat. 11:00 a.m.–5 p.m., Sun. noon–5 p.m., last Fri. night of every month 7–10 p.m. $

Hot Tip: If you're here on the last Friday of the month, call about the North Miami Gallery Walk starting at MoCA.

Rubell Collection

95 NW 29th St., Downtown Miami, 305-573-6090 • Arty Party

The Draw: One of the top collections of contemporary art in the U.S., from the Miami-based Rubell family (their late brother was Steve Rubell of Studio 54 fame).

The Scene: Newly expanded exhibition spaces show works of celebrated artists like Cindy Sherman, Jeff Koons, Purvis Young, Keith Haring, Damian Hirst, Richard Prince, and Charles Ray, many discovered by the Rubells in their emerging stages.
Open Wed.–Sun 10 a.m.–6 p.m., second Saturdays 10 a.m.–10 p.m. $

Hot Tip: This remarkable collection is open for viewing seasonally, so call first to make sure it's open.

Beaches

With 22 miles of beaches, Greater Miami has countless places for you to bask under the subtropical sun. While there are beaches for every taste—whether you're seeking out a party vibe, an athletic scene, a touch of seclusion, clothing optional, or pet friendly—these are the best of the bunch. Whichever you choose, don't forget to bring the sunscreen.

Bill Baggs Cape Florida State Park

1200 S. Crandon Blvd., Key Biscayne, 305-361-5811 • Outdoors

The Draw: It's one of the top ten beaches in the United States.

The Scene: When you need to recuperate from the highly social South Beach scene, the calm seas, quiet beaches, nature trails, picturesque historic lighthouse, and excellent seafood restaurant make this park an ideal destination.
Open daily 8 a.m.–sundown. $

Hot Tip: Show up a half-hour before tour times to sign up for tours of the historic lighthouse and keeper's quarters, held at 10 a.m. and 1 p.m. Thurs.–Mon.

Haulover Beach Park

10800 Collins Ave., Miami Beach, 305-944-3040 • Outdoors

The Draw: The beach for surfers, sunbathers, families, tourists, and locals looking for a fun day in the sun with lots to keep them busy.

The Scene: This mile-and-a-half stretch of sand delivers the total beach experience: sandy shores, open surf, picnic areas, dunes, plus a full-service marina, restaurant, tennis courts, golf course, and kite shops across the street.
Open daily sunrise–sunset. $

Hot Tip: You can find a section of this beach for every persuasion—there's a nude beach, a gay beach, a nude gay beach, a nude gay volleyball beach, and so on.

Lummus Park Beach

Ocean Dr. from 5th to 15th Streets, South Beach, 305-673-7714 • Clásico

The Draw: So this is the beach with those multicolored Art Deco lifeguard stands!

The Scene: Stretching across ten blocks of prime South Beach real estate, this is where locals go to the beach. Expect to see tourists, families, picnickers, rollerbladers, boombox-toting kids, derelicts, cyclists, and sun worshippers in every and any form.
Open daily sunrise–midnight.

Hot Tip: Topless bathing is pretty much everywhere here. (Thank the European visitors for bringing that time-honored tradition to South Beach.)

Classic Hotel Bars

While nearly every Art Deco hotel has its own version of a lobby bar, a choice few have bars that are especially memorable and worth going out of your way for.

D'Lounge

The National Hotel, 1677 Collins Ave., South Beach, 305-532-2311 • Arty Party

The Draw: Hollywood glamour, Beach style—you'll be tempted to show up in vintage 1940s dress, so perfect is this restored Deco landmark.

The Scene: No detail has been overlooked at this classic watering hole, from the massive oak bar to the original reupholstered barrel chairs and polished chrome light fixtures. Lounge and cabaret music set the mood for the low-key, handsome patrons. *Open daily 4 p.m.–1 a.m.*

Hot Tip: Ask Ed or Gloria—the National's extraordinary concierges—to show you the adjoining Press Room. Don't miss the terrazzo floor.

M-Bar

Mandarin Oriental, Miami, 500 Brickell Key Dr., Downtown Miami, 305-913-8288 • Outdoors

The Draw: Stylish business types and urbane grown-ups share discreet small talk over martinis against a backdrop of Asian tropical-chic décor.

The Scene: Sublime sophistication, as you might expect: rich dark-wood barstools and tables, cushioned couches, Japanese lanterns, and a bar topped with blue marble, with floor-to-ceiling windows revealing panoramic views of the skyline. *Open Mon.–Thurs. 5 p.m.–midnight, Fri.–Sat. 5 p.m.–1 a.m.*

Hot Tip: Order a martini. You decide—Cajun? Coffee Lover's? The menu lists 250 varieties, divided into categories such as sweet, naughty but nice, and oddballs.

Rose Bar

Delano, 1685 Collins Ave., South Beach, 305-672-2000 • Hot & Cool

The Draw: You might spot a celeb at this pink-hued fantasy bar, but more likely you'll see well-heeled young professionals and other business types.

The Scene: Bathed in a soft pink glow, with chess tables and billiards, the bar is tucked in the back of the Delano's dramatic high-ceilinged lobby. *Open Sun.–Thurs. noon–2 a.m., Fri.–Sat. noon–3 a.m.*

Hot Tip: After making the Rose Bar scene, head to the sultry pool bar where the crowd is often younger and hipper.

Cuban Food

You can't come to Miami without trying tasty Cuban cuisine. Countless restaurants with walkup counters serve up *cafecitos* and pastries, but these are the places that deliver the full cultural experience and the real flavor of Cuba.

La Carreta

3632 SW 8th St., Little Havana, 305-444-7501 • Clásico

The Draw: Without a doubt, one of the best places to get the whole *sabor cubano:* food, fellow diners, atmosphere.

The Scene: Cuban families and friends gather loudly for their beloved roast pork, black beans and rice, fried plantains, and flan.
Open Mon.–Thurs. 6 a.m.–2 a.m., Fri.–Sun. 24 hours. $

Hot Tip: Skip the Coke and order a Cuban soft drink, like Materva (made from an herb called maté) or Jupiña (pineapple).

Versailles

3555 SW 8th St., Little Havana, 305-444-0240 • Clásico

The Draw: This is where Cubans go: from working class folks getting a *cafecito* from the counter, to dressed-up families celebrating special occasions, to business types discussing deals to old men endlessly arguing about Castro.

The Scene: Noisy, gaudy diner staffed by crisply efficient waitresses accustomed to dealing with crowds.
Open Sun.–Thurs. 9 a.m.–1 a.m., Fri.–Sat. 9 a.m.–3:30 a.m. $

Hot Tip: The pressed *medianoche* sandwich (ham, pork, Swiss cheese, and pickles on a sweet Cuban roll) is a classic, but be daring and try the Elena Ruz: turkey, cream cheese, and strawberry preserves.

Yuca

501 Lincoln Rd., South Beach, 305-532-9822 • Clásico

The Draw: What happens when Cuban food gets a major facelift? You get the innovative upscale cuisine dubbed Nuevo Latino.

The Scene: More than a pit stop for fabulous mojitos, this elegant restaurant with a prime Lincoln Road location attracts a dressy crowd that does, in fact, include the Young Urban Cuban Americans it's named after (or was it named after the starchy tuber? Hmmm).
Open daily noon–11:30 p.m.$$

Hot Tip: End your meal with Cuban rice pudding, served in a sugar almond basket with homemade ginger wafers and cinnamon.

Dance Clubs

Maybe it's the Latin influence, maybe it's the heat—but this is one crazy dancing town, with places for salsa, house, hip-hop, disco, trance, swing, and everything else. Even laid-back lounges have cushions made to stand up on and boogie. These clubs are all about dance, with regular and guest deejays spinning on different nights.

crobar

1445 Washington Ave., South Beach, 305-672-8084 • Hot & Cool

The Draw: Packed with everyone from club kids to drag queens to dancin' fools, this steamy southern cousin of its Chicago and New York counterparts is the ultimate dance palace.

The Scene: South Beach's highest-energy dance club is located in the historic Cameo Theater, an Art Deco movie house. Inside, it's urban-industrial chic, with an intense, throbbing sound system worked by superstar deejays. Wave to the folks in the balcony, one of several VIP areas where the likes of Missy Elliott and Lil' Kim party. *Open Thurs.–Mon. 10 p.m.–5 a.m.* $$

Hot Tip: Arrive before 11:30 p.m. to avoid the long lines, and do dress up a bit.

Mansion

1235 Washington Ave., South Beach, 786-229-7857 • Hot & Cool

The Draw: Where does Dennis Rodman throw his July 4 shindig? Which hot spot does Outkast choose to host its MTV Video Music Awards party? Where does P. Diddy stop when he's in town? They all move into Mansion.

The Scene: From the same folks who brought you Opium/Privé comes this 40,000-square-foot two-level club whose concept is residence-meets-nightlife (no, that does not mean La-Z-Boys and litterboxes): sweeping staircases, exposed brick walls, crystal chandeliers, elaborate fireplaces, and Venetian glass mirrors. *Open Tues., Thurs.–Sat. 11 p.m.–5 a.m.* $$

Hot Tip: Go on, reserve a table. It'll cost you upwards of $200, but you'll be able to get your groove on in true Miami style.

Opium Garden

136 Collins Ave., South Beach, 305-531-5535 • Hot & Cool

The Draw: Open-air Asian-themed nightclub that is Miami's hottest weekend destination. Keep tabs on when Paris Hilton's going to make an appearance—just check the aerial advertising while you're sunbathing on the beach.

The Scene: Exotic accoutrements like golden Buddha statues, Chinese lanterns, pagodas, and lots of red add that must-have Oriental mystique, while a monster sound and lighting system keeps the crowd partying. *Open Tues., Thurs.–Sun. 11 p.m.–5 a.m.* $$

Hot Tip: Dress to impress and you should get past the velvet ropes with no problem—no jerseys, hats, tennis shoes, or shorts.

Dive Bars

You'll find no lemongrass saketinis on the cocktail menus here, and no cover charges or attitude either. Instead, stop in at one of these spots for a splash of local color, and chill with all the folks taking a breather from the stifling fabulousness elsewhere.

Jimbo's Place

Duck Lake Rd., Virginia Key, 305-361-7026 • Outdoors

The Draw: Aside from being a popular photo and video shoot location, this raggedy collection of shacks happens to be one of the town's friendliest casual beer-and-smoked-fish hangouts.

The Scene: Locals, politicians, models, and celebrities all gather here to watch bocce ball tournaments.
Open daily 6 a.m.–6:30 p.m. $

Hot Tip: It's not easy to find. Take the Rickenbacker Causeway to Virginia Key, turn left after the light at MAST Academy, then follow the road, staying to the right at the first fork in the road. When you come to the end of the road, stay to the left. You'll see the water treatment plant. Make a right and look for the driveway ahead on the right—you'll see cars parked along the road.

Mac's Club Deuce

222 14th St., South Beach, 305-531-6200 • Arty Party

The Draw: Pull up a barstool next to the barflies, actors, trannies, bikers, hookers, and socialite heiresses who go slumming here.

The Scene: Heavy with smoke and boozy perfume, the unmistakable eau-de-dive bar is so thick you can cut it with a stiletto—heel, we mean. Neon signs, posters, a pool table, and a jukebox are authentic props. (Well, yes, this bar was also a shooting location for *Miami Vice*).
Open daily 8 a.m.–5 a.m. $

Hot Tip: Drinks are two-for-one from 8 a.m.–7 p.m.

Tobacco Road

626 S. Miami Ave., Downtown Miami, 305-374-1198 • Outdoors

The Draw: If this dive bar was good enough for Al Capone, it's cool enough for you.

The Scene: Grimy, boozy, and dark, with one of the longest bars in the city, the Road has sensibly priced drinks and greasy-spoon food that's actually decent. It feels like a neighborhood bar, populated by yuppies, regulars, and occasional hipsters.
Open Mon.–Fri. 11:30 a.m.–5 a.m., Sat.–Sun. noon–5 a.m. $

Hot Tip: You never know what greats you'll see at The Road—B.B. King, Koko Taylor, Albert Collins, and Jr. Washington have all played here.

Best   Fine Dining

When the Thai-Peruvian-Inuit fusion tapas craze gets tiresome, count on these restaurants for flawless service, splendid décor, and a classic culinary experience that you'll remember long after you've returned home.

Azul

Mandarin Oriental, Miami, 500 Brickell Key Dr., Downtown Miami, 305-913-8254 • Outdoors

The Draw: Latin flavors blend with Asian, Caribbean, and classic French influence so artfully that Azul was named Miami's first AAA Five Diamond restaurant.

The Scene: Sleek and understated, Azul has unusual décor details, some subtle, like the water curtain in front of the open kitchen, and others dramatic, like the floor-to-ceiling windows affording bay and city views. But the expensively dressed business and special occasion guests are really here to experience the extraordinary food. *Open for lunch Mon.–Fri. noon–3 p.m.; dinner Mon.–Sat. 7–11 p.m.* $$$$

Hot Tip: If you get chilly, the restaurant keeps pashminas on hand in a wide array of colors. Reading glasses are available, too.

Norman's

21 Almeria Ave., Coral Gables, 305-446-6767 • Clásico

The Draw: If you want to know what New World cuisine is, head to guru Norman Van Aken's fine dining restaurant—he started it all.

The Scene: Norman's has three dining rooms, including a theater kitchen-dining room showcasing the chef and his brigade in action. His devotees range from connoisseurs who regularly indulge in the singular culinary experience here to regular folks who make this a treasured splurge. The consensus: big bucks, and worth every penny. *Open Mon.–Thurs. 6–10 p.m.; Fri.–Sat. 6–10:30 p.m.* $$$$

Hot Tip: With such an extensive array of dishes, Norman's offers a tasting menu that lets you experience a wide range of this distinctive cuisine's flavors.

Palme d'Or

The Biltmore Hotel, 1200 Anastasia Ave., Coral Gables, 305-913-3201 • Outdoors

The Draw: French nouvelle cuisine gets a facelift: it's less formal and more choices appear on the menu, so that you can build your own dining experience around more than 20 tasting dishes. Chef Philippe Ruiz' innovative flavors and ingredients remain.

The Scene: Elegant but not stuffy dining room has comfortable leather upholstery, Brazilian cherrywood floors, colorful frescoes, and vintage photographs. Expect a genteel and sophisticated older crowd made up of locals and business travelers. *Open Tues.–Thurs. 6–10:30 p.m., Fri.–Sat. 6–11:30 p.m.* $$$$

Hot Tip: Ask about suitable wine pairings for your tasting menu.

Gay Bars

Miami Beach—South Beach in particular—has long been known as a gay-friendly destination. In addition to the following gay clubs, many nightspots have gay-oriented party nights. Miami lesbians, on the other hand, have hardly any place to call their own, other than occasional girl-only parties.

Jade

1766 Bay Rd., South Beach, 305-695-0000 • Arty Party

The Draw: Stylish Balinese-Asian lounge has a variety of offerings: live music, deejay sounds, even poetry readings.

The Scene: Tucked away from the Washington Avenue madness on the quieter side of South Beach, Jade has a chic Zen vibe in its three lounge areas, and a second level art gallery. You'll find a young, good-looking mixed crowd of fun and friendly folks. *Open Wed.–Thurs. 9 p.m.–5 a.m., Fri. 7 p.m.–5 a.m., Sat. 10 p.m.–5 a.m., Sun. 9 p.m.–5 a.m. $*

Hot Tip: Euphoria Fridays is the one of the most popular gay hot parties in town; Siren on Saturdays is just for the girls.

Score

727 Lincoln Rd., South Beach, 305-535-1111 • Hot & Cool

The Draw: There's no better vantage point than this busy Lincoln Road sidewalk cafe for watching the endless stream of men and boys passing by.

The Scene: The outside cafe is only the tip of the iceberg. Inside, Score has three bars where muscle boys, out-of-towners, and locals looking for a good time hang out. Weekly fun includes karaoke night hosted by local drag queens, Latin night, and striptease night. *Open daily 1 p.m.–5 a.m.*

Hot Tip: No, the name does not suggest a sports bar. Rather, Score is a favorite gathering point after dinner or the movies.

Twist

1057 Washington Ave., South Beach, 305-538-9478 • Hot & Cool

The Draw: The longest established gay club on South Beach, Twist is a popular pit stop for locals and tourists, with multiple rooms and plenty of hunky studs.

The Scene: If you're looking for something special, you'll find it in Twist—the two-story building includes a video pub, garden area, Bungalow Bar with go-go boys, upstairs patio bar, main room with deejay, drag shows, frolic lounge, and game room with pool tables and video games. *Open daily 1 p.m.–5 a.m.*

Hot Tip: Drinks are two-for-one every day 1–9 p.m.

Best Golf Courses

Golfers, bring clubs. Among Greater Miami's 30+ public and private courses are some of the most challenging and most beautiful in the country. Weekend slots fill up quickly, so reserve your tee times well in advance.

Crandon Park Golf Course

6700 Crandon Blvd., Key Biscayne, 305-361-9129 • Outdoors

The Draw: Located on lush Key Biscayne, it's considered one of the most beautiful—and difficult—par-72 courses in Florida.

The Scene: Since 1987, it has hosted the Senior PGA Tour, attracting players including Lee Trevino, Chi Chi Rodriguez, Don Massengale, Ray Floyd, and Gary Player. Crandon Park features the world's largest tee, seven saltwater lakes, challenging sand traps, mangrove thickets, and many holes overlooking Biscayne Bay.
Open daily 7 a.m.–7 p.m. $$$$

Hot Tip: All golf carts use ParView, a sophisticated golf distancing and communications system that gives a graphical interpretation of the hole featuring distances to the landmarks, pro tips on how to best play the hole, and an elapsed timer to monitor pace of play.

Doral Golf Resort & Spa

4400 NW 87th Ave., Doral, 305-592-2000 • Clásico

The Draw: A must-visit for the serious golfer. Five 18-hole championship courses include the famous Blue Monster, host to the PGA Tour since 1962 and recently awarded Best of the World by *Golfer Magazine*.

The Scene: It's part of the Doral Golf Resort & Spa's 650 tropical acres west of Miami, which include the Jim McLean Golf School, a driving range, and the Arthur Ashe Tennis Center.
Open daily 6:30 a.m.–7 p.m. $$$$

Hot Tip: When you play the Gold course, bring a lot of golf balls. There's water on 16 of the 18 holes.

Miami Beach Golf Club

2301 Alton Rd., South Beach, 305-532-3350 • Hot & Cool

The Draw: Only blocks from South Beach action, the nifty complete redesign of former Bayshore Golf Course is getting rave reviews from visiting celebs and pro jocks for its challenging holes, tropical landscaping, and greens covered with a saltwater-tolerant grass called seaside paspalum.

The Scene: 128 acres of lush fairways designed by Arthur Hills, amid mangroves and tropical palms, this 18-hole, par-72 course is 6,800 yards from the back tees.
Open daily 7 a.m.–7 p.m. $$$$

Hot Tip: The Club is open 365 days a year. January through April are the busiest months, so plan accordingly.

Guided Tours

Get all the skinny on Miami from the people who know it best—just reserve your space on a guided tour. Whatever your interest—Deco architecture, celeb mansions, scandals past and present—you can explore it on foot, on bike, or on a jet ski.

Art Deco Welcome Center

1001 Ocean Dr., South Beach, 305-531-3484 • Clásico

The Draw: Sign up here for a guided Art Deco District walking tour or a self-guided audio tour.

The Scene: Formerly the Ocean Front Auditorium, this building on Ocean Drive houses the Welcome Center and the Miami Design Preservation League that spearheaded the efforts to save Beach hotels from being torn down in the 1970s.
Open daily 10 a.m.–7:30 p.m. $

Hot Tip: Need a pink flamingo for the folks back home? The Welcome Center gift shop is stocked with fun and funky souvenirs, books, and posters.

Dr. Paul George's Tours

305-375-1621 • Clásico

The Draw: Historian Dr. Paul George's fascinating tours are packed with local lore for fans of history and architecture, and those interested in the scoop on the colorful characters in Miami's past and present.

The Scene: Tours take place on foot, bike, boat, and coach and last two-plus hours. *Check the Historical Museum of Southern Florida website, www.historical-museum.org, for the current schedule. $–$$*

Hot Tip: If the timing works out, reserve your spot for the popular Mystery and Mayhem: Crime Coach Tour, offered twice a year.

Hector's Jetskis

South Beach, 305-318-9268 • Hot & Cool

The Draw: Wave to Gloria Estefan as you speed past her home on a waverunner.

The Scene: Hector leads groups of jet-skiers on tours around the Miami Beach islands where the rich and richer live, including Star, Palm, and Fisher Islands. *Tours daily from 7 a.m.–6:30 p.m. Call for reservations 24 hours in advance. $$$$*

Hot Tip: Even more fun than spotting a resident celeb is seeing the playful dolphins along the way.

Hotel Pools

Miami has so many spectacular hotel pools—from jungly spa pools, to massive shallow pools dotted with royal palms, to rooftop pools with underwater portholes—that you could spend your entire visit pool-hopping and still not see them all. These are the ones that are absolutely not to be missed.

The Biltmore Hotel

1200 Anastasia Ave., Coral Gables, 305-445-1926 • Outdoors

The Draw: The largest hotel pool in the continental United States, and a site where thousands of spectators in the 1920s and 1930s came to watch synchronized swimmers, bathing beauties, and alligator wrestlers.

The Scene: As dramatic as this enormous pool is, its history is even more intriguing. The 85-foot tropical waterfall was once a high diving tower from which four-year-old Jackie Ott dove as part of his act. And before his tree-swinging days in Hollywood, Johnny Weissmuller was a Biltmore swimming instructor and later broke swimming records here. While hotel guests bask in the sun, tourists gawk or eat lunch poolside. *Open daily 6:30 a.m.–6 p.m.*

Hot Tip: The tropical landscaping surrounding the pool works so well, don't be surprised to see indigenous egrets and anoles (lizards) joining you poolside.

Fontainebleau Hilton Resort

4441 Collins Ave., Miami Beach, 305-538-2000 • Clásico

The Draw: There are actually three outdoor pools here: an enormous free-form pool; a saltwater pool; and Cookie's World, an octopus water park for kids.

The Scene: Let's focus on the grown-up pools, a half-acre rock grotto with cascading waterfalls and lush tropical landscaping. Note that there's also a quieter saltwater pool for relaxing. *Open daily 6 a.m.–6 p.m.*

Hot Tip: Look familiar? The Fontainebleau's pool has been the backdrop for many movies, include *Scarface, The Bodyguard, The Specialist,* and *Goldfinger.*

Four Seasons Hotel Miami

1435 Brickell Ave., Downtown Miami, 305-358-3535 • Hot & Cool

The Draw: The two-acre Bahia Terrace on the hotel's seventh floor has not one, not two, but three large swimming pools.

The Scene: The standout pool is the Palm Grove, an enormous shallow pool neatly dotted with 20 or so tall royal palms. Guests can drag their beach chairs in the pool and seek some palmy shade. *Open sunrise to sunset.*

Hot Tip: Order a Latin-American beer and tapas from Bahia, the popular open-air bar.

Late-Night Eats

...or rather, early morning restaurants, since many South Beach clubs stay open till 5 a.m. After hours of clubbing, you'll want to stagger into one of these places for something decent to soak up some of those cosmos. Whichever you select, you're sure to have plenty of company.

11th Street Diner

1065 Washington Ave., South Beach, 305-534-6373 • Hot & Cool

The Draw: After a long, hard night of clubbing, the law says you must stop at this diner for a prehangover breakfast.

The Scene: Yup, this is a real, shiny 1948 stainless steel diner from Pennsylvania, plunked down on Washington Avenue. Locals and tourists alike crowd stools and booths for real diner food, like pot roast with mashed potatoes and string beans, and roast turkey with candied yams.
Open daily 24 hours. $

Hot Tip: Order the chocolate milkshake.

Big Pink

157 Collins Ave., South Beach, 305-532-4700 • Clásico

The Draw: It's big, and it's pink. It serves American comfort food, gourmet-style, in massive portions.

The Scene: Big Pink's Plexiglas pink barstools and communal tables are always occupied, so be prepared to make some new friends—models, families visiting from New Jersey, club kids feeding a hangover.
Open Sun.–Thurs. 9 a.m.–1 a.m., Fri.–Sat. 9 a.m.–2 a.m. $

Hot Tip: Big buckets of late-night snack food are favorites here: hand-cut fries, homemade chips and dips, sweet potato fries, chicken wings, onion rings, calamari, and state-fair corn dogs.

Cafeteria

546 Lincoln Rd., South Beach, 305-672-3663 • Arty Party

The Draw: When you're hungry for upscale comfort food, thirsty for a dirty martini, or just itching for someplace cool to go, Cafeteria is there for you 24/7.

The Scene: A onetime Cadillac showroom (check out the sign on the facade), this restaurant/lounge has a sleek white interior, with vinyl booths and a skylight ceiling, a buzzing Lincoln Road cafe scene, and a lounge in back for New York trendoids and South Beach night owls.
Open daily 24 hours. $$

Hot Tip: Meet to eat after clubbing at Cafeteria's Breakfast Club, a deejay/dance party held in the early morning hours 2–7 a.m.

Best · Latin Night Out

¡Ay, papi! Make it a salsa-and-*son* in the town that brought you Gloria Estefan. These are the best places to shake your bon-bon.

Bongos Cuban Cafe

AmericanAirlines Arena, 601 Biscayne Blvd., Downtown Miami, 786-777-2100 • Clásico

The Draw: Although this is a Disneyfied version of a Cuban nightspot, brought to you by Gloria and Emilio Estefan, you'll still have lots of fun. Plan on getting sweaty.

The Scene: Part of the bayfront AmericanAirlines Arena, Bongos' giant pineapple identifies this colorful restaurant-by-day, disco-by-night. Expect long lines outside on Friday and Saturday nights (and they're not of the conga variety).
Restaurant open for lunch Friday–Sun. 11:30 a.m.–5 p.m.; dinner Wed.–Sun. 5–11 p.m.; nightclub open Fri.–Sat. 11 p.m.–4 a.m. $$

Hot Tip: Break your rule of not ordering cocktails with cute names and have a Babaloo (Bacardi Añejo Rum, citrus juices, cream of coconut, and a touch of blue Curaçao).

Hoy Como Ayer

2212 SW 8th St., Little Havana, 305-541-2631 • Clásico

The Draw: This is real slice-of-life stuff, a grungy spot in Little Havana where Cubans gather to listen to Luis Bofill and Albita Rodriguez channeling Cuban greats Benny More and Celia Cruz.

The Scene: Old photos and newspaper articles bring on nostalgia for Cubans young and old, who are here for the rhythms they grew up with.
Open Thurs.–Sat. 9 p.m.–3 a.m. $

Hot Tip: Order a couple of Cuba libres, and you'll be feeling nostalgic too.

Tropigala

Fontainebleau Hilton Resort, 4441 Collins Ave., Mid-Beach, 305-672-7469 • Clásico

The Draw: The former La Ronde Room where Frank Sinatra once performed is now a Latin-flavored showplace where you dine while watching a glitzy show.

The Scene: Entertaining in a nostalgic way, Tropigala is a throwback to the nightclubs of the '50s and '60s, with gaudy props, an orchestra for dancing, and extravagant stage productions featuring barely clad showgirls. It may be touristy, but it's still great fun. If you're here for the top name Hispanic singers who occasionally turn up, the crowd is *puro* Latino.
Show times: Thurs. 8:30 p.m., Fri.–Sat. 8 p.m., 10 p.m., Sun 8:30 p.m. $$$$

Hot Tip: If you're staying at the Fontainebleau, you don't need to pay to get in to the show, unless there is a special performer.

Live Music Venues

Miami's known for hip-hop and Latin deejays, but there are a few live music nightspots where you can find real live musicians just about every night for jazz, rock, punk, blues, Latin music, and other tunes that defy categorization.

Churchill's Pub

5501 NE 2nd Ave., Little Haiti, 305-757-1807 • Arty Party

The Draw: Live indie rock—punk, hard rock, acoustical—'most every night in Miami's favorite English pub.

The Scene: Appropriately hole-in-the-wall décor: psychedelic parachutes, jukeboxes, pool tables, video games, soccer and rugby games on the telly. A grungy but affable mix of hard-core rock and punk lovers welcome newcomers to their neighborhood bar. *Open daily 11 a.m.–3 a.m.* $

Hot Tip: Try the traditional pub fare: shepherd's pie, scotch eggs, and the popular British restaurant–style curries.

Jazid

1342 Washington Ave., South Beach, 305-673-9372 • Arty Party

The Draw: Live music, every damn night—that's their motto. Downstairs, there's jazz, soul, Motown, and R&B, and Brazilian jazz monthly, played for performance lovers of all stripes: young, old, gay, straight, black, white, Hispanic, Anglo.

The Scene: Small, intimate, and candlelit, Jazid's been hosting local and national performers for seven years. Upstairs, there's a deejay den with overstuffed couches and a pool table.
Open nightly 9 p.m.–5 a.m. $

Hot Tip: Call to get on the guest list by 9 p.m., and you'll get in free from 9 to 11.

Upstairs at the Van Dyke Cafe

846 Lincoln Rd., South Beach, 305-534-3600 • Arty Party

The Draw: In a town where hip-hop rules, this cozy space delivers pure, unadulterated live straight-ahead jazz for aficionados who are dead serious about their music.

The Scene: The second floor of the always-packed Van Dyke Cafe is dark and inviting, with wooden floors and soft lighting—just as a jazz club should be. Regulars are twenty- to fifty-somethings who are there to listen.
Open daily 8 a.m.–2 a.m. Shows Mon.–Thurs. 9 p.m., 10:30 p.m., midnight; Fri.–Sat. 10 p.m., 11:30 p.m., 1 a.m. $

Hot Tip: Order a caipirinha, find a comfy loveseat, and settle back to hear live Brazilian jazz on Sundays.

Best

Meet Markets

Looking for Ms. Right...or just Mr. Right Now? You can always try your luck at various happy hour scenes, but these places are guaranteed to have lots of warm bodies and cold libations. The rest is up to you.

The Globe Cafe and Bar

377 Alhambra Circle, Coral Gables, 305-445-3555 • Outdoors

The Draw: Lawyers, architects, executives, doctors, and other stylish Miami urbanites show how they party after work.

The Scene: Sardine City. So many young professionals jam this handsome bar that cops put up barricades to keep them on the sidewalk and out of the street.
Open Mon.–Thurs. 11:30 a.m.–midnight, Fri.–Sat. 11:30 a.m.–2 a.m.

Hot Tip: Instead of the usual martini, go for a Bellini. They make them just like Harry's Bar in Venice does, with cold prosecco and white peach purée.

Gordon Biersch Brewery Restaurant

1201 Brickell Ave., Downtown Miami, 786-425-1130 • Outdoors

The Draw: Pretty much all of downtown Miami's young urban professionals make a beeline for this bar once the workday's over.

The Scene: Hundreds—maybe thousands—pack the inside restaurant and outdoor patio, brews in hand, getting buzzed. Some of these beers—Blonde Bock, for example—have a 7% alcohol content.
Open Mon.–Thurs. 11:30 a.m.–10:30 p.m., Fri.–Sat. 11:30 a.m.–midnight, Sun. 11 a.m.–midnight.

Hot Tip: If you don't see anyone interesting, you can always watch the beer brewing process in the glass-walled brewery.

Houston's

201 Miracle Mile, Coral Gables, 305-529-0141 • Outdoors

The Draw: A sleek watering hole for youngish professionals, who happily linger outside while waiting for a spot inside.

The Scene: You'll find plenty of urban sophisticates to chat up at the huge, oval bar that runs nearly the length of the restaurant. Fridays are the busiest nights.
Open Sun.–Mon. 11:30 a.m.–10 p.m., Tues.–Thurs. 11 a.m.–11 p.m., Fri.–Sat. 11:30–midnight.

Hot Tip: Powder your nose in the warm cinnamon terrazzo, mahogany, and stainless steel bathrooms—they're gorgeous.

Mojitos

Stroll down Lincoln Road on any Sunday afternoon and you'll see that everyone's drinking mojitos. This refreshing combination of rum, fresh mint, lime, simple syrup, and soda water is good just about anywhere, but the following places have elevated the mojito to the sublime.

OLA Restaurant

5061 Biscayne Blvd., East Side Miami, 305-758-9195 • Clásico

The Draw: This is where celebs Daisy Fuentes, Gloria and Emilio Estefan, and Jon Secada come for chef Douglas Rodriguez' sexed-up Latin-American dishes.

The Scene: Located in the work-in-progress East Side, OLA's two-story building includes a ceviche bar, a communal table, and an expansive main dining area that attracts local politicos, television anchors, and refugees from South Beach.
Open for lunch Mon.–Fri. 11 a.m.–3 p.m.; dinner Mon.–Thurs. 6–11 p.m., Fri.–Sat. 6 p.m.–midnight, Sun. 6–10:30 p.m. $$$

Hot Tip: Lots of mojitos to try here—watermelon, martini, coconut—but go for broke with the $13 mojito, made with Bacardi O, mint, white grapes, and champagne.

Ortanique on the Mile

278 Miracle Mile, Coral Gables, 305-446-7710 • Clásico

The Draw: Hot chef Cindy Hutson's "Cuisine of the Sun" draws heavily on Caribbean and tropical flavors, including some of the best ceviche in town.

The Scene: Cheerful and colorful, with handpainted walls, Caribbean gingerbread designs, and gauzy curtains throughout. Attractive youngish professionals network at the long wooden bar where islandy rum drinks are poured freely.
Open for lunch Mon.–Fri. 11:30 a.m.–2:30 p.m.; dinner Wed.–Thurs. 6–10:30 p.m., Fri.–Sat., 6–11 p.m., Sun. 5:30–9:30 p.m. $$$

Hot Tip: Ortanique's mojitos use Cuban mint leaves and sugarcane swizzle sticks.

Wish

The Hotel, 801 Collins Ave., South Beach, 305-531-2222 • Hot & Cool

The Draw: Experience the dreamy garden setting and ethereal cuisine of this Todd Oldham–designed restaurant and hotel.

The Scene: Lush colors, airbrushed tiles, and vivid stripes and checkered patterns set the stage for the refreshing indoor-outdoor spaces. Couples looking for a romantic hideaway love the enchanting umbrellas, while scenesters get the bigger picture from the new rooftop Spire Bar overlooking the bustling Collins Avenue scene.
Open for lunch daily 11:30 a.m.–3 p.m.; dinner daily 7 p.m.–midnight. Spire Bar open Thurs.–Sun. 7 p.m.–1 a.m. $$$

Hot Tip: Get your buzz on with a frozen mojito—it comes with electronic ice cubes.

Of-the-Moment Dining

Make your reservations immediately for these hot spots—this year's must-dine-at tickets might be next year's lambada. But right now, slip your concierge a 20 to get reservations for these trendy tables.

Barton G

1427 West Ave., South Beach, 305-672-8881 • Hot & Cool

The Draw: Leave it to an extravagant party planner and former set designer to come up with a restaurant with wildly original presentations and a playful delivery, ideal for special occasions.

The Scene: Diaphanous ceiling-to-floor curtains, a wall of fresh orchids, and a tropical garden patio provide a low-key backdrop for eye-popping dishes. Expect to join in on lots of "Happy Birthday" choruses—everyone here seems to be celebrating something. *Open for dinner Sun.–Thurs. 6–10 p.m., Fri.–Sat. 6 p.m.–midnight. $$$*

Hot Tip: By all means, gawk at what everyone else is ordering before you decide. But keep in mind that the Big Top Cotton Candy and Over-the-Top Popcorn Surprise are musts for dessert.

Casa Tua

1700 James Ave., South Beach, 305-673-1010 • Hot & Cool

The Draw: You'll feel like a houseguest (well, a paying one) invited to dinner in an elegant Italian farmhouse hidden behind high hedges.

The Scene: Romantic and elegant, with a cozy brick outdoor terrace and linen-topped tables, and a quietly happening upstairs bar where the well-heeled party crowd, chic Europeans, and Latin-American government and business honchos mingle. *Open for lunch Mon.–Sat. 11 a.m.–3 p.m.; dinner Mon.–Thurs. 6:30–10 p.m., Fri.–Sun. 6:30–11 p.m. $$$$*

Hot Tip: Take the houseguest idea a step further and ask about staying in one of Casa Tua's five suites. You can also sign up for cooking classes on Saturday mornings.

Vita

1906 Collins Ave., South Beach, 305-538-7855 • Hot & Cool

The Draw: Star power—owner Nicola Siervo's also part of hot clubs Mynt and RokBar—and fabulous Northern Italian cuisine, plus a stellar wine list.

The Scene: Noisy but comfortable, with cozy white-and-blue striped cushioned banquettes and a charming candlelit outdoor garden. *Open Sun.–Thurs. 7 p.m.–midnight, Fri.–Sat. 7 p.m.–1 a.m. $$$$*

Hot Tip: After dinner, head to Mynt or RokBar right across the street.

Outdoor Dining

Miami is one of the few places where you can dine outdoors year-round, so make the most of the balmy evenings with a meal under the stars, illuminated by a flickering candle, accompanied by a frangipani-scented breeze, and perhaps some moonglow.

Baleen

Grove Isle Hotel and Spa, Four Grove Isle Dr., Coconut Grove, 305-858-8300 • Outdoors

The Draw: This splendid bayside restaurant on Grove Isle, a private island, is not only one of Miami's dreamiest settings, but delivers a memorable selection of seafood.

The Scene: Casually luxurious, Baleen's décor is tropical with whimsical monkey-motif chandeliers, while outdoors tables are perched on whitewashed terraces framed by white curtains and palms. Fellow diners are starry-eyed lovers and locals treating guests to Miami's twinkling waterfront.
Open daily for breakfast 8–11 a.m.; lunch 11 a.m.–2 p.m.; dinner Sun.–Thurs. 7–10 p.m., Fri.–Sat. 7–11 p.m. $$$

Hot Tip: Try to get one of the romantic waterfront tables for two (it's one of Miami's most popular places to pop the question).

Boater's Grill

Bill Baggs Cape Florida State Park, 1200 S. Crandon Blvd., Key Biscayne, 305-361-0080 • Outdoors

The Draw: First-rate fresh seafood and Cuban cuisine, in casual surroundings overlooking No Name Harbor.

The Scene: This rustic eatery is part of Cape Florida State Park, one of South Florida's most scenic parks because of its historic lighthouse and award-winning beaches. Boaters and in-the-know locals stop here for a superlative and affordable meal and an excellent wine selection.
Open daily 9 a.m.–9 p.m. $

Hot Tip: Come here after sunset, and you won't need to pay the park entrance fee.

Grass Restaurant & Lounge

28 NE 40th St., Design District, 305-573-3355 • Arty Party

The Draw: A hip escape from South Beach craziness where you can kick back under the stars with a watermelon mojito listening to deep house music.

The Scene: This green open-air oasis in the heart of the Design District, with a huge thatched roof and lots of fans and hanging lanterns, attracts artsy types from the neighborhood, low-profile professionals, and an attractive young crowd.
Open Tues.–Thurs. 8 p.m.–3 a.m., Fri. 6 p.m.–4 a.m., Sat. 8 p.m.–4 a.m. $$$

Hot Tip: On weekends, you won't get past the doorman without reservations—or so they claim.

Best Power Lunches

Deals are made and broken over pricey expense-account lunches at these restaurants. Just take a look at the crowd: these suits represent Miami's power brokers, politicians, big-business types, entertainment moguls, and Latin-American government bigwigs.

Capital Grille

444 Brickell Ave., Downtown Miami, 305-374-4500 • Clásico

The Draw: It's located in the heart of the Financial District, so your fellow diners include international business suits, politicians, and even, once in a while, visiting basketball teams.

The Scene: Deals go down daily at this clubby Brickell Avenue spot as players enjoy New York strip steaks and outstanding wines.
Open for lunch Mon.–Fri. 11:30 a.m.–3 p.m.; dinner Mon.–Thurs. 5–10:30 p.m., Fri. 5–11 p.m., Sat. 6–11 p.m., Sun. 5–10 p.m. $$$

Hot Tip: Get buzzed on their signature cocktail, the Stoli Doli, a pineapple-infused vodka martini.

Joe Allen

1787 Purdy Ave., South Beach, 305-531-7007 • Hot & Cool

The Draw: Power brokers and savvy locals hang out at this unpretentious bar and restaurant, where the waitstaff does know their name.

The Scene: Though Joe Allen has locations in New York's theater district, London, and Paris, don't mistake this locale for a chic big-city venue—the decor is low-key and austere, and dress is casual.
Open daily 11:30 a.m.–11:30 p.m.; Sunday brunch 11:30 a.m.–3:30 p.m. $$

Hot Tip: Bartenders make a mean martini here. (Note: that does not mean a saketini, lycheetini, or anything other than gin and vermouth.)

The Palm

Village of Merrick Park, 4425 Ponce de Leon Blvd., Coral Gables, 786-552-7256 • Outdoors

The Draw: This Palm has only been open for a few years, but already the local mayor—among other movers and shakers—holds his weekly power lunch here.

The Scene: Classic and elegant steakhouse, with white tablecloths and caricatures on the walls that are a signature of this family-owned chain based in New York City.
Open for lunch Mon.–Fri. 11:30 a.m.–3 p.m.; dinner Mon.–Fri. 3–10:30 p.m., Sat.–Sun. 5–10:30 p.m. $$$$

Hot Tip: Order the cheesecake—it is delivered daily from the same bakery in the Bronx that has been supplying it for 70 years.

Restaurant/Lounges

The restaurant that transforms into a lounge may not have been invented in Miami, but there is no question that it has been perfected here.

B.E.D.

929 Washington Ave., South Beach, 305-532-9070 • Arty Party

The Draw: The granddaddy of the restaurant/lounges, B.E.D. serves you dinner in bed, followed by the best parties in town. (No need to wear your pj's, but do wear something dressy you can recline in, and shoes that are easy to kick off.)

The Scene: Queen-size beds with long curtains line the space, and meals are brought out on exotic trays. After dinner, when the club starts rocking, you get to jump on the bed. Don't be surprised when you see anyone from Carmen Electra to Britney Spears to Andy Roddick here—this is a popular pit stop for visiting celebs.
Open Mon., Wed.–Sun. 8 p.m.–5 a.m. $$$

Hot Tip: Make reservations for dinner at the 10 p.m. seating for a front-row view of the transformation from dinner to club. Your reservation also gets you first option to stay on the bed for bottle service from midnight to 5 a.m. (Or give up the bed and stay for the party anyway).

Pearl Restaurant & Lounge

Nikki Beach Club, One Ocean Dr., South Beach, 305-538-1111 • Hot & Cool

The Draw: Pearl, the luxury component of Nikki Beach Club, is more than champagne, caviar, and the high rollers hanging out at the bar; the food is top-rate.

The Scene: White fur-lined curtains and warm orange walls cast a warm, otherworldly glow around the champagne bar lined with Beautiful People.
Open Wed.–Thurs. 7 p.m.–1 a.m., Fri.–Sun. 7 p.m.–5 a.m. $$$$

Hot Tip: Choose the outdoor seating for dinner—the terrace has a great ocean view.

Rumi

330 Lincoln Rd., South Beach, 305-672-4353 • Arty Party

The Draw: Named after a 13th-century mystic, Rumi has good food, an intimate vibe, and an impressive list of celebrity clients: Janet Jackson, Seal, and Erykah Badu, among many others.

The Scene: Enormous boxy lights cast a sensuous glow on this warm, narrow supper club, where after dinner, a giant Murphy bed comes down to provide lounging space.
Open Tues.–Sat. 7 p.m.–5 a.m. $$$

Hot Tip: Because it's a favorite with musicians and entertainment industry types, don't be surprised if you happen upon an impromptu live concert.

Best Romantic Dining

Intimate candlelit nooks, fine wine and food, discreetly attentive service all help kindle romance. Sometimes aphrodisiac cuisine works too.

Restaurant St. Michel

Hotel Place St. Michel, 162 Alcazar Ave., Coral Gables, 305-444-1666 • Outdoors

The Draw: Intimate Old World inn and restaurant serving sophisticated New American cuisine in candlelit setting, especially popular with thirty- and forty-somethings looking for traditional appeal.

The Scene: Vine-covered walls frame lace-curtained cafe windows, with dainty sidewalk tables under twinkle-lit red awnings conjuring up a French country inn. Inside, there's a working brass elevator, parquet floors, gorgeous antiques, and a piano bar. *Open for breakfast Mon.–Fri. 7–9:30 a.m.; lunch and dinner Sun.–Thurs. 11 a.m.–10:30 p.m., Fri–Sat. 11 a.m.–11:30 p.m.; Sunday brunch 11 a.m.–2:30 p.m. $$$*

Hot Tip: Two words—chocolate soufflé.

Tamara

The National Hotel, 1677 Collins Ave., South Beach, 305-532-2311 • Arty Party

The Draw: Exquisite French fusion cuisine served in a tiny but elegant restaurant space within the magnificently restored National Hotel.

The Scene: Style-setters and music and film industry types have discovered this plush jewel of a restaurant, named after Art Deco portraitist Tamara de Lempicka, whose mosaic mural decorates the ceiling. Expect to find all the necessary intoxicating elements here: soft candlelight, lavish flower arrangements, and tantalizing cuisine. *Open daily 6 a.m.–midnight. $$$*

Hot Tip: Sit outside overlooking the National's dramatic 205-foot infinity pool.

Tantra Restaurant & Lounge

1445 Pennsylvania Ave., South Beach, 305-672-4765 • Arty Party

The Draw: If your definition of "romantic" means sensual, exotic, or primal, then this too-hot-to-handle restaurant/lounge is for you.

The Scene: It's sensory titillation: fresh-cut grass under your feet, scented candles, groovy deejay music, gauzy décor, and Middle Eastern and Indian–inspired aphrodisiac cuisine. After dinner, your sweet nothings may be drowned out by the music when Tantra turns into one of South Beach's hottest and most seductive nightclubs. *Open nightly for dinner 7 p.m.–1 a.m. Lounge open till 5 a.m. $$$$*

Hot Tip: Ask for the chimney, the most romantic spot in the house. It has a cloistered feel with a curtain you can close if the mood is right.

See-and-Be-Seen Clubs

You'll need to get past the velvet ropes at these terminally haute spots. If you do, maybe you'll see your picture next to Beyoncé's in next month's *Ocean Drive* magazine. Here are a few tips for getting in: Be sure to go early, dress well, and bring an attractive date.

Mynt Lounge

1921 Collins Ave., South Beach, 786-276-6132 • Hot & Cool

The Draw: The club that tops the list for A-listers.

The Scene: Minty green in decor and fragrance (an aromatherapy system fills the air with scent), Mynt doesn't have a VIP area—meaning you might actually get to hang out with Leonardo DiCaprio, Missy Elliott, Enrique Iglesias, or Vin Diesel. *Open Wed.–Sat. 11 p.m.–5 a.m. $$*

Hot Tip: This is one of the toughest velvet ropes to get past. Have your concierge get you on the guest list.

Privé

136 Collins Ave., South Beach, 305-531-5535 • Hot & Cool

The Draw: If über is the new ultra (or is it the other way around?), this VIP lounge is all that, created specifically for celebs, jet-setters, and Miami scenesters.

The Scene: Part of the Opium Garden complex with a separate entrance, Privé is streamlined modern, with illuminated Lucite fixtures, columns, and Helmut Newton photography. Prepare to rub—uh, shoulders—with scary cleavage-wielding young things, hip-hop moguls, rock stars, heiresses, and the usual Page Six names. *Open Thurs.–Sun. 11 p.m.–5 a.m. $$*

Hot Tip: Once you're in, celebrate with a Privé Kiss: Bacardi Coco, Tequila, Bacardi O, sour, and pineapple.

Skybar

The Shore Club, 1901 Collins Ave., South Beach, 305-695-3100 • Hot & Cool

The Draw: Like its LA counterpart, this poolside nightspot attracts some boldface names (does Tara Reid still count?), models, and plenty of eye candy.

The Scene: Intensely colorful with lanterns and Moroccan accents, Skybar is made up of different areas with lots of poolside daybeds and cushions for lounging. On a typical night, you'll see models (male and female), bachelorettes on a night out, and local hotties; visiting celebs like Queen Latifah and Owen Wilson stop here too. *Open Mon.–Wed. 4 p.m.–2 a.m., Thurs.–Sat. 4 p.m.–3 a.m., Sun. 4 p.m.–2 a.m.*

Hot Tip: It isn't easy to get past the door. If you're a hotel guest, you're in. Or have dinner at Nobu or Ago. Otherwise, try coming early.

Best Spas

Make sure you budget time for the hottest must-do component of any vacation. Pampering yourself Miami-style includes all kinds of tropical treatments, plus the all-important before-and-after detox.

The Ritz-Carlton Spa, South Beach

One Lincoln Rd., South Beach, 786-276-4090 • Hot & Cool

The Draw: You'll find all the latest, directly from Paris: the spa features La Maison de Beauté Carita from Paris, using their signature techniques, which take a holistic approach to beauty.

The Scene: With an eye toward practical pampering, treatments at this 16,000-square-foot Temple of Beauty are geared toward dealing with South Beach excesses, through cleansing and massage therapies, Zen waters, pre- and post-sun facials, and a full range of grooming and glamour services.
Open daily 9 a.m.–7 p.m. $$$$

Hot Tip: Go all the way before a night on the town with the five-and-a-half hour Avant SoBe treatment, followed by the three-hour Après SoBe detox therapy.

The Spa at Mandarin Oriental

500 Brickell Key Dr., Downtown Miami, 305-913-8288 • Outdoors

The Draw: Gorgeous three-level holistic spa overlooking the water features a variety of treatments: Ayurvedic, Chinese, Balinese, Thai, and European, in splendid luxury.

The Scene: Lots of Zen serenity in this 15,000-square-foot spa: bamboo, rice paper, glass, and linen are part of the treatment room decor. The top floor houses six specially designed spa suites.
Open daily 9:30 a.m.–9:30 p.m. $$$$

Hot Tip: Top treatments include Ayurvedic Holistic Body treatment and Balinese synchronized massage, for which you are advised to book well in advance on weekends.

The Spa at Ritz-Carlton, Key Biscayne

455 Grand Bay Dr., Key Biscayne, 305-365-4500 • Outdoors

The Draw: Consistently rated one of the top spas in North America, this 20,000-square-foot spa uses tropical botanicals like coconut, mango, gardenia, and bay rum in many of its treatments.

The Scene: Tropical and airy, with West Indies colonial-style decor, the spa makes the most of its island setting, with an oceanfront massage cabana and a variety of classes on the ocean terrace or in the pool.
Open daily 9 a.m.–8 p.m. $$$$

Hot Tip: Pamper those piggies in the private VIP Pedicure Suite featuring a plasma television, signature champagne cocktail, fruit kabobs, aroma neck rest, and 15-minute hand and foot massage.

Steakhouses

There's more to a steakhouse than steak, and these fine independent establishments go out of their way to present their specialty with élan and great attention to detail in a distinctive and stylish setting.

Christy's

3101 Ponce de Leon Blvd., Coral Gables, 305-446-1400 • Outdoors

The Draw: A classic clubby steakhouse that's been serving steaks and signature Caesar salads for more than 20 years.

The Scene: Conservatively elegant, with crisp white table linens, wood paneling and leather chairs, and formally attired waiters, Christy's looks like the power brokers' headquarters it is.
Open for lunch Mon.–Fri. 11:30 a.m.–4 p.m.; dinner seating Sun.–Thurs., till 10 p.m., Fri.–Sat. till 11 p.m. $$$$

Hot Tip: Save room for the baked Alaska for two, finished tableside with a glass of flaming cherry liqueur poured on top.

Prime 112

The Browns Hotel, 112 Ocean Dr., South Beach, 305-532-8112 • Hot & Cool

The Draw: The hottest new entry in the South Beach dining scene is—surprise!—all about the food.

The Scene: This see-and-be-seen restaurant is a contemporary take on the traditional steakhouse, with leather banquettes, warm amber lighting, tabletop lamps on the bar counter, Sinatra playing in the background, and flawless service. In season, it's so difficult to get in, you can count on diners being famous, monied, or well connected.
Open for lunch daily noon–3 p.m.; dinner Sun.–Thurs. 6:30 p.m.–midnight., Fri.–Sat. 6:30 p.m.–1 a.m. $$$$

Hot Tip: Reservations are absolutely essential. If you can't book well in advance of your trip, have the concierge work on this as soon as you check in.

Tuscan Steak

433 Washington Ave., South Beach, 305-534-2233 • Arty Party

The Draw: Feast family-style on luscious steak as though you were in Italy. Features unusual variations on the classics, such as Parmesan-crusted New York sirloin steak.

The Scene: Think Florentine decor, not masculine steakhouse, with Tuscan colors such as burnt sienna and burnt umber, rough-hewn stone walls, and a long granite bar. It's inviting and comfortable, and allows for formal Tuscan service. You'll see tourists and locals, dressed to the nines or casually chic, at this pricey eatery.
Open Sun.–Thurs. 6–11 p.m., Fri.–Sat. 6 p.m.–midnight. $$$

Hot Tip: A must-order: white truffle garlic bread.

Sunday Brunches

One of the reasons Sunday brunch is so darn popular here is timing—after all, you likely rolled in at 6 a.m. after clubbing on a Saturday night, and probably need to fortify yourself. These lavish brunches are sure to get you going all over again.

1200 Restaurant & Courtyard

The Biltmore Hotel, 1200 Anastasia Ave., Coral Gables, 305-445-1926 • Outdoors

The Draw: One of the most sumptuous brunches in town, with nine stations set up around a captivating Mediterranean courtyard while classical musicians entertain you.

The Scene: Follow the fragrance of melting butter wafting through the palms. Nosh in luscious abundance on sushi, caviar, seafood, waffles and eggs made to order, salads, paella, barbecue, bananas Foster, crepes, and sundaes, and wash it down with unlimited champagne. *Open daily 6:30 a.m.–10:30 p.m.; Sunday brunch 10:30 a.m.–2:30 p.m. $$–$$$$*

Hot Tip: If you're a hotel guest, you're guaranteed seating. If not, book the 10:30 a.m. seating to make sure you won't have to wait for a table at this popular brunch spot.

Bleau View

Fontainebleau Hilton Resort, 4441 Collins Ave., Mid-Beach, 305-674-4670 • Clásico

The Draw: Grand hotel dining at its most extravagant in a Tuscan piazza setting. Prepare to feast.

The Scene: White-toqued chefs stand at the ready behind tables heaped with raw bar, caviar, and sushi; carving tables; pasta; salads; and over-the-top desserts. Hotel guests and locals trying to impress out-of-town visitors have no trouble standing in line for this sumptuous buffet.
Open daily 6:30 a.m.–midnight; Sunday brunch 10 a.m.–3 p.m. $$$$

Hot Tip: Sit next to one of the floor-to-ceiling windows to enjoy the best views of the garden and grotto pool.

Metro Kitchen + Bar

Hotel Astor, 956 Washington Ave., South Beach, 305-672-7217 • Arty Party

The Draw: An enticing menu, to be savored in a groovy neo-Deco setting, against a backdrop of glorious gospel sounds.

The Scene: The sleek downtown dining area and lounge in the extremely cool Hotel Astor becomes an intimate Sunday happening with gospel diva Maryell Epps.
Open for lunch Sat. 11:30 a.m.–2:30 p.m.; dinner Mon., Wed., Thurs. 7–11 p.m., Tues. 7 p.m.–12:30 p.m., Fri. 7 p.m.–midnight, Sat. 7 p.m.–12:30 a.m., Sun 7–10:30 p.m.; Sunday brunch noon–3 p.m. $$$

Hot Tip: Arrive early to get a good seat; the show starts at 1 p.m.

Sunday Parties

Somewhere, someone got the idea that a hotel pool should be more than a place for lounging around. So they decided to hire a deejay, invite cool people, set up some cabanas, serve frosty cocktails, and call it a party. Consider yourself invited to these hot weekend events.

DiLido Beach Club

The Ritz-Carlton, South Beach, One Lincoln Rd., South Beach,
786-276-4000 • Hot & Cool

The Draw: Page Six mainstays, E! Channel regulars, notorious jet-setters, and tabloid fodder are among the crowd for the Sunday pool party at the DiLido Beach Club at the Ritz-Carlton, South Beach.

The Scene: White-curtained cabanas and fluffy futons surround the sleek ocean-facing pool, while deejays spin music mixed especially for the Ritz-Carlton.
Open 4 p.m.–sunset. $$

Hot Tip: Snack on goodies like grilled naan bread sandwiches and mezze from this happening oceanfront restaurant in South Beach.

Nikki Beach Club

One Ocean Dr., South Beach, 305-538-1111 • Hot & Cool

The Draw: It all began here: Nikki Beach is South Beach's original beach party club, with tepees and bamboo beds, and the gorgeous bodies to fill them.

The Scene: There's no pool here, so imagine *Beach Blanket Bingo,* only with deejays playing chill music, surgically enhanced thong-clad beautiful women posing on outdoor beds, and champagne flowing endlessly. Okay, forget it, this isn't anything like *Beach Blanket Bingo.*
Open Thurs.–Sun. 11 a.m.–5 a.m. $$

Hot Tip: Weekend brunch is a lavish, all-day affair featuring pastries and pancakes.

Sunday Soiree at the Raleigh

The Raleigh, 1775 Collins Ave., South Beach, 305-534-6300 • Arty Party

The Draw: Hipsters wouldn't miss these beach parties at the glamorous Raleigh—they're hosted by South Beach's hottest promoters.

The Scene: The party revolves around the distinctive scalloped-edge pool with its fat black inner tubes, and the beach area with its retro black-and-white striped lounge chairs. Visiting celebs sometimes show up.
Open Sundays noon–midnight. $

Hot Tip: This is too hip a hotel to order something sweet and sticky. Ask the bartender for a Negroni instead.

Sushi

Miami's love affair with sushi is only logical, with fresh fish so readily available. Top-quality sushi is served at many Thai, Japanese, and pan-Asian restaurants. These places go above and beyond, with presentation, ambience, and panache.

Bond St. Lounge

TownHouse Hotel, 150 20th St., South Beach, 305-398-1806 • Arty Party

The Draw: Cool South Beach outpost of the extremely cool New York sushi joint.

The Scene: Loud and crowded with hipsters who jam the low tables in this lower-level restaurant/lounge in the adorable Townhouse.
Open Mon.–Wed. 6–11 p.m., Thurs.–Sun. 6 p.m.–midnight. $$

Hot Tip: Have their signature Green Tea Martini.

Nobu

The Shore Club, 1901 Collins Ave., South Beach, 305-695-3232 •
Hot & Cool

The Draw: Nobu Matsuhita's Peruvian-infused Japanese cuisine has packed 'em in from the moment this restaurant in the oh-so-trendy Shore Club opened—just ask Madonna, one of the first guests.

The Scene: Noisy, crowded, and oddly nondescript (think generic Japanese) décor for such a pricey place. Servers can help you decipher the menu, or just splurge on the *omakase,* or chef's choice.
Open for dinner Mon.–Thurs. 7 p.m.–midnight., Fri.–Sat. 7 p.m.–1 a.m., Sun. 7–11 p.m. Lounge open Mon.–Thurs. 6 p.m.–midnight., Fri.–Sat. 6 p.m.–1 a.m., Sun. 6–11 p.m. $$$$

Hot Tip: Have a pisco sour and some appetizers in the lounge while you're waiting for your table, preferably no earlier than 10 p.m. when the cool crowd shows up—note that they don't take reservations for fewer than six people.

SushiSamba Dromo

600 Lincoln Rd., South Beach, 305-673-5337 • Hot & Cool

The Draw: South Beach edition of the hot Brazilian-Japanese-Peruvian restaurant that started in Manhattan.

The Scene: Gorgeous orange-and-red Carnaval-inspired decor and a sexy Brazilian beat on a prime Lincoln Road people-watching corner make this a sizzling destination for seeing and being seen.
Open Sun.–Thurs, noon–midnight, Fri.–Sat. noon–2 a.m.; Sunday brunch noon–5 p.m. $$$

Hot Tip: Accompany your sushi with a caipirinha, Brazil's national drink, a potent potion consisting of fresh lime, sugar, and cachaça.

Tapas Bars

Spain's tasty tidbit trend has taken on a life of its own, with tapas menus so extensive that you can make a meal out of them. These tapas spots serve finger food that's worth every pretty penny.

Chispa

225 Altara Ave., Coral Gables, 305-648-2600 • Clásico

The Draw: High-profile chef Robbin Haas' sizzling new contemporary Latin restaurant ignites passion for creative ceviches, flatbreads, and appetizers. Haas has a knack for attracting Miami's good-looking movers and shakers to his scorching bar scene.

The Scene: Look up at the lights: huge "spark" fixtures and goatskin shades cast a warm glow, and more than 100 hanging oil lamps illuminate the 40-foot bar.
Open for lunch Mon.–Sat. 11:30 a.m.–3:30 p.m., Sun. noon–3:30 p.m.; dinner Sun.–Thurs. 5:30–10:30 p.m., Fri.–Sat. 5:30 p.m.–12:30 a.m. $$

Hot Tip: Order the best reason to go loco over Nuevo Latin cuisine: guava cheesecake.

Mundo

Village of Merrick Park, 325 San Lorenzo Ave., Coral Gables,
305-442-6787 • Hot & Cool

The Draw: Mango Gangster Norman Van Aken's latest creation, featuring his inventive New World dishes in an earthier, bite-size form. It's a winner—his passionate fans, plus demanding Gables and Pinecrest residents, can't get enough.

The Scene: Located in Coral Gables' smart new retail and dining center, the Village of Merrick Park, Mundo is warm and friendly, with dark walnut floors, a zinc and copper bar, and an open kitchen that invites diners to watch the action.
Open for lunch Mon.–Sat. noon–3 p.m.; dinner Mon.–Sat. 5:30–10:30 p.m., Sun. 1–9 p.m. $$$

Hot Tip: For dessert, order the ginger crusted tiny fruit cheesecakes, creamy mouthful-size morsels that fittingly wrap up a meal of tapas.

Tapas y Tintos

448 Espanola Way, South Beach, 305-538-8272 • Clásico

The Draw: Part of Espanola Way's arty scene, this quaint little tapas restaurant serves up tantalizing Spanish specialties and an authentically Spanish experience.

The Scene: A Spanish cultural outpost as well as a hangout for South Beach bohemians, showcasing traditional culinary delicacies, good wines, music, poetry, and even soccer on Sundays.
Open Mon.–Thurs. 4 p.m.–midnight, Fri.–Sun. noon–2 a.m. $

Hot Tip: Nightly entertainment includes tango classes, salsa and merengue dancing, jazz sessions, and flamenco shows.

Theme Bars

Disney these ain't. But there's nothing wrong with a little gimmickry to go with your gimlet. Each of these places reveals a different slice of the Miami scene, so give one of these fine institutions a try.

Automatic Slims

1216 Washington Ave., South Beach, 305-695-0795 • Hot & Cool

The Draw: The trailer-trash ambience that runs counter to South Beach's fabulousness.

The Scene: Old neon signs, chicken wire, and a mechanical bull are the props; the crowd is a goofy mix of dressed-up and dressed-down—what they have in common is that they're all ready to get rowdy.
Open daily 8 p.m.–5 a.m.

Hot Tip: Buxom bartenders call and pour the shots here; pull up a seat at the bar and you'll figure it out.

Laundry Bar

721 N. Lincoln Lane, South Beach, 305-531-7700 • Arty Party

The Draw: Their motto: get washed while you get sloshed.

The Scene: State-of-the-art stainless steel front-loading washing machines and different parties every night! It's straight-friendly, and good, uh, clean fun.
Open daily 7 a.m.–5 a.m. Bar open noon–5 a.m.

Hot Tip: Laundry Bar hosts one of the longest happy hours in town—it starts at 4 p.m., and it's still going strong at 9 p.m. Be sure to get there in time to partake of the free hors d'oeuvres.

Playwright Irish Pub & Restaurant

1265 Washington Ave., South Beach, 305-534-0667 • Arty Party

The Draw: Leave behind the pastel Deco glitz and head into this Irish pub, where you'll find a traditional dark wooden bar, photos of Joyce, Guinness and Harp, and an easygoing vibe.

The Scene: Expats order up pints, shoot pool, and catch up on all the soccer matches on television here.
Open daily 11 a.m.–5 a.m.

Hot Tip: In addition to decent pub food, you can get a full Irish breakfast here, something to remember if you're out till dawn and seeking sustenance.

Views of Miami

Miami is rightfully proud of its picturesque skylines and postcard-perfect bay views. Here are some prime vantage points that show off the city's most comely assets.

Big Fish

55 SW Miami Avenue Rd., Downtown Miami, 305-373-1770 • Outdoors

The Draw: Savvy locals, executives, and the occasional tourist know about this hard-to-find seafood restaurant with great views of downtown Miami, the neon rainbow on the Metrorail tracks, and the busy comings and goings on the Miami River.

The Scene: Watching huge freighters navigate the river is always fun; speculating just what's on those boats—now, that's entertainment! (The U.S. Customs building is located just up the river east of the Brickell Avenue Bridge).
Open for lunch Mon.–Fri. noon–3:30 p.m.; dinner Mon.–Fri. 6 p.m.–midnight; Sat.–Sun. noon–1 a.m. $$

Hot Tip: Getting here is tricky: from Brickell, head west on SE 5th St. and go under the bridge, and it's on your right.

Rusty Pelican

3201 Rickenbacker Causeway, Key Biscayne, 305-361-3818 • Outdoors

The Draw: Primo location off the Rickenbacker Causeway takes in the bay, the downtown Miami skyline, and the cruise ships.

The Scene: Yes, it's a tourist trap, where locals bring out-of-town visitors to show off the city. Snag one of the outside tables and enjoy a drink or two.
Open Mon.–Thurs., Sun. 5–11 p.m., Fri.–Sat. 5 p.m.–midnight. Bar open until 1 a.m. daily. $$

Hot Tip: Skip dinner here—the food is mediocre and overpriced.

Smith & Wollensky

One Washington Ave., South Beach, 305-673-2800 • Outdoors

The Draw: Perched on the tip of South Beach, this steakhouse has picture windows revealing breathtaking views of the ocean, downtown Miami, and the parade of cruise ships coming into port.

The Scene: The décor suggests turn-of-the-century New York. But the waterfront vistas are undeniably Miami, attracting transplanted New Yorkers, tourists, and locals.
Open Mon.–Sat. noon–2 a.m., Sun. 11:30 a.m.–2 a.m. $$$

Hot Tip: If you can't do dinner here, at least stop for drinks at the Friday happy hour, one of the hottest in town.

Waterfront Joints for a Cold Beer

A briny breeze off the water, streaky clouds overhead, and an ice-cold bottle of brew evoke the ol' things-just-don't-get-better-than-this cliché. Here's where to live that lovely dream.

Monty's Raw Bar and Outdoors Restaurant

2550 S. Bayshore Dr., Coconut Grove, 305-856-3992 • Outdoors

The Draw: On the bay in Coconut Grove, this popular raw bar and fish restaurant is a couple of cuts above a seafood shack.

The Scene: Mellow live reggae sets the scene midweek through weekends, while the 4–8 p.m. happy hour is one of the Grove's busiest.
Open Mon.–Thurs. 11:30 a.m.–11:30 p.m.; Fri. 11:30 a.m.–1:30 a.m.; Sat.–Sun. noon–1:30 a.m. $$

Hot Tip: If you've got a hankering for stone crabs, order them here—they'll certainly cost less than at Joe's. Fresh claws are in season October–May; the rest of the year, they serve the slightly less succulent Jonah crabs.

Scotty's Landing

3381 Pan American Dr., Coconut Grove, 305-854-2626 • Outdoors

The Draw: Grovey bayside hideaway where the conch fritters are meaty, the music is real, and there isn't a tourist within shouting distance.

The Scene: Old salts, drunken sailors, yuppies, colorful characters, Labrador retrievers...hey, are we in Key West?
Open Mon.–Thurs. 11 a.m.–10 p.m., Fri.–Sat. 11 a.m.–11 p.m., Sun. 11 a.m.–10 p.m. $

Hot Tip: If you get a bucket of six beers, one bottle's free.

Sunday's on the Bay

5420 Crandon Blvd., Key Biscayne, 305-361-6777 • Outdoors

The Draw: Sunday's not only has lovely bayside views, but is the perfect vantage point for Miami's gorgeous sunsets.

The Scene: Boaters come out here to dock and eat, while landlubbers come to check out the boats.
Open Mon.–Thurs. 11 a.m.–10 p.m., Fri.–Sun. 11 a.m.–11:30 p.m. $$

Hot Tip: Live reggae and salsa on Sundays draw big crowds.

Watersports

Throw on your suit—you've got some great grownup toys to take out for a spin. Take your pick: waverunners, sailboards, catamarans, kayaks, banana boats, water bikes, and kiteboards.

El Club

425 Grand Bay Dr., Key Biscayne, 305-361-9191 • Outdoors

The Draw: In the waters surrounding Key Biscayne—among South Florida's calmest and most beautiful—you may spot dolphins, rays, sharks, and other sea creatures.

The Scene: Conveniently located on the beach between the Sonesta Beach Resort and the Ritz-Carlton, El Club rents waverunners, sailboats and catamarans, kayaks, and other watersports equipment. They can also teach you to fly an ultralight.
Open daily 10 a.m.–6 p.m. $$

Hot Tip: Sign up for a two-hour snorkeling trip via inflatable boat to the wreck of the Half Moon for an up-close look at corals, sponges, and other marine life.

Miami Catamarans

Rickenbacker Causeway, Key Biscayne, 305-345-4104 • Outdoors

The Draw: Picture yourself flying across the Biscayne Bay aboard a sleek catamaran.

The Scene: Conditions at so-called Hobie Beach (aka Dog Beach) are ideal for those hankering to try some new watersports for the first time because the winds are steady, the sea is generally calm, and there are no heavy currents.
Open daily 10 a.m.–6 p.m. $$$$

Hot Tip: Seems obvious, but we'll say it anyway: use lots of sunscreen. The subtropical rays are brutal, and a burn will spoil the rest of your trip.

Sailboards Miami

Rickenbacker Causeway, Key Biscayne, 305-361-7245 • Outdoors

The Draw: Join the rest of the jocks windsurfing Biscayne Bay, or learn how to handle its extreme new sibling, the kiteboard.

The Scene: Instructors guarantee that anyone can learn to windsurf in only two hours. If you've got that skill mastered, you can progress to kiteboarding, a combination of wakeboarding and windsurfing.
Open Thurs.–Tues. 10 a.m.–6 p.m. $$–$$$$

Hot Tip: No wind? No problem. Rent a kayak and take a self-guided tour past Vizcaya, celebrity homes, and Key Biscayne.

The Miami Experience

Dive into the Miami of your choice with one of four themed itineraries: *Hot & Cool* (p. 70), *Arty Party* (p. 100), *Outdoors* (p. 130), and *Clásico* (p. 158). Each is designed to heighten your fun-seeking experience by putting you in the right place at the right time—the best restaurants, nightlife, and attractions, and even the best days to go there. While the itineraries, each followed by detailed descriptions of our top choices, reflect our very top picks, a few additional noteworthy options are included in the listings. So, whether you're looking for the steamiest new club and the hottest crowd or the best waterfront seafood shack in town, you'll find it all right here.

Hot & Cool Miami

It's South Beach at its most sizzling. Expect hot bodies, warm beaches, ice-cold martinis. This itinerary will keep you out on the town from morning till night and morning again at the party palaces Britney, Paris, Ashton, and P. Diddy visit when they're in town. These activities are heavy on hedonism, the restaurants are A-list hot spots, and the hotels are among the hottest on the planet. So throw on your dancing shoes, and get ready to soak up one of the steamiest, sexiest scenes in America.

Hot & Cool Miami:
The Itinerary

Our Hotel Choice: The Ritz-Carlton, South Beach, because this gorgeous resort is right on the beach, hosts hot weekend pool parties, and has an over-the-top spa.

Prime Time: Fri.–Sun.

Morning: Order your morning coffee from room service before heading down to the pool to *catch a few rays* and get that healthy going-out glow. Then head over to the **Bass Museum of Art**, a 1930 Art Deco building that houses an outstanding collection of 3,000 works including Renaissance and Baroque paintings by such masters as Botticelli and Rubens. Plan to spend at least two hours here.

Lunch: After sating your cultural appetite, drive over to *Lincoln Road* for an al fresco lunch. Look for the huge orange umbrellas of **SushiSamba Dromo**, whose inventive Brazilian-Japanese-Peruvian–inspired cuisine includes sushi, ceviche, and samba-style churrasco. Or head for the austere pan-Asian **World Resource Cafe** for Japanese and Thai specialties.

Afternoon: It's time for some shopping. Lincoln Road has countless *shops and galleries*, and you could easily spend your entire vacation here. Chain stores like Anthropologie, Williams-Sonoma, and Victoria's Secret have branches here, but the real treasures are the wide array of independent shops. Some highlights are **Base**, an eclectic mixture of home, gift, footwear, and accessory items plus a popular CD lounge; **Dog Bar**, packed with the latest accoutrements for your canine; and **Books & Books**, home to an impressive collection of art, design, fashion, and architecture books and international magazines. Another must-visit is **Brownes & Co.**, a cozy apothecary stocking hard-to-find beauty products. Upstairs, at **Some Like It Hot**, pop in for a margarita pedicure involving zesty limes and salt or a Japanese silk facial.

After all that shopping, it's break time. By that, we mean *mojito time*. Have yours at one of the outdoor tables of the lively **Van Dyke Cafe**—it's the best vantage point for taking in the pedestrian parade. Or go to **Score**, Lincoln Road's most centrally located gay bar.

Dinner: Dress for the paparazzi tonight—you'll be at some of the best see-and-be-seen joints in town. Take your pick of The Shore Club's two high-profile restaurants: **Nobu**, part of chef Nobu Matsuhisa's culinary empire, a noisy, jam-packed space where you're guaranteed A-list sightings; and Robert De Niro's **Ago**, where you might spy a model or B-lister dining on traditional Tuscan cuisine overlooking the hotel's hip Skybar. Or go to **Barton G**, special occasion venue extraordinaire where folks come to be dazzled by *over-the-top creations*, like shrimp cocktail, a colossal martini glass heaped with king crab legs and other crustaceans.

Nighttime: The *hottest lounge action* gets under way at The Shore Club's exclusive **Skybar**, a Moroccan-inspired complex that includes tropical gardens, the glowing Redroom, and poolside bars with gauzy curtains and cushions for lounging. You may even share a daybed with some of the gorgeous crowd. If it's dancing you're after, make tracks to **crobar**, in the old Cameo Theatre on Washington Avenue. When you stagger out in the early hours, follow the crowds to **Pizza Rustica** for a slice of arugula-and-potato pizza to absorb the evening's cocktails. Thus fortified, stop by **Automatic Slims**, a divey-by-design bar that is the perfect antidote to excessive fabulousness. Or try out another late-night option, the new **Onda Lounge**, with its special dance-on-the-seat banquette cushions.

Day 2

Morning: It wouldn't be a true South Beach experience without breakfast at Ocean Drive's **News Cafe**, where you can sip a *morning cappuccino* while catching up on the headlines in the *South China Morning Post*. Golfers will want to tee up minutes away at the freshly revamped **Miami Beach Golf Club**, where celeb jocks rave about the layout and greens. Those of you who want to sweat with the stars indoors should jog over to **Crunch** for your workout. And if you'd rather burn your energy taking your credit card out of your wallet, drive up to the posh **Bal Harbour Shops**, a longtime luxury destination with shops like Giorgio Armani, Prada, and Chanel. Or visit its newest competitor, the open-air **Village of Merrick Park**, Coral Gables' shopping and dining hangout for the chic and well-heeled.

Lunch: For lunch, superstar chef Norman Van Aken's **Mundo** serves *tapas*, New World style. Or head back to the Beach to local favorite **Joe Allen**, a gem of a place in South Beach that serves up homespun dishes like meatloaf and pork tenderloin to local movers and shakers and in-the-know folks like Rosie O'Donnell and Janet Reno.

Afternoon: After lunch, head to the spa to cleanse your system of last night's excesses—and to get ready for tonight's. **The Ritz-Carlton Spa, South Beach** houses the Maison de la Beauté Carita, the only spa outside Paris to offer avant and après clubbing treatments. Or indulge in some *aromatherapy* at **Agua**, the white-on-white rooftop spa at Delano, or the Zen-like spa at the Shore Club. Or head back to your hotel pool to enjoy some time in the sun. Make sure to take advantage of all the spiffy poolside gimmicks on offer, like the tanning butler at the Ritz-Carlton whose sole duty is to spritz you with lotion. Ahh...bring on another glass of Cristal, doll.

Dinner: Squeeze in a disco nap before slipping into your skimpiest dress-up finery this evening. You want to look like you belong when you settle down with a *pre-dinner lycheetini* at the oh-so-cool Philippe Starck–designed **Rose Bar** at Delano. Or head over to **Spire Bar & Lounge** at The Hotel for a Glowing Green Apple Martini, or another of their electronic cocktails illuminated with colorful plastic ice cubes. For dinner, you will have tipped your concierge nicely to secure a reservation at either the unassuming **Prime 112** housed in the historic Browns Hotel—hands-down the hottest steakhouse to catch the attention of fickle South Beach trendsters—or **Casa Tua**, the elegant house-turned-restaurant serving exquisite Italian cuisine to a Euro-chic crowd. Finally, there's the A-list staple, **Blue Door** at Delano, with French culinary delights from Claude Troisgros and company—at the very least, expect to see pro athletes and couples on a big date in this surreal setting.

Nighttime: Continue your night on the town at the *inimitable hot spot* **Opium Garden** (and, if you can manage it, the inner VIP lounge **Privé**). Or you may prefer trying to slip past the velvet ropes into the sleek pale green **Mynt Lounge,** or its hot pink rock neighbor, **RokBar.** For the gay scenester, **Twist** has it all—multiple bars for drinking, dancing, cruising, lounging, whatever your heart desires. Afterward, stop at the 24-hour **11th Street Diner** for a post-club snack or early breakfast or the tiny **La Sandwicherie** for a croissant sandwich.

Morning: If you're up early, get some fresh air by taking a guided tour—on *jetskis*. **Hector's Jetskis** will set you up, just as he has Anna Kournikova and other jet-setters, so you can admire the stunning waterfront mansions and beautiful yachts.

Afterward, it's time to switch gears and prepare to settle in for a delightfully *leisurely meal*, since the fabulous brunches that follow linger well into the afternoon. **Mark's South Beach,** in the stylish Hotel Nash, showcases the highly original fare of award-winning chef Mark Militello, attracting serious foodies to this smart wood-paneled eatery; and **Emeril's Miami Beach** at the Loews serves loud tourists things like Grand Marnier–citrus French toast and smoked gulf shrimp cakes as part of their Cajun haute cuisine.

Afternoon: Slip your pampered self into a swimsuit, because it's time to head to *a beach party*. The longtime favorite is **Nikki Beach Club**, with cozy tepees and bamboo beds for lounging beneath the palms. The hottest new pool party in town is the **DiLido Beach Club** at the Ritz-Carlton, South Beach, which hosts a St. Tropez scene complete with deejays and percussionists. And the Sunday pool party at the Delano always attracts celebs who are in town for the weekend.

Dinner: Dress for romance this evening, as these are among South Beach's dreamiest restaurants. **Wish** in The Hotel features a candlelit patio dining area under huge umbrellas—an enchanting backdrop for classic American–haute Asian cuisine with inventive surprises. At **Pearl Restaurant & Lounge**, the very elegant *restaurant/champagne lounge* of Nikki Beach Club, you will dine on sophisticated world fare. Be sure to save room for Cristal and caviar at the mod orange-and-pink glowing lounge. Or find **Nemo**, a longtime favorite, with inventive American dishes, all presented in dramatically textured spaces—artsy tiles, cool lighting—populated by an eclectic crowd.

Nighttime: Head to **Mansion**, all plush banquettes, chandeliers, and sweeping staircases, for *an evening of dancing*. You'll find all varieties of dance music at **Amika Loft Lounge & Discotheque**. Or hit the bubbly till sunrise at romantic **Flute Champagne Lounge,** and walk barefoot along the beach back to your hotel.

Hot & Cool Miami:
The Hotels

Delano

1685 Collins Ave. (17th St.), South Beach, 305-672-2000 /
800-606-6090
www.morganshotelgroup.com

This is the hotel that dazzled the South Beach hotel scene when it opened
in 1995 with its surreal Philippe Starck–designed indoor-outdoor lobby;
pristine (though small) all-white guest rooms; cool pool; and trendy bar and
restaurant areas. Since then, a number of other drop-dead-gorgeous spaces
targeting celebs and scenesters have opened in South Beach, but folks never
get tired of talking about this 16-story 1947 beachfront property, or gawking
about the lobby in search of Madonna or Queen Latifah. The 208 guest
rooms, lofts, suites, and duplex poolside bungalows have white wide-plank
wood floors with cork underneath for insulation, oversize pillows, and tropi-
cal-weight cotton duvets. In the suites and poolside bungalows, new luxurious bathrooms have monolithic marble bathtubs, multi-head showers, and
bath amenities from their signature bathhouse. All rooms have color televisions with VCR and cable; an in-house video library; fresh flowers; newspapers delivered to your door; and a 24-hour concierge. For a prime view of the
Atlantic, ask for an oceanfront (not oceanview) room. In the lobby you'll find
the popular Rose Bar (see p. 93), the Blue Door restaurant (see p. 81), and
Blue Sea, serving caviar, oysters, and sushi. You may want to indulge in a
spa treatment at Agua (see p. 95), located on the rooftop. Note that the
Sunday pool parties are a hot ticket. $$$$

Four Seasons Hotel Miami

1435 Brickell Ave. (SE 14th St.), Downtown Miami, 305-358-3535 /
800-332-3442
www.fourseasons.com
Best Hotel Pools

The Four Seasons chain barged into the Miami luxury hotel market in a big,
big way: its sleek 70-story building is the tallest in the city, while a 2,000-
pound Botero bronze nude clearly dominates the expansive lobby. The sculpture is just part of the hotel's impressive art collection, which focuses strong-
ly on Latin-American artists who work in Miami. The Four Seasons' 221
rooms include 39 suites with bay and city views; DVD/CD players; luxurious
bathrooms with L'Occitane toiletries; and, in most rooms, cushioned window

seats for taking in the views. Working out is a glorious experience: the dramatic Sports Club/LA is 40,000 square feet of state-of-the-art fitness facilities, flooded with light from floor-to-ceiling windows. The hotel's seventh-floor Bahia Terrace is a remarkable two-acre space with lush landscaping and three large swimming pools—one a shallow pool studded with huge royal palms, meant for shady sunbathing. Also on the terrace is the Latin-themed Bahia Bar, a loungey watering hole next to a 22-foot water wall, that's turned out to be such a draw that scenesters drive over from South Beach to check it out. Inside, an elegant martini bar caters to the quieter crowd, and the restaurant Acqua serves Northern Italian cuisine. $$$$

The Hotel

801 Collins Ave. (8th St.), South Beach, 305-531-2222 / 877-843-4683
www.thehotelofsouthbeach.com

The Hotel Formerly Known as The Tiffany (a trademark infringement suit by the jewelry retailer is responsible for the name foolishness) really is one of South Beach's precious gems. Fashion designer Todd Oldham designed the interior, and what a treat! Hand-airbrushed tiles, mosaic door pulls, dyed velveteen sofas, crush-dyed cabana curtains, woven throw pillows, even the casual shirts worn by the staff reflect Oldham's lush color sense. There's no art, just framed mirrors (you're the art). The four-story boutique hotel has four suites and 48 deluxe rooms that are small but sunny, each with bathroom amenities by The White Company of London; cable television, VCR, CD, and video library; and wireless Internet. Ask for room 224 or 324 overlooking the pretty restaurant courtyard. The rooftop deck has an emerald-shaped pool, bar, and cabanas overlooking the ocean; a fitness facility; and the Spire Bar & Lounge (see p. 93) on the rooftop underneath the Tiffany sign. Downstairs you'll find Wish (see p. 88), one of South Beach's top restaurants; and an adorable gift shop where you can buy original Todd Oldham designs, including tie-dyed robes, woven satin ribbon cushions, and earthenware plates from Wish. $$$

Hotel Victor

1144 Ocean Dr. (11th St.), South Beach, 305-428-1234
www.hotelvictorsouthbeach.com

If minimalist design isn't your thing, head to Ocean Drive's newest entry: the extravagant Hotel Victor next door to Casa Casuarina, better known as the former Versace mansion, now a private party palace. Designed by Parisian Jacques Garcia and operated by Hyatt, this luxurious 91-room boutique property—a redo of the 1937 Art Deco hotel—is aiming for chic opulence and glamour. Each room has panoramic views of the ocean or South Beach;

custom-designed furniture; 350-thread-count Egyptian cotton linens; infinity soaking tubs; wide-screen plasma and LCD panel TVs; DVD and CD players; and surround sound. The 6,000-square-foot Spa V and Fitness Club has not only first-rate fitness equipment, but a Turkish hammam with a unisex steam room, rainwater showers, heated marble slabs at massaging stations, and seven treatment rooms. Outside, a raised, rimless pool overlooks the Atlantic, and includes a bar and outdoors VIP lounge. Inside, you'll find their signature restaurant VIX with culturally inspired cuisine, and a sleek oval-shaped bar overlooking the garden terrace. VUE is the informal dining spot, featuring ceviche and satays, while deejays and vibe managers make sure everything is groovy. As if all this were not enough: the V Bar and Lounge features a musical live jellyfish tank. $$$

Mandarin Oriental, Miami

500 Brickell Key (Brickell Ave.), Downtown Miami, 305-913-8288 / 866-888-6780
www.mandarinoriental.com

When this contemporary 327-room luxury waterfront hotel opened in 2000, it did more than add another stylish silhouette to the skyline. It dramatically kicked up the level of service in Greater Miami, where customer service even at top hotels could be tactfully described as wretched. Enter the Mandarin Oriental, the hotel of choice for business travelers, international visitors, and celebrities like Luciano Pavarotti, Michael Jackson, and Michael Jordan, where the staff considers it their job to delight you. Located on Brickell Key, an island just off Downtown's Financial District, the Mandarin Oriental's sweeping curved profile and Asia-meets–South Florida décor fit perfectly, providing guests spectacular views of the downtown skyline and bay. There's beauty in the details: leather-covered staircase railings, the sleek aluminum that keeps champagne cold at the bar, the silk cushions offered for added comfort at the lobby bar sofas. The hotel is not on the beach, so they hauled in 260 tons of sand and built their own beach, adding hammocks and exotic canopy beds for outdoor massages. Other draws include their tri-level Spa at Mandarin Oriental (see p. 156), world-class restaurant Azul (where hotel guests get priority reservations, see p. 139), and outstanding waterfront Cafe Sambal (see p. 141). There's not a bad room here—all guestrooms have water views and niceties like Bose Wave stereos and Molton Brown ameni-ties—but the deluxe rooms on the sixth floor have private verandas. $$$$

The Ritz-Carlton, South Beach

One Lincoln Rd. (Collins Ave.), South Beach, 786-276-4000
www.ritzcarlton.com

When the Ritz-Carlton announced it was restoring the Morris Lapidus–
designed DiLido Hotel, folks got curious. The Ritz-Carlton, doing over a
1953 Art Moderne/Miami Modern property? And when it was done, the transformation surprised even the skeptics. It's a stunner. The lobby includes
unusual design materials never used before in a Ritz-Carlton, like the original black terrazzo floors; a grand staircase; and a dramatic curved wall of
polished cherrywood with 72 polished domed wall sconces. A multimillion-
dollar art collection on loan to the hotel includes an original Joan Miró etch-
ing in the lower lobby. The décor of the 375 rooms, inspired by the state-
rooms on a luxury liner, features dark cherry furniture and nautical colors.
The elevated pool, which overlooks the Atlantic, is flanked by 72 poolside
and oceanview lanai rooms and suites, spacious cabanas, including VIP
cabanas outfitted with four-poster beds and plush pillows. Another surprise:
the beachside DiLido Beach Club (see p. 90) has become the hot gathering
place for celebs and local socialites on weekends. Check out the 16,000-
square-foot spa; signature restaurant; mezzanine lounge; and frivolities like
synchronized swim shows, tanning butlers, and custom-spun lounge music.
Request an oceanview room—they all have balconies. $$$$

The Shore Club

1901 Collins Ave. (19th St.), South Beach, 305-695-3100 /
800-606-6090
www.shoreclub.com

Like its companion property Delano, the Shore Club aims for shock and awe
in design. With its highly polished terrazzo floors, white sheer curtains, and
white-jacketed hotel staff, you'll feel like you're checking into an asylum for
the terminally hip. Behind the lobby, vivid Matisse-inspired colors frame
tropical gardens with hundreds of potted plants and two elevated infinity-
edge pools. Tufted beds and pillows adorn eclectic seating areas, all lighted
with Moroccan lanterns hung from trees. There are 325 rooms, 73 suites, an
oceanfront beach house, and a triplex penthouse with rooftop sundeck and
private pool. All rooms have Bose CD players-radios, 400-thread-count
Egyptian linens, Ric Pipino bath products, and newspapers delivered to your
door. If you're looking for quiet, ask for a room on one of the upper floors
away from the pool bar. The rooftop spa attends to your beauty treatment
needs. Two of South Beach's hottest restaurants, Nobu (see p. 85) and Ago
(see p. 80), are here, as is the trendy Skybar (see p. 93). If all that were not
enough, there's a co-ed Scoop boutique and Me & Ro jewelry store. $$$$

The Tides

1220 Ocean Dr. (12th St.), South Beach, 305-604-5070 / 866-438-4337
www.thetideshotel.com

The self-dubbed diva of Ocean Drive, The Tides has a cool aura that's evident in every fabulous detail. The lobby's casual white linen slipcovered sofas and chairs and polished chrome details have a Gatsby-ish elegance, and the guests at the bar exude that same low-key, chic vibe (well, not counting celeb clients J-Lo or Ben Affleck). Despite its location on frenetic Ocean Drive, this 1936 L. Murray Dixon–designed hotel is a quiet oasis, cleverly laid out so that each of its 45 rooms and suites has an ocean view. Among the most spectacular are the Terra Nova penthouse, which has 360-degree views of the city and an outdoor terrace with a Jacuzzi. The creamy white rooms are warm rather than stark, and come with an unusual amenity: each room is equipped with a Bushnell telescope. White 500-count Frette linens cover pillow-top beds, and there's a chalkboard for messages—perhaps to let the maid know she needs to clean that fogged-up telescope lens. The pool has a fountain that doubles as a shower, and a large canvas awning over one end so that guests can avoid the blazing sun while taking a dip. The outstanding restaurant, 1220 at The Tides (see p. 80), takes up part of the lobby and the terrace steps out front and serves excellent international bistro cuisine. $$$$

Hot & Cool Miami:
The Restaurants

11th Street Diner
1065 Washington Ave. (11th St.), South Beach, 305-534-6373
www.sobediner.com
Best Late-Night Eats

When you're hankering for meat loaf, pancakes, or patty melts, follow the crowds day and night to this sleek stainless steel diner—its booths and swivel stools are just as jammed early in the morning with post-club people as they are in the afternoon for the lunch bunch. You can order a cherry coke or a Jack and coke, and from the terrace watch the slightly seedy parade of humanity on Washington Avenue. If this diner looks familiar, it may be because it was featured on MTV's *The Real World*. *Open daily 24 hours.* $

1220 at The Tides
The Tides, 1220 Ocean Dr. (12th St.), South Beach, 305-604-5070

You may even neglect the fabulous people-watching in the overwhelmingly elegant 1220 at The Tides, just off the lobby and on the terrace steps of this Ocean Drive boutique hotel, because the food is so distracting. New executive chef Paul Blouin has introduced an international bistro menu of uncomplicated classics: French onion soup, Maine lobster bisque, Maryland crab cakes, mixed grill, and veal Oscar. 1220 at The Tides has an impressive selection of international wines and specialty beverages, including single malt scotches and grappa, and a cigar menu. *Open daily for breakfast 7–11 a.m.; lunch 11 a.m.–6 p.m.; dinner 6 p.m.–midnight.* $$$

Ago
The Shore Club, 1901 Collins Ave. (19th St.), South Beach, 305-695-3226

This outpost of Robert De Niro and Agostino Sciandri's famed Hollywood restaurant overlooks the celeb-infested pools and garden of the Shore Club, providing an only slightly quieter setting than the Shore Club's other hangout, Nobu. Ago flies well under the celeb radar—the best you can hope for is a sighting of someone booted off *The Apprentice*. Ask for a table on the lovely outdoor patio. Order traditional Northern Italian pasta, pizzas, and seafood. A wood-burning oven adds smoky flavor to fish and meats. Service is polished and gracious. *Open for breakfast Mon.–Thurs. 7–11:30 a.m., Fri.–Sun. 7 a.m.–1 p.m.; lunch Mon.–Sun. 11:30 a.m.–4 p.m.; dinner Mon.–Thurs. 7 p.m.–midnight, Fri.–Sat. 7 p.m.–1 a.m., Sun. 7 p.m.–midnight.* $$$

Barton G

1427 West Ave. (14th Terr.), South Beach, 305-672-8881
www.bartong.com
Best Of-the-Moment Dining

Don't be fooled by the sedate, tasteful setting of event planner extraordinaire
Barton G. Weiss' restaurant. This is special-occasion dining at its most spectacular. Start with a Sabrinatini, named after one of his pet chimpanzees,
then progress to other acts in this fine culinary circus: popcorn shrimp atop
real popcorn spilling out of a red-and-white paper box; watermelon-colored
sashimi snow cones; a foie gras short stack, served with savory pancakes and
syrup. The swordfish épée is breathtaking—visualize chunks of fish speared
on a four-foot gentleman's sword. Even homely fried chicken (well, Texan
pecan and honey fried chicken) is piled imaginatively in a ceramic rooster.
Over the top? Absolutely, and the well-trained staff is proud of it. *Open for
dinner Sun.–Thurs. 6–10 p.m., Fri.–Sat. 6 p.m.–midnight.* $$$

Blue Door

Delano, 1685 Collins Ave. (17th St.), South Beach, 305-674-6400
Best Always-Trendy Tables

Try this recipe for a magical night out: savoring the fresh cool cuisine from
celebrated chef Claude Troisgros in a surreal setting of white sheer and vel-
vet drapery, and curvy white leather banquettes and sofas. This is the place
to come when you want to add a playful twist to a special occasion. Choose
from inspired dishes like marinated loin of venison with juniper berry and
peppercorn red wine sauce, or so-called sexy sides like potato foam with
black truffle. Desserts are splendid. Save room for Crepe Passion, a passion
fruit pancake crepe soufflé. In fact, you'll be so busy savoring your
Chocopistachio, a melted bittersweet chocolate cake with caramelized pista-
chio ice cream, that if you're not paying attention you'll totally miss seeing
Tobey Maguire or Naomi Campbell walk by. *Open for breakfast daily 7–11:30
a.m.; Sunday brunch 10:30 a.m.–2:30 p.m.; lunch 11:30 a.m.–4 p.m.;
dinner 7–11:30 p.m.* $$$$

Casa Tua

1700 James Ave. (17th St.), South Beach, 305-673-1010
www.casatualifestyle.com
Best Of-the-Moment Dining

They don't advertise. There's no sign in front of the 1925 Mediterranean
Revival house concealed behind a tall hedge. In fact, the only clue that
you've found one of South Beach's hottest restaurants is the limo in front
dropping off some very young, very beautiful, and very well-dressed people.

Casa Tua claims to be more home than restaurant or hotel (there are five suites here, too)—witness the elegant bowls of roses, original artwork, family photos, and cozy sofas. The haute Italian menu changes often, but usually includes specialties like carpaccio, veal tenderloin, and exquisite pastas. Service is gracious and attentive. There's no better place to splurge on a special occasion, but do book as far in advance as possible. *Open for lunch Mon.–Sat. 11 a.m.–3 p.m.; dinner Mon.–Thurs. 6:30–10 p.m., Fri.–Sun. 6:30–11 p.m.* $$$$

Emeril's Miami Beach

Loews Miami Beach Hotel, 1601 Collins Ave. (16th St.), South Beach, 305-695-4550
www.emerils.com

Designer Chef Emeril Lagasse's ninth restaurant—in the historic St. Moritz building that's part of the Loews Miami Beach Hotel—looks both frivolous and serious, and maybe that's the idea. Both the food and décor let you know you're here to experience fine dining with a playful attitude. Loyal fans and tourists pack the main dining room, a huge banquette tricked out in colorful stripes, while nearby stand two vault-size wine towers with beaded chandeliers emerging from the center. Likewise, the new New Orleans cuisine combines classics like Creole bouillabaisse and andouille-crusted redfish with the inspired whimsy of Cuban coffee-chocolate flan and sumptuous strawberry-guava cheesecake. Sunday brunches feature fun old-school Southern libations like brandy milk punch, mint juleps, and Sazerac, to a backdrop of live jazz. *Open for lunch Mon.–Sat. 11 a.m.–2:30 p.m.; dinner Sun.–Thurs. 5:30–10:30 p.m., Fri.–Sat. 5:30–11 p.m.; Sunday brunch 11 a.m.–2:30 p.m.* $$$$

A Fish Called Avalon

700 Ocean Dr. (7th St.), South Beach, 305-532-1727

It's not clear why all the touristy Ocean Drive restaurants tout their fare by displaying plastic-wrapped dishes of seafood under the hot sun. But at A Fish Called Avalon, a longtime favorite with both tourists and locals, you can rest assured that the seafood is fresh and cleverly prepared. Try their jerk-grilled grouper with roasted tomato grits and mango relish or their bang-bang shrimp with cucumber slaw and orange mint sauce. If you don't want to watch sunburned tourists from the terrace, try the intimate dining space inside. *Open nightly 6–11 p.m.* $$

Joe Allen

1787 Purdy Ave. (18th St.), South Beach, 305-531-7007
www.joeallenrestaurant.com
Best Power Lunches

One of Miami's best-kept secrets is Joe Allen, out of the mainstream South Beach parade near the residential west side of South Beach. Despite other locations in sophisticated world cities like New York, London, and Paris, Joe Allen maintains a totally unpretentious atmosphere and is a favorite with networking business types and clued-in visitors. The huge, wide-ranging menu is loaded with down-home favorites like meatloaf with mashed potatoes and gravy, sautéed calf's liver, pizzas, and warm date pudding with hot toffee sauce. Reservations, taken up to a week in advance, are a must. *Open daily 11:30 a.m.–11:30 p.m.; Sunday brunch 11:30 a.m.–3:30 p.m.* $$

Joia Restaurant Bar/Upper Lounge

150 Ocean Dr. (1st St.), South Beach, 305-674-8871
www.joiamiami.com

One of the pioneer restaurant/lounges in South Beach when it opened in the late 1990s, Joia was once co-owned by Madonna's bud Ingrid Casares, so celeb sightings here were a dime a dozen. Today Joia has mellowed into a chic neighborhood spot with a gorgeous outdoor terrace. Newly face-lifted, the restaurant feels like a luxurious home, with sand-colored floors and plush red banquettes, a canopied terrace, and silver chandeliers. The world cuisine features influences from the South Pacific, Latin America, and the Mediterranean, and there's a ceviche and tempura bar. Expect a friendly, sophisticated crowd. *Open Tues.–Wed. 7–11:30 p.m., Thurs.–Sun. 7 p.m.– 1 a.m.; Upper Lounge open weekends 11 p.m.–5 a.m.* $$$

La Sandwicherie

229 14th St. (Washington St.), South Beach, 305-532-8934
www.lasandwicherie.com

This little outdoor lunch counter has provided countless clubbers with healthy late-night snacks since 1988. Open from early morning till 5 a.m., La Sandwicherie serves tasty fruit shakes, veggie juice combos, French bread and croissant sandwiches, coffee, teas, and ice cream. It's a fine place for a snack break after dancing at 4 a.m., but in case you happen to be passing by during the hot daytime, you'll be happy to know that mist fans blow cool relief, while the fruit smoothies are a bright and tropical pick-me-up. *Open daily 9 a.m.–5 a.m.* $

Mark's South Beach

Hotel Nash, 1120 Collins Ave. (11th St.), South Beach, 305-604-9050
www.chefmark.com

Award-winning chef Mark Militello—another member of Miami's "Mango
Gang" of chefs developing New World cuisine—shows off his culinary inno-
vations at this chic restaurant in the lobby of the historical Hotel Nash. (His
other restaurants are located in Boca Raton, Fort Lauderdale, and West Palm
Beach). You'll join his followers and a chic crowd enjoying offbeat seafood
dishes like cracked conch, ceviche style, with vanilla and rum; orange car-
damom glazed salmon; and Pacific shrimp with saffron fennel risotto. The
choices are daunting—the daily chef's tasting menu might be the answer.
*Open for breakfast for hotel guests only Wed.–Sun. 7–11 a.m.; lunch noon–
3 p.m.; dinner Wed.–Thurs. 7–11 p.m., Fri.–Sat. 7 p.m.–midnight.;
Sunday brunch noon–3 p.m.* $$$$

Mundo

Village of Merrick Park, 325 San Lorenzo Ave. (Ponce de Leon Blvd.),
Coral Gables, 305-442-6787
www.mundorestaurant.com
Best Tapas Bars

This new tapas restaurant from New World cuisine master Norman Van Aken
is more than just a light (and much less pricey) version of Norman's, his outstanding serious foodie haunt. Casual and convivial, Mundo starts with flavors from Latin America, the Caribbean, Spain, and Asia, and transforms
them into fabulous little dishes: baby back barbecued ribs with sugarcane
chutney, or duck, caramelized onion, and Chinese sausage wood-oven pizza.
Even humble corn tortillas with guacamole are elevated to earthy elegance,
served tiny and light as blintzes with pork and piquant avocado salsa. The
idea here is to order and share dish after dish, accompanied by choices from
the extensive wine list, until you've made a most satisfying culinary journey
around the world. *Open for lunch Mon.–Sat. noon–3 p.m.; dinner Mon.–Sat.
5:30–10:30 p.m., Sun. 1–9 p.m.* $$$

Nemo

100 Collins Ave. (1st St.), South Beach, 305-532-4550
www.nemorestaurant.com

Warm and appealingly low-key, Nemo has been charming diners with its
fresh, inventive cuisine since 1995. Located on the slightly less frenzied
south end of South Beach, Nemo has several lovely dining areas: an interac-
tive food bar, drink bar and lounge, dining room, loggia, terrace, garden, and
courtyard, some decorated with jeweled lamps and rich textures. It's very

convivial, all the better to complement the food, described as creative New American. Grilled local black grouper comes with shaved hearts of palm, avocado, blue crab, and chimichurri; the Indian spiced pork chop is accompanied by sticky black rice, caramelized onion, and papaya salsa. Their desserts, made in-house, are unforgettable, like the Meyer lemon crème brûlée with south Philly lemon ice and wild huckleberry tart. *Open for lunch Mon.–Fri. noon–3 p.m.; brunch Sun. 11 a.m.–3 p.m.; dinner Mon.–Sat. 7 p.m.–midnight, Sun. 6–11 p.m.* $$$

News Cafe

800 Ocean Dr. (8th St.), South Beach, 305-538-6397
www.newscafe.com

What started in 1988 as a charming sidewalk cafe and hangout for the international set has ended up an enduring symbol for South Beach's transformation into a see-and-be-seen destination. Though the model scene isn't what it used to be, News Cafe remains the place on the Beach to enjoy a leisurely breakfast and the daily paper (with numerous national and international choices, this is a first-class newspaper shop), and discreetly check out who's hiding behind that *La Gazzetta dello Sport*. The food is okay—straightforward breakfast fare, sandwiches, salads, pasta, Mediterranean appetizers—but your main reason for being here is to see the parade of people passing by on Ocean Drive. *Open daily 24 hours.* $

Nobu

The Shore Club, 1901 Collins Ave. (19th St.), South Beach, 305-695-3232
www.noburestaurants.com
Best Sushi

One of the world's finest sushi chefs, Nobu Matsuhisa joined actor Robert De Niro to open this South Beach hot spot at the fab Shore Club. Visiting celebs like Madonna and Michael Jordan, along with well-heeled sushi lovers, show up for Nobu's cutting-edge Japanese cuisine with Peruvian influences, like the spicy yellowtail and jalapeño rolls and new-style sashimi. Don't expect to savor your sea urchin tempura in quiet contemplation; you'll barely be able to make your order heard. Never mind. There will be plenty of time to talk about your splendid meal, and all the A-listers at the next table, the following morning. *Open for dinner Mon.–Thurs. 7 p.m.–midnight, Fri.–Sat. 7 p.m.– 1 a.m., Sun. 7–11 p.m. Lounge open Mon.–Thurs. 6 p.m.–midnight, Fri.–Sat. 6 p.m.–1 a.m., Sun. 6–11 p.m.* $$$$

Pearl Restaurant & Lounge

Nikki Beach Club, One Ocean Dr. (1st St.), South Beach, 305-538-1111
www.pearlsouthbeach.com
Best Restaurant/Lounges

The '60s orange and white-fur decor is a little kooky, but the food is dead serious at this trendy restaurant/lounge in the Nikki Beach complex. Savory dishes like Moroccan spiced cuttlefish calamari or Jamison Farm lamb two ways reveal a great culinary sophistication. After dinner, Pearl has a busy lounge scene where the Cristal flows freely. *Open Wed.–Thurs. 7 p.m.–1 a.m., Fri.–Sun. 7 p.m.–5 a.m.* $$$$

Pizza Rustica

863 Washington Ave. (8th St.), South Beach, 305-674-8244

Fans rave about the plate-size crispy pizza squares laden with rosemary-scented potatoes or spinach and blue cheese that are served up at this take-out stand, but what wouldn't taste good at four in the morning after you've been slamming back Grey Goose–and-pineapple cocktails all night? Still, Pizza Rustica does turn out excellent, massive country-style slices for under five bucks, with toppings like four cheese, and bufala mozzarella with Roma tomatoes and fresh basil. There are two Washington Avenue locations, at 9th and at Espanola Way, and a third on Lincoln Road. Don't be surprised if you have to wait in line for your slice at 4 a.m. *Open daily 11 a.m.–6 a.m.* $

Prime 112

The Browns Hotel, 112 Ocean Dr. (1st St.), South Beach, 305-532-8112
www.prime112.com
Best Steakhouses

Located in the newly restored eight-suite 1915 Browns Hotel, this modern steakhouse is far from the usual clubby, masculine den you'd expect—it's sleek yet warm, with homey touches of old wood and tile. But it's the food that everyone talks about: dry-aged prime steaks, potato dishes like house-made tater tots, and desserts like Granny Smith apple pie with candied walnut streusel and caramel sauce. Even the bar snacks are strips of tasty bacon rather than the usual peanuts. Prime 112's philosophy is simple: use the best ingredients, such as butter (from Vermont) and bacon (Applewood Smoked). Other menu items include Kobe beef hot dogs ($20) and hamburgers ($30), and warm chocolate chunk cookies with a glass of milk. Try for a table on the tiny terrace, but be forewarned: this is currently the hottest restaurant in town for visiting celebs and fashion and music industry bigwigs—so book well in advance. *Open for lunch daily noon–3 p.m.; dinner Sun.–Thurs. 6:30 p.m.–midnight, Fri.–Sat. 6:30 p.m.–1 a.m.* $$$$

SushiSamba Dromo

600 Lincoln Rd. (Pennsylvania Ave.), South Beach, 305-673-5337
www.sushisamba.com
Best Sushi

Far from a typical sushi bar, SushiSamba Dromo is the Miami branch of the
hip New York City restaurant group, attracting foodies, professionals, and
models to its flamboyant surroundings. They combine bold Brazilian flavors
with Japanese technique and Peruvian culinary tradition, coming up with
recipes like sashimi ceviche and inventive samba rolls. The fusion works
wonderfully—you can order fresh, well-prepared sushi and tempura and mix
it up with traditional Brazilian barbecue and Peruvian street food. Wash it
down with a Pisco sour or an exotic shochu martini, and it's sayonara, amigo.
*Open Sun.–Thurs. noon–midnight, Fri.–Sat. noon–2 a.m.; Sunday brunch
noon–5 p.m.* $$$

Talula

210 23rd St. (Collins Ave.), South Beach, 305-672-0778

High-profile culinary couple Andrea Curto-Randazzo and Frank Randazzo
bring their creative American cuisine to this rustic dining room with garden
patio. They've won all kinds of awards (she was named one of *Food & Wine*
magazine's best cooks, among many other accolades), but their restaurant is
a little off the beaten path, so it's more populated with local fans and the
occasional tourist. Crispy-skin yellowtail snapper, soft-shell crabs, grilled foie
gras with caramelized figs, and marinated grilled stuffed pork chop are
standouts. Not to be missed: the chocolate bread pudding. *Open for lunch
Tues.–Fri. noon–2:30 p.m.; dinner Tues.–Thurs. 6:30–11 p.m., Fri.–Sat.
6:30–11:30 p.m., Sun. 6–10 p.m.* $$

Van Dyke Cafe

846 Lincoln Rd. (Jefferson Ave.), South Beach, 305-534-3600

Brought to you by the same folks who started News Cafe—Ocean Drive's
people-watching headquarters—the Van Dyke's sidewalk cafe is a Lincoln
Road mainstay, housed in the imposing 1924 former Van Dyke Hotel. The
eclectic cafe fare is decent, but you're not here for culinary rapture. Pull up
a seat under one of the big red umbrellas, order a mojito, and enjoy the
pedestrian parade. *Open daily 8 a.m.–2 a.m.* $

Vita

1906 Collins Ave. (19th St.), South Beach, 305-538-7855
Best Of-the-Moment Dining

Club impresario Nicola Siervo has his hand in a lot of successful South
Beach ventures—Mynt, Rok Bar, Metro Kitchen + Bar—and this latest effort
is a winner too. Models and scenesters fill the comfy banquettes and candlelit outdoor garden for socializing and filling their pretty faces with this
top-notch Italian cuisine. Regional Italian specialties like *strozzapreti alla
romagnola* (pasta with smoked salmon and asparagus) and Chianti-braised
quail are rarely found on menus, and they're a special treat. *Open
Sun.–Thurs. 7 p.m.–midnight, Fri.–Sat. 7 p.m.–1 a.m.* $$$$

Wish

The Hotel, 801 Collins Ave. (8th St.), South Beach, 305-531-2222
Best Mojitos

Classic American cooking melds with haute Asian cuisine at this outstanding
restaurant, distinctively designed by Todd Oldham, that's been a proving
ground for top culinary talents. Dishes like braised beef short ribs with wild
mushroom risotto, and truffle-roasted turbot served with littleneck clams and
artichokes, consistently delight. Huge white umbrellas lend the garden terrace a cool, chic, and comfortable ambience. This gorgeous place has
attracted the likes of Mick Jagger, Madonna, and Rupert Everett. *Open for
lunch daily 11:30 a.m.–3 p.m.; dinner daily 7 p.m.–midnight. Rooftop Spire
Bar & Lounge (see p. 93) open Thurs.–Sun. 7 p.m.–1 a.m.* $$$

World Resource Cafe

719 Lincoln Rd. (Meridian Ave.), South Beach, 305-535-8987

Satisfy your cravings for sushi and Thai food in one stop at this Lincoln Road
cafe. The menu includes savory noodle dishes, aromatic curries, traditional
Japanese preparations, and fresh sashimi. Sit outdoors so you can take full
advantage of their excellent people-watching location. *Open Sun–Thurs.
noon–11 p.m., Fri.–Sat. noon–midnight.* $$

Hot & Cool Miami:
The Nightlife

Amika Loft Lounge & Discotheque

1532 Washington Ave. (15th St.), South Beach, 305-534-1499
www.amikamiami.com

One of the newest entries in South Beach combines two clubland buzz-words—loft and lounge—with that old-school moniker, discotheque. And it didn't take Amika long to lure a fun party crowd for hip hop, R&B, funk, and house music. The club has a main room, a laid-back lounge, and a loft that gives everyone a chance to scan the crowd below. It's all been done up in a slick, slightly retro '60s look with wood veneers and warm and cool colors. *Open Thurs.–Sun. 9 p.m.–5 a.m.*

Automatic Slims

1216 Washington Ave. (13th St.), South Beach, 305-695-0795
Best Theme Bars

The theme here is "where beautiful people come to get ugly," and the look is faux gritty, with campy old neon signs and a chopper out front. Cheeky female bartenders pour shots for rowdy customers. Karaoke night, '80s rock, and bull-riding, among many other enticements, keep things loud and rowdy. *Open daily 8 p.m.–5 a.m.*

crobar

1445 Washington Ave. (Espanola Way), South Beach, 305-672-8084
www.crobar.com
Best Dance Clubs

The lines are long in front of the historic Cameo Theater every weekend with crowds waiting to get into their favorite throbbing mega-dance club. This Chicago import (there's also a New York location) gets 'em all: locals, tourists, celebs, drag queens, club kids, Prada-clad socialites, and even some buttoned-down suits. Superstar deejays spin house, R&B, hip-hop, rock, retro, and funk. Monday nights host the popular Back Door Bamby circuit party. *Open Thurs.–Mon. 10 p.m.–5 a.m.* $$

DiLido Beach Club

The Ritz-Carlton, South Beach, One Lincoln Rd. (Collins Ave.),
South Beach, 786-276-4000
www.ritzcarlton.com
Best Sunday Parties

The Ritz-Carlton, South Beach raised a few eyebrows when it jumped into
the A-list party scene by bringing in a top party promoter and deejays, and
making sure all the hammocks and daybeds passed muster. The next thing
you know, Johnny Knoxville is asking the tanning butler to take care of his
back and Andre 3000 from Outkast is tooling around the property in a
Segway. Welcome to the DiLido Beach Club, where deejays spin thumping
techno while you sip cocktails accompanied by Mediterranean tidbits.
Scenesters show up on Sunday afternoons for their beach parties; on
Thurs.–Sat. evenings at 6 p.m., costumed swimmers go all Esther Williams
and dive into the infinity pool for a synchronized swimming performance.
Open 4 p.m.–sunset. $$

Flute Champagne Lounge

500 S. Pointe Dr. (Collins Ave.), South Beach, 305-674-8680
www.flutebar.com

Plush velvet banquettes and intimate nooks bring a romantic elegance to
Miami's edition of this Manhattan champagne bar on the tip of South Beach.
A dramatic crystal chandelier hangs high over the horseshoe-shaped bar,
where champagne and Petrossian's caviar are the preferred intoxicants at
this posh spot. Deejays spin nightly, and there's live jazz on Wednesdays.
Open Sat.–Thurs. 8 p.m.–5 a.m., Fri. 5 p.m.–5 a.m.

Mansion

1235 Washington Ave. (12th St.), South Beach, 786-229-7857
www.mansionmiami.com
Best Dance Clubs

The latest party palace from the Opium folks, Mansion's gimmick is called
"residence-meets-nightlife"—meaning this huge club has staircases, fire-
places, Venetian glass mirrors, crystal chandeliers, brick walls, and all sort of
homey touches (if your home is a mansion, that is). Located in a building
that was first built as the French Casino in 1936, Mansion has six bars and
two levels that attract the same kind of crowd as Opium: well-known names,
Miami hotties, and the usual group of fashionistas, models, and club kids.
Open Tues., Thurs.–Sat. 11 p.m.–5 a.m. $$

Mynt Lounge

1921 Collins Ave. (19th St.), South Beach, 786-276-6132
www.myntlounge.com
Best See-and-Be-Seen Clubs

The cool green place for the social elite, Mynt has a casually chic clientele that includes the insanely wealthy and the exaggeratedly beautiful—which would certainly account for a guest list that includes Britney Spears and Hugh Grant. Downstairs is the Grand Lounge with house music; the Ultra Lounge features hip-hop, with occasional appearances by celebrity deejays like Paul Oakenfold and DJ Reche from Ibiza. Step up to the 40-foot bar for the signature drink, the Mynt-tini (of course), a vodka martini with fresh-squeezed lime juice and mint leaves. *Open Wed.–Sat. 11 p.m.–5 a.m.* $$

Nikki Beach Club

One Ocean Dr. (1st St.), South Beach, 305-538-1111
www.nikkibeach.com
Best Sunday Parties

The quintessential beach club where beautiful people lounge languidly on bamboo beds drinking champagne at noon, Nikki Beach is blessed with a fabulous oceanfront location that makes all this hedonism possible. In fact, this complex has now become a franchise, with locations in Marbella, St. Tropez, St. Barth, and Puerto Vallarta. Success hasn't spoiled Nikki Beach, however; the vibe remains friendly, the music moody, and the food sophisticated. New at Nikki Beach is the Zen Tea Garden, serving traditional Chinese high tea, food, music, Zen dance, meditation, and other cultural programs. *Open Thurs.–Sun. 11 a.m.–5 a.m.* $

Onda Lounge

1248 Washington Ave. (12th St.), South Beach, 305-674-4464

Cool blue décor, a loungey groove, and tasty tapas are what this new nightspot is all about. Onda, which means wave in Italian, is happy and playful with a New York vibe, and with principals connected to glitzy mag *Ocean Drive,* the celeb quotient is high and guaranteed. Even the chef consultant, Kerry Simon, is high-profile. Keep in mind that the leather banquette cushions were designed to be sturdy enough for guests to dance on while ogling A-listers. So don't be shy. *Open Thurs.–Sat. 11 p.m.–5 a.m.* $

Opium Garden

136 Collins Ave. (1st St.), South Beach, 305-531-5535
www.opiummiami.com
Best Dance Clubs

Picture the scene: golden Buddhas, towering palm trees, Oriental lanterns, Asian pagodas, and hundreds of scantily clad party people getting their groove on under the stars to sexy house music. This is Opium Garden on any weekend. You should be able to get past the doorman if you dress nicely. Or be a big spender (be prepared to shell out between $200 and $2,000, depending on the size of your group) and reserve a table in advance to skip the whole velvet rope nonsense. *Open Tues., Thurs.–Sun. 11 p.m.–5 a.m.* $$

Pearl Restaurant & Lounge

Nikki Beach Club, One Ocean Dr. (1st St.), South Beach, 305-538-1111
www.pearlsouthbeach.com
Best Restaurant/Lounges

See Hot & Cool Restaurants, p. 86 for description.
Open Wed.–Thurs. 7 p.m.–1 a.m., Fri.–Sun. 7 p.m.–5 a.m. $$$$

Privé

136 Collins Ave. (1st St.), South Beach, 305-531-5535
www.opiummiami.com
Best See-and-Be-Seen Clubs

It seems Miami's celebs needed a club-within-a-club, so Privé was born. Part of the Opium Garden compound, but with its own separate entrance, the space has two bars, with streamlined sofas, Lucite fixtures, and sleek Helmut Newton photography. Have your concierge get you on the guest list, dress to impress, and you could be sharing a bottle with Jessica Simpson, Missy Elliott, or Cameron Diaz. *Open Thurs.–Sun. 11 p.m.–5 a.m.* $$

RokBar

1905 Collins Ave. (19th St.), South Beach, 305-538-7171
www.rokbarmiami.com

Rocker Tommy Lee's entry into the South Beach club scene, next door to the too-hot Mynt Lounge, brings a hip rock-'n'-roll vibe into a town known more for hip-hop and dance music. Big-hair '80s rock and punk blasts amid the blinding fluorescent pink, yellow, black, and white décor. The crowd is sassy, including both those who grew up with the music and those barely old enough to know who ZZ Top is. Hot tip for guys: bathrooms feature stylish Rolling Stone tongue urinals. *Open Tues.–Sat. 10 p.m.–5 a.m.*

Rose Bar

Delano, 1685 Collins Ave. (17th St.), South Beach, 305-672-2000
Best Classic Hotel Bars

Although there is now an impressive list of hopelessly hip lobby bars in South Beach, the bloom is still not off the original, the Rose Bar at Delano, where bona fide beautiful people mingle with wannabes. Yes, you will over-pay dearly for a cosmo in return for lounging around in this Philippe Starck–designed space with fully upholstered pink walls and Venetian chandeliers. Get over it. *Open Sun.–Thurs. noon–2 a.m., Fri.–Sat. noon–3 a.m.*

Score

727 Lincoln Rd. (Meridian Ave.), South Beach, 305-535-1111
Best Gay Bars

From the outside, Score looks like just another Lincoln Road sidewalk cafe. Inside, however, you'll find a huge main bar, an upstairs bar, and a gay video dance bar. Every night there's a different themed party: cabaret shows, progressive Latin parties, striptease night, hip-hop, and live jazz and blues. *Open daily 1 p.m.–5 a.m.*

Skybar

The Shore Club, 1901 Collins Ave. (19th St.), South Beach, 305-695-3100
Best See-and-Be-Seen Clubs

Known for its intensely hued décor, lush gardens, and sensual lantern-lit lounge areas—and its snotty door policy—Skybar manages to attract some celebs and models, though the crowd seems to include more than its fair share of girls-night-out groups and bachelorette parties. Still, the ambiance is cool enough for folks like Sting, Calvin Klein, and Whitney Houston. There are multiple components at work here: the Red Room, all crimson and hip-hop, and its tropical garden, with hanging lanterns and loungey cushions; the poolside Rumbar; and the Sandbar, where you can kick off your Manolo Blahniks and soak up the festive atmosphere barefoot in the sand. *Open Mon.–Wed. 4 p.m.–2 a.m., Thurs.–Sat. 4 p.m.–3 a.m., Sun. 4 p.m.–2 a.m.*

Spire Bar & Lounge

The Hotel, 801 Collins Ave. (8th St.), South Beach, 305-531-2222
www.thehotelofsouthbeach.com

Chill out under The Hotel's distinctive neon Deco "Tiffany" sign, a reminder of the property's former name, ditched after the jeweler got its panties in a bunch over trademark infringement. Amid the glittering backdrop of South Beach's low-rise skyline, this rooftop oasis gets you buzzed with its signature electronic cocktails—including the new champagne mojito—and sated via a light tapas menu. Head here after dinner at Wish downstairs to join the chic thirty-something cocktail crowd lounging on designer Todd Oldham's playful overstuffed sofas and chairs. *Open Thurs.–Sat. 7 p.m.–1 a.m.*

State

320 Lincoln Rd. (Washington Ave.), South Beach, 786-621-5215
www.statesouthbeach.com

Nightlife impresarios Gerry Kelly and Maxwell Blandford's latest venture is this upscale lounge and club on Lincoln Road. Its theme is Hollywood Baroque, sort of, with imported velvets, taffetas, silks, and mahogany and a Belle Epoque chandelier as the centerpiece. Over-the-top events and after-parties for fashion and music industry confabs are frequently staged here; otherwise, deejays spin house, rock, hip-hop, and sexy R&B for a wildly attractive young crowd. *Open Fri.–Sun. 11 p.m.–5 a.m.*

Twist

1057 Washington Ave. (10th St.), South Beach, 305-538-9478
www.twistsobe.com
Best Gay Bars

This is the consummate gay club, all in one big package: seven bars, including a video pub, garden area, tropical Bungalow Bar with go-go dancers, upstairs patio bar, main room with deejay, frolic lounge, and game room with pool tables and video games. Come early for two-for-one drinks every day 1–9 p.m. *Open daily 1 p.m.–5 a.m.*

Hot & Cool Miami:
The Attractions

Agua

Delano, 1685 Collins Ave. (17th St.), South Beach, 305-672-2000

They don't quite call this a spa—it's a rooftop bathhouse and solarium with a health bar. Overlooking the ocean and South Beach, Agua offers massages, facials, aromatherapy body treatments, and special services such as guided meditation, acupuncture, and natural health consultations using iridology (analyzing the condition of the eyes—evidently this goes one step further than bloodshot and bleary from last night's partying). Some of the services can be performed in your hotel room if you're a guest. $$$$

Bal Harbour Shops

9700 Collins Ave. (96th St.), Bal Harbour, 305-866-0311
www.balharbourshops.com

Fashionistas, socialites, and the likes of Beyoncé, J-Lo, Cher, and Will Smith head here to check out haute couture amid flora, fauna, and fountains. Not your cookie cutter upscale mall, Bal Harbour Shops is the real deal when it comes to luxury shopping, anchored by elegant department stores Neiman-Marcus and Saks Fifth Avenue and populated by a heady list of world-class designer boutiques that include Christian Dior, Emanuel Ungaro, Escada, Luca Luca, Ermenegildo Zegna, Dolce & Gabbana, Gianfranco Ferre, Gianni Versace, Prada, Valentino, Bulgari, Tiffany, Marc Jacobs, and Pratesi. When your credit card needs a break, stop for freshly brewed tea at Lea's Tea Room or a salad at the Bal Harbour Bistro. Mall hours: *Open Mon.–Fri. 10 a.m.–9 p.m., Sat. 10 a.m.–7 p.m., Sun. noon–6 p.m.*

Base

939 Lincoln Rd. (Jefferson Ave.), South Beach, 305-531-6470
www.baseworld.com

If restaurant/lounges are the current trend, then retail/lounges must be next. This entertaining hybrid carries an unusual array of merchandise—men's and women's clothing, footwear, decorative home accessories, fragrance, and gifts—with a cool CD bar. The concept is terrific, and so is the crisp, edgy execution: sportswear is functional, footwear is designed for urban trekkers, books and magazines are stylish and stylized, and the jewelry and decorative accessories are enticing. The CD bar offers the best chill-out music available. *Open Mon.–Thurs. 11 a.m.–10 p.m., Fri.–Sun. 11 a.m.–11 p.m.*

Bass Museum of Art

2121 Park Ave. (Collins Ave.), South Beach, 305-673-7530
www.bassmuseum.org
Best Art Spaces

Freshly expanded and renovated, the Bass Museum of Art maintains a collection of 3,000 works encompassing European fine arts and decorative arts, Renaissance tapestries, modern and contemporary design objects, and photos and drawings that document Miami Beach's unique design history. The cafe serves light lunch, snacks, and afternoon tea. *Open Tues., Wed., Fri., Sat. 10 a.m.–5 p.m.; Sun. 11 a.m.–5 p.m.; Thurs. 10 a.m.–9 p.m. Closed holidays.* $

Books & Books

933 Lincoln Rd. (Jefferson Ave.), South Beach, 305-532-3222
www.booksandbooks.com

When Bill or Hillary Clinton come to town to promote their books, they come to Books & Books. With two locations (the other is at 265 Aragon Ave. in Coral Gables), these bookstores have exactly what they ought to: lots and lots of books and periodicals; friendly, knowledgeable help; and a roster of interesting events year-round. Owner Mitchell Kaplan is also one of the movers behind the highly popular Miami Book Fair International each November. The Lincoln Road store, located in the historic Sterling Building, has a noteworthy collection of books on art, design, fashion, and architecture, plus a large international magazine collection. *Open Sun.–Thurs. 10 a.m.–11 p.m., Fri.–Sat. 10 a.m.–midnight.*

Brownes & Co./Some Like It Hot

841 Lincoln Rd. (Jefferson Ave.), South Beach, 305-538-7544

Uh-oh...you're out of that special lip balm. Maybe you need relief in the form of a facial after too much sun at that pool party. Or perhaps you're craving a power yoga break to clear your mind and body. This Lincoln Road beauty emporium is the place to go. The apothecary, an inviting mélange of antique cases and shelves, stocks a huge variety of beauty products amid a cozy, friendly vibe. Brownes Beauty Lounge handles the usual—cuts, colors, blowouts, and manicures—and the unusual—treatments like bamboo lemongrass exfoliating scrubs and frangipani body-nourishing wraps. Packages for guys include the 007: a shave, haircut, and manicure, accompanied by a shaken-not-stirred martini. The Yoga Room on the second floor offers a full slate of classes throughout the week in a tranquil, comfortable setting. *Salon open Mon.–Sat. 9:30 a.m.–8 p.m., Sun. noon–6 p.m.; store open Sun.–Wed. 10 a.m.–8 p.m., Thurs.–Sat. 10 a.m.–9 p.m.*

Crunch

1259 Washington Ave. (12th St.), South Beach, 305-674-8222
www.crunch.com

Not all of South Beach's perfect bods come from Drs. Nip and Tuck. Quality workout time is part of the obsession, and even guests staying in hotels with cool gyms end up at Crunch. The South Beach version of this big-city chain is a huge facility with a boxing ring, sun deck, and classes ranging from Aerobics with Attitude to Zumba. Perhaps you'll be motivated to shape up by signing up for Whipped—in which a patent leather–clad diva struts around the studio in thigh-high boots carrying a menacing riding crop. Or maybe the thought of pumping iron next to celebs like Tyson Beckford gets your adrenaline going. Whatever your motive, sweat never looked so good. (VIP passes are provided for many hotel guests at this gym.) *Open Mon.–Fri. 6 a.m.–midnight, Sat. 8 a.m.–9 p.m., Sun. 9 a.m.–8 p.m.* $$

Dog Bar

723 N. Lincoln Lane (Euclid Ave.), South Beach, 305-532-5654 /
866-436-4227
www.dogbar.com

You can't return home without a trinket for Lucy the lab. Stop at the Dog Bar, just off Lincoln Road, for those canine essentials like jewel-encrusted gold-tasseled dog dishes, all-natural peanut-butter gingerbread men, and herbal eyewash kits. You'll also find animal-related artwork by local and national artists, some of whom can be commissioned for pet portraits. Because nothing is too good for Lucy, is it? *Open daily 10 a.m.–10 p.m.*

Hector's Jetskis

South Beach, 305-318-9268
Best Guided Tours

Sure, you could sit in a bus and listen to a guide tell you about South Beach's past and present. Or you could throw on your bathing suit and take a waverunner tour with Hector, and get some sun at the same time. He'll take you past all those fab mansions and yachts on Star, Palm, and Fisher Islands. When you call, he'll tell you where to meet. *Tours daily from 7 a.m.–6:30 p.m. Call for reservations 24 hours in advance.* $$$$

Miami Beach Golf Club

2301 Alton Rd. (W. 23rd St.), South Beach, 305-532-3350
www.miamibeachgolfclub.com
Best Golf Courses

Freshly face-lifted to the tune of $10 million dollars, the Miami Beach Golf Course aims to bring world-class golf back to the Beach. Known as the Bayshore Golf Course when it opened in 1923, the course was completely redone by Arthur Hills, one of America's foremost course designers: all the grass and most of the trees were replaced, and the hills and bunkers were entirely resculpted. The result: 18 holes and 6,800 yards to test golfers that include celebs like Matt Damon and NFL Hall-of-Famer Jim Brown. Best of all, it's located right in the heart of Miami Beach, just a few minutes down the road from South Beach and its countless attractions. *Open daily 7 a.m.–7 p.m.* $$$$

The Ritz-Carlton Spa, South Beach

One Lincoln Rd. (Collins Ave.), South Beach, 786-276-4090
www.ritzcarlton.com
Best Spas

Paris flair, plus South Beach sensibility, are behind the Ritz-Carlton's 16,000-square-foot spa, featuring La Maison de Beauté Carita, a French regimen developed by the Carita sisters, known for inventing such chic hairstyles as Brigitte Bardot's ponytail and Maria Callas' chignon 50 years ago. These treatments are designed for clients who are indulging in a night on the town, including therapies for before and after extreme partying. The Après SoBe, for example, includes the Power Shower—the spa equivalent of sobering up under cold and hot showers—while the Oxygen Inhalation Session has five aromatherapeutic scents that relieve post-party headaches. And the Oxygen Butler is standing by for those hangover emergencies. In the only full-service spa on South Beach, other offerings include a fitness center, oceanfront exercise classes, relaxation lounges, a full-service salon, and two couples' suites, one with a floor-to-ceiling window overlooking South Beach. *Open daily 9 a.m.–7 p.m.* $$$$

Village of Merrick Park

358 San Lorenzo Ave. (Ponce de Leon Blvd.), Coral Gables, 305-529-0200
www.villageofmerrickpark.com

Staid Coral Gables got a boost of high fashion and hot nightlife when this impressive open-air shopping, dining, and entertaining complex opened in 2003, aiming to save upscale shoppers the drive to the Bal Harbour Shops. Anchored by Neiman Marcus and Nordstrom and 100 boutiques and retailers, Merrick Park has a collection of major-league designer boutiques, a floor devoted to home furnishing stores, original restaurant/bars meant to linger in, and a serene Asian garden and fountains, perhaps for a moment of meditation in between spending sprees. It's already got a reputation for its fine shoe stores—Jimmy Choo, Moreschi, and Donald Pliner Couture, among others—and designer boutiques like CH Carolina Herrera, Roberto Cavalli, Gucci, and Hugo Boss. But what sets this center apart from other South Florida malls is its concentration of outstanding casual restaurants and cafes—Mundo and OLA Steaks, among others—that have created a burgeoning nightlife scene. *Open Mon.–Sat. 10 a.m.–9 p.m., Sun. noon–6 p.m.*

Arty Party Miami

Hipsters know that Miami isn't just about the beach. There's a sophisticated and diverse arts scene that includes Latin-American and Caribbean artists, fine established museums and galleries, young bohemians, and world-class events like the annual Art Basel. This itinerary serves up stylish South Beach spots and visits to the area's best artsy hangouts, including the up-and-coming Design District, Wynwood, and East Side neighborhoods. You'll dine at Miami's hippest restaurants, party at restaurant/lounges with a very hot cool factor, and chill at fabulous pool parties alongside the glitterati.

Arty Party Miami:
The Itinerary

Our Hotel Choice: **The National Hotel**, because it is the most splendid of the many examples of Art Deco restoration, with details like a vintage bar and lounge, a 205-foot pool, cabana suites, and impeccable service.

Prime Time: Thurs.–Sat.

Day 1

Morning: Get this party off to the right start. Head to **Lincoln Road Mall**, which—be very clear about this—is not an enclosed structure, but an open-air pedestrian mall. Known as the Fifth Avenue of the South in the 1950s, this vibrant strip of galleries, shops, and restaurants is now the site of South Beach's best people-watching. Start with some eggs Benedict or a breakfast burrito at the groovy London brasserie import, **Balans**. Then it's time to check out *the art scene*. **ArtCenter/South Florida** occupies three separate buildings of galleries and studios showcasing local talent. Another gallery worth a visit is **Britto Central**, featuring the work of Brazilian pop artist Romero Britto, whose colorful art cheerfully adorns everything from vodka bottles to cars. Don't miss the vivid mosaic fountain at Euclid Avenue. Make your way over to Washington Avenue to one of South Florida's museum treasures, **The Wolfsonian—FIU**, a remarkable collection of design art and artifacts housed in an exquisite 1927 storage facility.

Lunch: Sup on some *dim sum* at the intentionally kitschy **Miss Yip Chinese Cafe**, or dig into a thin-crusted pizza at **Spris**.

Afternoon: Spend some time browsing the *shops and galleries* along Lincoln Road. With any luck, you'll be treated to some fine performance art along the way—a favorite is the platform-shoed disco guy getting down to Gloria Gaynor on his boom box.

After shopping, it's likely you've worked up a thirst. It's *cocktail time*, and the beverage of choice is the mojito, that refreshing lime, rum, and mint concoction that is de rigueur on Lincoln Road on a balmy afternoon… well, any afternoon, actually. A favorite is the always-popular Italian **Segafredo**, where sophisticated European scenesters watch the passing parade from the barstools. Or head to the straight-friendly but gay-oriented **Laundry Bar**, designed to get you loaded while washing a load. If you're in the mood for a sweet pick-me-up, join the other Europeans for an espresso and a slice of tiramisu at **Paninoteca European Eatery**.

Dinner: Sexy restaurant/lounges—places that turn into clubs after dinner—are a hot ticket in South Florida. And none is as blatantly *aphrodisiac* as **Tantra Restaurant & Lounge**, with grass on the floor, gauzy booths, erotic videos, and Middle Eastern fusion cuisine aimed at igniting romance. Or head across the causeway to the **Grass Restaurant & Lounge**, a Balinese-inspired oasis of chic tranquillity, specializing in Asian fusion food in a Zen setting. For a really festive evening, dine at **Taverna Opa**, where—after a tasty Mediterranean dinner of meze and fresh seafood—napkins rain from the ceiling, Greek disco music is cranked up, and waiters and belly dancers dance on the tables. Before you know it, you'll be up there too. *Opa!*

Nighttime: To wind down afterward, try **Jazid**, smoky and cool with live jazz and Latin music, or chill out on the water sofas at the **Rooftop Lounge** at the TownHouse Hotel. Or wind down shooting some pool at stylish **Felt Billiards Club**. For an alternative scene, **Jade** serves up Oriental chic with a bar, dance floor, and lounge. Late night, refuel at **Cafeteria** where you can indulge in comfort food 24/7, and where a *cool lounge* scene lingers till early in the morning.

Day 2

Morning: Wake up Miami-style with the motley crowd of locals and tourists jamming the counters of **Puerto Sagua** for Cuban *café con leche* and *pan tostado.* If you came here to golf, make your way to **Don Shula's Golf Club** in Miami Lakes. Otherwise, it's time to head on to some of Miami's most *cutting-edge art* collections. Your first stop is the **Museum of Contemporary Art—MoCA—**in North Miami, a Charles Gwathmey–designed building filled with works by some of the country's most noteworthy contemporary artists. Next, drive to the up-and-coming Wynwood neighborhood roughly north and west of downtown Miami. It's home to two outstanding private collections open to the public: the **Rubell Collection**, with important works from such artists as Jean-Michel Basquiat and Keith Haring; and the **Margulies Collection** at the Warehouse, an extensive collection that includes avant-garde contemporary and vintage photography, video, and sculpture.

Lunch: Finally showing up on the hip-o-meter are Miami's **Design District** and the adjoining East Side Miami, where restaurants, nightspots, and galleries are premiering faster than new reality television shows. For lunch, try **Soyka**, one of the first restaurants to open in this *happening 'hood* and a busy hangout for area professionals and artsy types, or the groovy gourmet hot-dog stand, **Dogma Grill.**

Afternoon: Afterwards, check out the Design District's numerous galleries and decorative design stores. Or make your way back to the hotel for a relaxing *poolside massage* and perhaps a disco nap before getting dolled up for a night on the town.

Dinner: Slip into that bare little number and those Jimmy Choos—you've got a night full of partying ahead. Begin with martinis at the *stylish hotel bar* of your choice: the gorgeous **D'Lounge** at the National Hotel; the oh-so-stark **Bar at Sagamore Hotel**; or the sleek urban **Fallabella Bar** at The Albion, where models and entertainment types are often busy networking. Now, it's time to tuck into **B.E.D.**—which stands for Beverage, Entertainment, Dining. It means you get to kick off those stilettos and climb into a queen-size bed while the pajama-clad waitstaff serves fine fusion cuisine. After dinner, the whole place turns into one of the hottest, most celeb-infested lounges in South Beach. If you prefer something even more incendiary, go to **Touch** for modern international cuisine served up with belly dancers, percussionists, and flame twirlers. Another hip option is **Rumi**, where the decor is '70s modern, the food sophisticated New World, and the after-dinner vibe sultry and hot.

Nighttime: All of the above hot spots magically morph into fab lounges that stay open very late. But if you're still craving *after-hours fun*, make like a sardine with the other friendly locals at the tiny but very cool **Blue** lounge on Espanola Way or the authentic dive bar **Mac's Club Deuce.**

Day 3

Morning: If you need a quiet scene to help nurse that hangover, **A La Folie Cafe Français,** tucked away on Espanola Way, will make you some crepes that should fit the bill quite nicely while you read the Sunday paper at a sidewalk table. Then take a drive to the **Lowe Art Museum** at the University of Miami campus for a look at their diverse collection of *classical and* *international art*, then pop by the bright red new **Miami Art Central** a few blocks away and see works by contemporary artists of Latin-American and Hispanic descent.

Lunch: Back on the Beach, the **Playwright Irish Pub & Restaurant** serves up fine Irish fare, while the **IceBox Cafe** has stylish brunchy dishes and *fabulous cakes* and cobblers in the dessert case.

Afternoon: It's time to get mobile and do a little *sightseeing* aboard one of those spiffy little scooters available for rent from **Beach Scooter Rental**. As you cruise around the Art Deco Historic District, make a point of stopping at the west end of the Miami Beach Convention Center, to tour the moving **Holocaust Memorial** and the **Miami Beach Botanical Garden**. Over on funky **Espanola Way**, the Weekend Market is under way, a low-key affair where vendors sell jewelry and oddball collectibles. Cool down with an Indian mango ice cream cone from **The Frieze Ice Cream Factory**, or an icy *dulce de leche* espresso refreshment at **Dulcianna Coffee & Gelato**.

Dinner: Dress up in something bare and flirty to show off your Sunday-in-the-sun glow with A-listers at **China Grill**, one of South Beach's venerable hot spots with a *hot new sushi den*, the Dragon Room. Or make your way to **Tuscan Steak**, a chic Florentine steakhouse from the same folks who run China Grill. For a low-key but very hip sushi scene, head to **Bond St. Lounge** in the basement of The TownHouse Hotel.

Nighttime: If you want to *dance all night*—literally—the place to go is **Space** in Downtown Miami, where the deejays spin long past sunrise. Or check out the new **Pawn Shop Lounge** downtown, with its authentically gritty facade (yes, this was a pawn shop once) and its wacky interior. Another fine choice is the always-cool **Bar at the Marlin** in the rock-'n'-roll Marlin Hotel, a slick subterranean nightspot that attracts hipsters and celeb rockers.

The Day After: You're just in time for salvation at the Sunday Gospel Brunch at **Metro Kitchen + Bar** at Hotel Astor. Get into party mode at one of South Beach's many cool Sunday afternoon poolside shindigs, where in-the-know locals and It people congregate while deejays spin and cosmos intoxicate. The hippest ticket to hedonism is the **Sunday Soiree at the Raleigh**, while the **Zee Lounge** at the National Hotel is all about chilling. (Handy tip: Use the new beachside promenade to party-hop.)

Arty Party Miami:
The Hotels

The Albion

1650 James Ave. (Lincoln Rd.), South Beach, 305-913-1000 /
877-782-3557
www.rubellhotels.com

It's hard not to admire a hotel where management lists "sincere" and "smiling" among its attributes, while vowing not to be arrogant, intimidating, or snobby—and leaves lollipops and good-night notes on the pillows at turndown. The cool and unpretentious Albion, a 1939 Nautical Art Deco property off Lincoln Road, is a favorite with hip New Yorkers, models, and entertainment and media industry folks. Its monochromatic industrial-chic decor belies its colorful past as the grungy local headquarters for Abbie Hoffman and Students for a Democratic Society during the 1972 Democratic National Convention in Miami. The 96 rooms are minimalist but comfortable, custom-designed by contemporary architect Carlos Zapata. If you reserve one of the corner rooms overlooking Lincoln Road, you'll have more windows from which to enjoy the streetside promenade. The second-level pool provides more than watery fun. you can watch swimmers underwater through portholes. Be sure to stop in for a drink at the Fallabella Bar (see p. 120), their stylish watering hole. $$

Hotel Astor

956 Washington Ave. (10th St.), South Beach, 305-531-8081 /
800-270-4981
www.hotelastor.com

Quite simply one of the most suave and delightful of South Beach's many Deco hotels, the 1936 Hotel Astor combines stunningly preserved design elements with modern comfort, and throws in top-flight service. The striking minimalist lobby, in browns and seafoam, with modern white leather furniture, features nifty original wall panels done in Vitrolite, a pigmented glass popularly used in the 1930s. The 42 guest rooms are sleek and warm, in soothing shades of taupe and brushed chrome, with blond oak furnishings. Waffle-weave bathrobes, Frette linens, and Molton Brown amenities are there for your comfort, and natural canvas blinds block out harsh sunlight. Marble bathrooms have oversize bathtub-showers with glass doors, and brushed chrome fixtures. The Astor's restaurant, the Metro Kitchen + Bar (see p. 113), serves modern American fare and hosts an energetic Sunday gospel brunch, while the bar patio is the scene of hip weekly parties. The beach is a couple of blocks away, and the Astor sacrificed their swimming pool to add lounge space for their popular shindigs. If you can deal with life sans pool, then by all means book a room at this stunning property. $$

The Marlin
1200 Collins Ave. (12th St.), South Beach, 305-604-3595
www.marlinhotel.com

The Hotel Marlin—aka the rock-'n'-roll hotel—only has 12 oversize suites, but what stories they harbor! Room 306, a one-bedroom suite, is where Aerosmith's Steven Tyler wrote "Pink." Beyoncé Knowles stayed in Room 205, the Honeymoon Suite, while recording her last CD. There's also the suite where former owner and Island Records founder Chris Blackwell lived, site of wild parties in the '90s. Even when rock stars don't stay here, they visit—Missy Elliott held court with Jimmy Fallon in the mezzanine lounge during the MTV Video Music Awards weekend in Miami, and Anna Kournikova and Enrique Iglesias stopped by when his father was recording here. It's just that kind of place. There's no pool, but the beach is across the street. All suites have fully equipped kitchens, TVs with VCRs, CD players and CD libraries, bathrobe and slippers, Aveda hair and skin care products, and—unfortunately—walls that do not talk. $$

The National Hotel
1677 Collins Ave. (17th St.), South Beach, 305-532-2311 /
800-327-8370
www.nationalhotel.com

If you want to step back in time, when movie stars were glamorous and refined (or at least seemed that way), then book a room at the National Hotel, which has been meticulously restored to its 1940 grandeur. It's a current favorite of people in the movie and entertainment industry (glam star Gwen Stefani of No Doubt is a regular client). The owners have won awards for their outstanding restoration work here, which includes original furnishings, such as the chairs in the lounge and lobby; polished chrome light fixtures; and the carpeting and chandelier in the Oval Room. The 151 guest rooms, including 7 one-bedroom suites and a three-level penthouse suite, occupy the historic tower and the new cabana wing overlooking the 205-foot infinity pool. Rooms include plush linens and 27-inch flat screen televisions with DVD and VCR. The National's glamorous setting encourages nonguests to hang out here in their lobby bar, D'Lounge (see p. 120); the new Zee Lounge pool bar (see p. 124); and Tamara (see p. 116), their French fusion restaurant. $$$$

The Raleigh

1775 Collins Ave. (18th St.), South Beach, 305-534-6300 /
800-848-1775
www.raleighhotel.com

Built and designed in 1940 by famed Beach architect L. Murray Dixon, the Raleigh was heralded as a jewel of modernist design. It still is, only now it has the added cachet of hot poolside parties and a cool fashion and entertainment industry clientele. Hidden behind lush foliage, the sleek hotel shows its age wonderfully in the beautifully preserved lobby, coffee shop, and legendary martini bar (check out the photo gallery out front). A key prop in Esther Williams movies, the scalloped pool, filled with fat black inner tubes, is one of the world's most photographed. The corny-but-cool nautical-motif pool bar and stylish black-and-white striped cushions in the poolside lounge are the setting for hip Sunday soirees (see p. 123). The 104 rooms and suites have 1940s period furnishings; terrazzo floors and cedarwood closets; and modern conveniences like in-room stereos, two-line speaker phones, and high-speed Internet access; a nice touch is linen duvets, 400-thread-count Egyptian cotton sheets, and Kiehls bathroom amenities. Note that the seventh-floor rooms all have terraces. Chef Eric Ripert is at the helm of the hotel restaurant's French- and Latin-inspired cuisine, served on the balmy outdoor terrace surrounded by palm trees and hanging lanterns. $$$

Sagamore Hotel

1671 Collins Ave. (17th St.), South Beach, 305-535-8088 /
877-242-6673
www.sagamorehotel.com

Nowhere is the current trend of hotels doubling as art galleries so dramatic as in the lobby of the Sagamore Hotel. The stunning white lobby is a Deco-flavored canvas for the exquisite contemporary art collection that's displayed in the public spaces and guest rooms. The interior of this 1948 hotel—one of the first examples of postmodern architecture on the Beach—was demolished during renovation, but many charming details were preserved, including the neon hotel signs, terrazzo floors, and original mail and security boxes at the front desk. The austere design sensibility extends to the simple lawn stretching from the back terrace to the beach, and a zero-entry L-shaped pool, bar, and second-story sundeck. All 92 guest suites, tastefully contemporary (and compatible with the postmodern era), are in shades of beige and cream, with fully equipped kitchens, king-size beds with pillow-top mattresses, and at least two televisions. Consider splurging on one of the spacious poolside bungalows. Stylish guests have included Adrien Brody and Kate Moss, among others from the worlds of art, fashion, and entertainment. $$$

TownHouse Hotel

150 20th St. (Collins Ave.), South Beach, 305-534-3800
www.townhousehotel.com

Never mind that this groovy hotel doesn't have a pool—the beach is only a block away. Or you may opt to lounge on the queen-size waterbeds at the cool Rooftop Lounge (see p. 123). Everything about TownHouse is designed to make you smile: the flowered lamp shades, bright red telephones, exercise equipment at the end of the hallways, minimalist-mod décor, and laid-back lobby with board games and comic books. The gift shop—the opposite of the typical overpriced, uninspired hotel shop—stocks beer, wine, water, and fun snacks for your in-room fridge, in addition to its signature red-and-white beach accessories. TownHouse is home to the popular sushi bar and hipster hangout, the Bond St. Lounge (see p. 110). Service is cheerful and mellow. You could pay a lot more money to stay at the nearby Shore Club or Delano, but it won't buy the we-don't-take-ourselves-seriously ambience that's truly fun here. Ask for one of the corner rooms, as they're the sunniest. $$

Arty Party Miami:
The Restaurants

A La Folie Cafe Français
519 Espanola Way (Euclid Ave.), South Beach, 305-538-4484
www.alafoliecafe.com

You'll smell the aroma of butter melting on the grill and hear guests chatting in French long before you set foot in this romantic sidewalk cafe on Espanola Way. What to choose? Buckwheat crepes with pears, brie and walnuts, sweet crepes with chestnut purée and whipped cream, cheesy croque-monsieur sandwiches, salade niçoise, quiche lorraine, croissants, and toasted baguettes are all very French and all very good. Hot drinks include all forms of espressos and teas, plus those big bowls of café au lait that go so nicely with your morning newspaper. *Open daily 9 a.m.–midnight.* $

Balans
1022 Lincoln Rd. (Michigan Ave.), South Beach, 305-534-9191
www.balans.co.uk

A Lincoln Road European import with a fun British vibe, Balans serves cafe dishes and offers a great vantage point for people-watching. The breakfast menu includes burritos, French toast, pancakes, eggs benedict, and the like, while the eclectic day menu features salads, grilled meats and seafoods, pasta, wraps, and the occasional British specialty like bangers and mash. The lobster club sandwich and banoffi pie with toffee sauce are worth every carb. *Open Sun.–Thurs. 8 a.m.–midnight, Fri.–Sat. 8 a.m.–1 a.m.* $

B.E.D.
929 Washington Ave. (10th St.), South Beach, 305-532-9070
www.bedmiami.com
Best Restaurant/Lounges

B.E.D.—it stands for Beverage, Entertainment, Dining—was a forerunner of the restaurant/lounge movement. Its gimmick—dinner served on trays in big beds—caught on quickly, and the post-dinner party scene remains one of the hottest in town. Don't dismiss the outstanding French and globally influenced cuisine, and do make sure to order the *dulce de leche* soufflé for dessert. Visiting celebs party here—among them, J-Lo, George Clooney, Will Smith, Matt Damon, and Ben Affleck—and stories about their late-night capers are the stuff of legends. The best part of all: for all the hype, there's not a speck of attitude here. *Open Mon., Wed.–Sun. 8 p.m.–5 a.m.* $$$

Bond St. Lounge

TownHouse Hotel, 150 20th St. (Collins Ave.), South Beach, 305-398-1806
Best Sushi

Fresh new spins on sushi are served at this South Beach location of the wildly popular Manhattan restaurant by the same name. At this basement restaurant/lounge at the TownHouse Hotel, you can savor sesame-crusted shrimp rolls with orange curry and balsamic honey, and sun-dried tomato and avocado rolls with garlic ponzu oil and green tea salt. The scene is hip and loud, and the overstuffed chairs cozy. *Open Mon.–Wed. 6–11 p.m., Thurs.–Sun. 6 p.m.–midnight.* $$

Cafeteria

546 Lincoln Rd. (Pennsylvania Ave.), South Beach, 305-672-3663
Best Late-Night Eats

As New York City's southernmost suburb, South Beach shares a fair number of restaurants and nightspots. Cafeteria is one of the most recent, and most welcome, additions with its 24-hour designer comfort cuisine, bar, lounges, and prime Lincoln Road location. The menu has fun takes on diner fare—upscale macaroni and cheese, fried chicken salad, meatloaf, banana vanilla wafer pudding—while the lounge scene unfolds amid the futuristic white vinyl booths. If you come between 2 and 7 a.m., you can join the revelers at Cafeteria's Breakfast Club, a deejay/dance party. *Open daily 24 hours.* $$

China Grill

404 Washington Ave. (5th St.), South Beach, 305-534-2211
Best Always-Trendy Tables

China Grill was one of the very first restaurants in South Beach where diners could play hey-isn't-that-Jack-Nicholson? while dining on chic pan-Asian fusion cuisine. And after nearly a decade, the place still demands a long wait on weekends. But it's worth it—the grill and wok-prepared dishes are beautiful and lavishly presented on oversize plates, meant for sharing. Entrées include Shanghai lobster with ginger, curry, and crispy spinach, and sizzling whole fish served with Chinese black bean and red chili sauce. The bar scene is one of the hottest in town, and the newest hangout is the intimate Dragon Room, a separate room within China Grill, for sushi and sake. *Open for lunch Mon.–Fri. 11 a.m.–6 p.m.; dinner Mon.–Fri. 6 p.m.–midnight, Sat.–Sun. 6 p.m.–1 a.m.* $$$

The District Restaurant Lounge

35 NE 40th St. (N. Miami Ave.), Design District, 305-576-7242
www.thedistrictmiami.com

Yet another indicator that the Design District is an ever-growing blip on the
hip radar, The District has opened, an easygoing, indoor-outdoor restaurant
and lounge located on the site of longtime favorite Piccadilly Garden. The
wide-ranging New American cuisine is inspired by different culinary
"districts"—New Orleans, Little Italy, and the Pacific Northwest, among others—all of which are represented on the lunch and dinner menus. The best
deal is Nite Bites, a snack menu served during happy hour and late at night,
when scenester cliques from the neighborhood order cocktails by the pitcher
and graze on treats like buttermilk-soaked chicken wings and Italian pear
and cheese *fiocchi. Open for lunch Tues.–Sat. 11:30 a.m.–4 p.m.; dinner
5:30–11 p.m.; happy hour Thurs.–Fri. 5–8 p.m.* $$

Dogma Grill

7030 Biscayne Blvd. (NE 70th St.), East Side Miami, 305-759-3433
www.dogmagrill.com

Part of Miami's Upper East Side renaissance, this hip hot-dog stand (motto:
A Frank Philosophy) lets you choose your dogma: natural beef franks, Polish
sausage, or veggie dogs gone gourmet. Hipsters from the 'hood crowd the
outdoor tables for choices that include the Pushcart, with spicy brown mus-
tard and New York–style sautéed onions; the Chili Cheese Dog, slathered in
L.A. chili, yellow mustard, onions, and cheddar cheese; and the Athens,
heaped with chopped cucumbers, tomatoes, onions, kalamata olives, fresh
oregano, and feta cheese. There are also freshly made corn dogs, sandwiches
and salads, sides like garlic fry-chips, and fresh mint lemonade. *Open daily
10 a.m.–10 p.m.* $

Dulcianna Coffee & Gelato

532 Lincoln Rd. (Pennsylvania Ave.), South Beach, 305-532-1101

There's a nice Argentinian twist to this friendly snack stop on Lincoln Road,
and it comes in the form of caramelized milk called *dulce de leche.* This
sweet, rich spread is part of delectable coffee-based drinks like iced *dulce
de leche café,* and appears in their gelati. It also shows up in *alfajores,*
addictive foil-wrapped chocolate sandwich confections that you can buy by
the piece or by the box. Sweet and definitely not low-carb, these goodies are
a favorite with models and Latinos. *Open Sun.–Thurs. 8:30 a.m.–12:30 a.m.,
Fri.–Sat. 8:30 a.m.–1:30 a.m.* $

Frieze Ice Cream Factory

1620 Michigan Ave. (Lincoln Rd.), South Beach, 305-538-2028

Instead of ordering some overwrought restaurant dessert after dinner, head to The Frieze for a scoop or two of their housemade ice creams and sorbets. The chocolate, caramel, and toffee variations are superb, but the exotic tropical fruit sorbets are sublime: Indian mango, tamarind, and guanabana are just a few. Flavors change seasonally; summer sorbets feature watermelon, cantaloupe, and honeydew, and you might happen upon interesting experiments like root beer, red wine, and pickled ginger. We're cool with that. *Open Sun.–Thurs. noon–midnight, Fri.–Sat. noon–1 a.m. $*

Grass Restaurant & Lounge

28 NE 40th St. (N. Miami Ave.), Design District, 305-573-3355
www.grasslounge.com
Best Outdoor Dining

Nestled among the Design District's eclectic furniture and design shops, this Asian-inspired restaurant/lounge is a laid-back alternative to frenetic South Beach. Mostly open-air with tiki huts and lots of stone and bamboo, Grass presents a Bali-style vibe for local hipsters and low-key A-listers. There are two dinner seatings for the outstanding Peruvian-Asian cuisine, and then the lounge scene takes over. The tough door policy suggests excessive attitude (reservations on weekends are a must), but once you're in and you've thrown back a pineapple lemongrass martini, everything looks copacetic. *Open Tues.–Thurs. 8 p.m.–3 a.m., Fri. 6 p.m.–4 a.m., Sat. 8 p.m.–4 a.m. $$$*

IceBox Cafe

1657 Michigan Ave. (Lincoln Rd.), South Beach, 305-538-8448
www.iceboxcafe.com

Tucked away on a side street off Lincoln Road, this tidy silver eatery serves excellent cafe fare and a beautiful weekend brunch—chive pancakes with smoked salmon and spicy red-pepper omelets with chimichurri and hash browns, for example. But the best items to emerge from its stainless steel open kitchen are the desserts: cobblers, tartlets, old-fashioned layer cakes, icebox cakes, and other homespun goodies lined up in the display cases. Even the buff male-model types and svelte models who hang out here can't resist. *Open Tues.–Thurs., Sun. 11 a.m.–11 p.m., Fri.–Sat. 11 a.m.–1 a.m. $*

Metro Kitchen + Bar

Hotel Astor, 956 Washington Ave. (10th St.), South Beach, 305-672-7217
Best Sunday Brunches

The Hotel Astor does everything right. It has a gorgeous understated lobby, a happening party scene at the bar, and a restaurant that meshes urban style with tropical lushness. Cuisine is modern American jazzed up with hints of French, Italian, and Asian influence. Seared foie gras is served with grilled lychees, boniato, and aged balsamico; slow-cooked chicken comes with sun-dried tomato mash and pomegranate jus. Hipsters and savvy business types have discovered this jewel. Note that the bar is especially packed on Tuesday and Saturday nights. *Open for lunch Sat. 11:30 a.m.–2:30 p.m.; dinner Mon., Wed., Thurs. 7–11 p.m., Tues. 7 p.m.–12:30 a.m., Fri. 7 p.m.– midnight, Sat. 7 p.m.–12:30 a.m., Sun. 7–10:30 p.m.; Sunday brunch noon–3 p.m.* $$$

Miss Yip Chinese Cafe

1661 Meridian Ave. (Lincoln Rd.), South Beach, 305-534-5488
www.missyipchinesecafe.com

Miss Yip's is a campy-by-design take on Chinese takeout or eat-in, and you should definitely choose to take a seat here. You don't want to miss the jars of Chinese herbs and oddities lining the windows, or the flashy crimson-and-gold décor. And you won't find trendy pan-Asian-fusion cuisine here, just good traditional Chinese, including homemade dim sum, moo shoo wraps, barbecued duck, and General Tsao's chicken, all served with friendly feng shui. Luckily, in true South Beach style, there are lychee mojitos. *Open Mon.–Thurs., Sun. noon –11 p.m., Fri.–Sat. noon–midnight.* $

Paninoteca European Eatery

809 Lincoln Rd. (Meridian Ave.), South Beach, 305-538-0058

The pleasures of simple fare and good ingredients can never be underestimated. Paninoteca's European menu hits that tender spot and for scenery offers the entertaining backdrop of Lincoln Road. Join the many Italians who seek out panini—grilled, pressed sandwiches on rustic ciabatta, baguettes, or croissants—as basic as fresh tomato, mozzarella, greens, and basil, or as complicated as Le Roti (medium rare roast beef, gorgonzola, onion confit, baby greens, mayo, dijon, white wine vinegar, and olive oil). Individual pizzas, salads, and hot open-faced panini are on the menu, along with pasta and more substantial entrées after 5 p.m. In between meals, pop in for an espresso and a slice of tiramisu, or perhaps the banana chocolate chunk bread pudding with vanilla ice cream. *Open Mon.–Thurs. noon–11 p.m., Fri.–Sun. 11 a.m.–1 a.m.* $

Puerto Sagua

700 Collins Ave. (7th St.), South Beach, 305-673-1115

There's nothing trendy about this longtime diner, and that's just fine with its devoted clientele of old Cubans, young club kids, and anyone else looking for decent Cuban food. The pressed medianoche sandwiches are fresh, the platanos sweet, and the flan creamy and golden. Red snapper, *zarzuelas de mariscos* (seafood casseroles), and paella are menu highlights. Among the restaurant's kitschy "art" are the nifty three-dimensional paintings by the Scull sisters, twin artists whose whimsical art portrays Old Havana and South Beach. *Open daily 7:30 a.m.–2 a.m.* $

The Raleigh Coffee Shop

The Raleigh, 1775 Collins Ave. (18th St.), South Beach, 305-534-6300
www.raleighhotel.com

You'll find the gorgeously restored Deco breakfast counter off the lobby—just follow the scent of cinnamon. Pull up the old diner stools or snag an outdoor seat and try banana bread French toast, buttermilk pancakes with fresh mango and warm maple syrup. Or splurge on the black truffle and fontina omelette. There are lunch and dinner menus, too, equally enticing, all favorites of the Raleigh's cool fashion industry crowd for a quick bite. *Open for breakfast 6 a.m.–noon; lunch noon–4 p.m.; dinner Mon.–Thurs. 6–11 p.m., Fri.–Sun. 6 p.m.–midnight.* $

Rumi

330 Lincoln Rd. (Collins Ave.), South Beach, 305-672-4353
www.rumimiami.com
Best Restaurant/Lounges

This stylish Lincoln Road hot spot considers itself a modern version of a supper club. With cool earth-toned decor and soft glowing overhead lights, Rumi—named after a Middle Eastern poet and mystic—is a restaurant serving progressive cuisine in the earlier part of the evening. Dishes include orange and black pepper dusted lamb loin, rillettes of jerked pork, and the unforgettable molten coffee cake with sweet cream. Then, around midnight, the lounge takes over and the scene starts swinging (literally—there's a swing to play on). Expect occasional live entertainment and—thanks to management's ties with the music industry—surprise concerts from visiting VIPs like Erykah Badu. *Open Tues.–Sat. 7 p.m.–5 a.m.* $$$

Sage on Fifth
425 Washington Ave. (5th St.), South Beach, 305-672-3737

Intimate and comfortable, this newcomer to the South-of-Fifth neighborhood serves up eclectic New American cuisine, like grilled rack of lamb with black bean strudel, house-made pastas, and fresh seafood. Desserts really shine here: the Key lime cheesecake soufflé with mojito sorbet, and the meringue-crusted jumbo strawberries with bitter orange coulis and mango-coriander sorbet are standouts. There's a cozy neighborhood ambience here, and outdoor tables let you watch the Prada-carrying crowd waiting to get into China Grill across the street. *Open for lunch Mon.–Fri. 11 a.m.–3 p.m.; dinner nightly 6 p.m.–midnight.* $$$

Segafredo
1040 Lincoln Rd. (Lenox Ave.), South Beach, 305-673-0047

If you have any doubt about which Lincoln Road sidewalk cafe to choose for your afternoon cocktail, just look for the red umbrellas under which you'll find a cosmopolitan crowd sipping—well, cosmopolitans. Segafredo, one of the area's most European outdoor cafes, is always crowded with Italians gossiping over a glass of wine, while house music keeps the mood mellow. Small and cozy, with barstools and comfy loveseats, the lounge is next to the historic Colony Theatre. Snack on panini by day, or settle in late night for after-dinner drinks and tiramisu. *Open daily 11 a.m.–1 a.m.* $

Soyka
5556 NE 4th Ct. (Biscayne Blvd.), East Side Miami, 305-759-3117

From Mark Soyka, owner of South Beach's popular News Cafe and the Van Dyke, comes this huge dining spot in on-its-way East Side Miami. The industrial chic space—terrazzo floors, exposed girders, and concrete walls—sets the stage for comfort food, steaks, and fish. Regulars include area businessfolks and resident hipsters. *Open Mon.–Thurs., Sun. 11 a.m.–11 p.m., Fri.–Sat. 11 a.m.–midnight.* $$

Spris
731 Lincoln Rd. (Meridian Ave.), South Beach, 305-673-2020

Italian visitors head to Spris to sit at sidewalk tables under blue umbrellas and savor authentic thin-crusted quattro formaggi pizza, and so should you. The wood-burning oven renders the crust perfectly charred, and toppings are delivered with a deft Italian touch. Pastas, carpaccini, salads, and tiramisu are on the menu too, but when the pizza is this good, do you really need to order anything else? *Open daily noon.–1 a.m.* $

Tamara

The National Hotel, 1677 Collins Ave. (17th St.), South Beach, 305-532-2311
www.nationalhotel.com
Best Romantic Dining

This tiny, chic restaurant tucked away in the back of the National Hotel's
impressive lobby is a well-kept secret. A favorite romantic hideaway, Tamara
is a splendid discovery. Its rich French fusion cuisine doesn't stint on the
flavor. Dishes include Maine lobster, shelled and sautéed in European butter
on truffle-infused potato purée; and vol au vent, jumbo shrimp and scallops
with a puff pastry shell filled with morels and asparagus. The fitting end:
chocolate volcano. *Open daily 6 a.m.–midnight.* $$$

Tantra Restaurant & Lounge

1445 Pennsylvania Ave. (Espanola Way), South Beach, 305-672-4765
www.tantrarestaurant.com
Best Romantic Dining

There's nothing subtle about this restaurant/lounge, which aims to provide
a sensual environment to enhance your senses. A real grass floor, scented
candles, exotic music, plush couches, and a cuisine that leads you to culi-
nary ecstasy by relying heavily on oysters, lobster, truffles, and chocolate are
sure to titillate. Start off with their signature martini, the Tantric Kiss (vodka,
pineapple, cranberry, peach schnapps), and follow it up with a Tantra Plate
that includes some potent aphrodisiacs—Prince Edward Island oysters,
jumbo shrimp, eel, and ahi tuna sashimi with lychee sorbet. Then it's on to
the lamb pomegranate or sea bass Aphrodite, and a chocolate dessert. After
your meal, Tantra turns into a sexy lounge that keeps going till very late. Ask
your server about hookah service. All in all, it's good fun, and remains one of
South Beach's hottest tickets for visiting celebs and local big names. *Open
nightly for dinner 7 p.m.–1 a.m. Lounge open till 5 a.m.* $$$$

Taverna Opa

36–40 Ocean Dr. (1st St.), South Beach, 305-673-6730
www.tavernaoparestaurant.com

Let's call it My Big Fat Greek Night o' Fun. This exuberant restaurant and
party hot spot starts out the evening as a casual Greek seafood restaurant,
then explodes into mayhem. Begin with tasty meze—tzatziki, stuffed grape
leaves, spanakopita—and continue with excellent grilled fish and seafood.
Before you know it, the Greek disco music is amped up, a hunky waiter
jumps up on the table and starts dancing, belly dancers join in, napkins fly
from the ceiling, and soon after, you're up there dancing too. They close
when the ouzo runs out. *Open daily 4 p.m.–3 a.m.* $

Touch

910 Lincoln Rd. (Jefferson Ave.), South Beach, 305-532-8003
www.TouchRestaurant.com

Well, as Gypsy reminded us, ya gotta have a gimmick. Here it's fire twirlers, barely clothed pole dancers, and live percussionists to spice up the new "modern-influenced grill"—luxurious cuisine where Kobe rib-eye steaks, lobster, and foie gras figure prominently. Bartenders—uh, sorry, professional mixologists—take their jobs very seriously and come up with enticing specialty drinks every season, like lemontinis, prickly pear margaritas, and chocolate martinis. Petrified palm trees, luxurious silks and suede, and a theatrical setting draw well-dressed, beautiful revelers of all ages, including the occasional VIP (Rosie O'Donnell and Janet Jackson have partied here). A new lounge out front serves drinks and tapas for those who prefer the slightly less volatile entertainment on Lincoln Road. *Open for dinner Sun.–Thurs. 7 p.m.–midnight, Fri.–Sat. 7 p.m.–1 a.m. Lounge open Sun.–Thurs. till 1 a.m., Fri.–Sat. till 2 a.m.* $$$

Tuscan Steak

433 Washington Ave. (5th St.), South Beach, 305-534-2233
Best Steakhouses

If you think Italian family-style dining means sharing platters of mushy ziti and grapefruit-size meatballs, Tuscan Steak will change your mind. This posh and pricey Florentine grill is part of China Grill Management, which lists Blue Door at Delano and China Grill among its Miami properties. High rollers looking to impress dates and expense-account businesspeople are among the clientele. Yes, you order dishes to share, and the choices are savory indeed: antipasti like Tuscan bean salad with grilled rare tuna or prosciutto di Parma with tropical fruit; and variations on staples like pasta, risotto, polenta, and gnocchi. And then there is the steak: T-bone steak with roasted garlic purée; grilled filet mignon with Tuscan roasted potatoes, topped with gorgonzola and a Barolo sauce; or Parmesan-crusted New York sirloin steak. Naturally, the extensive wine list features many Italian wines, including Tuscans and Super Tuscans. Super, indeed. *Open Sun.–Thurs. 6–11 p.m., Fri.–Sat. 6 p.m.–midnight.* $$$

Arty Party Miami: The Nightlife

Bar at the Marlin

The Marlin, 1200 Collins Ave. (12th St.), South Beach, 305-604-3595
www.marlinhotel.com

Music industry types, a faithful New York and L.A. contingent, and people from the film and fashion worlds join savvy locals at this classic bar in the rock-'n'-roll Marlin Hotel. It's gotten a redo of sorts, without compromising its roots—the lower level, where live bands occasionally perform, keeps its speakeasy feel. New additions include a second bar, comfy banquettes, lounge chairs, and areas suited to dining, and a funky restaurant serving American bistro fare with Asian flair. Despite the clientele, the Bar at the Marlin is still a casual hangout that welcomes everyone, rock star or not. *Open Mon.–Tues., Sat. 10:30 p.m.–5 a.m., Wed.–Thurs. 10:30 p.m.–3 a.m., Fri. 5 p.m.–5 a.m., Sun. 6 p.m.–5 a.m.*

Bar at Sagamore Hotel

Sagamore Hotel, 1671 Collins Ave. (17th St.), South Beach, 305-535-8088
www.sagamorehotel.com

The stark all-white Sagamore feels more like a big-city modern art museum than a lobby bar, but you'll warm up to the high-drama environs after snagging a seat on one of their saddle barstools and slamming back a vodka Red Bull or two. You are surrounded by top-flight contemporary art and furnishings, so by all means take the time to check them out while you're here. *Open nightly 6 p.m.–1 a.m.*

B.E.D.

929 Washington Ave. (10th St.), South Beach, 305-532-9070
www.bedmiami.com
Best Restaurant/Lounges

See Arty Party Restaurants, p. 109 for description.
Open Mon., Wed.–Sat. 8 p.m.–5 a.m. $$$

Blue
222 Espanola Way (Washington Ave.), South Beach, 305-534-1009

The name comes from the deep color that makes up the décor of this long, narrow, unpretentious bar. Known for its laid-back vibe and deep house music, Blue's simply one of those friendly places with no cover charge and no nonsense. Resident deejays mix it up—hip-hop, R&B, tropical house, Latin—on different nights. Come early, or you may not get in—this small place fills up quickly. *Open nightly 10 p.m.–5 a.m.*

Cafeteria
546 Lincoln Rd. (Pennsylvania Ave.), South Beach, 305-672-3663

See Arty Party Restaurants, p. 110 for description.
Open daily 24 hours. $$

China Grill
404 Washington Ave. (5th St.), South Beach, 305-534-2211

See Arty Party Restaurants, p. 110 for description.
Open for lunch Mon.–Fri. 11 a.m.–6 p.m.; dinner Mon.–Fri. 6 p.m.–midnight,
Sat.–Sun. 6 p.m.–1 a.m. $$$

Churchill's Pub
5501 NE 2nd Ave. (NE 55th St.), Little Haiti, 305-757-1807
www.churchillspub.com
Best Live Music Venues

Look for the old double-decker buses parked by this indie rock institution located in a dicey Miami neighborhood. Part neighborhood bar, part live music venue, Churchill's hosts touring bands regularly, and no two nights are the same. It can be punk, hard rock, acoustical music, rap, even jazz. The British pub food is decent, and you can come here to catch soccer and rugby games on TV. *Open daily 11 a.m.–3 a.m.* $

The District Restaurant Lounge
35 NE 40th St. (N. Miami Ave.), Design District, 305-576-7242
www.thedistrictmiami.com

See Arty Party Restaurants, p. 111 for description.
Open for lunch Tues.–Sat. 11:30 a.m.–4 p.m.; dinner 5:30–11 p.m.; happy
hour Thurs.–Fri. 5–8 p.m. $$

D'Lounge

The National Hotel, 1677 Collins Ave. (17th St.), South Beach, 305-532-2311
www.nationalhotel.com

The ambience is timeless chic at the National Hotel's vintage bar and lounge, a glamorous space dominated by an exquisite oak bar and original design details like chrome light fixtures and barrel chairs. So devoted is the National to its painstakingly perfect restoration that its lounge and cabaret-style music make you feel as though you've stepped right into another era, and the well-dressed clientele of fashion and entertainment industry professionals fits right in. Friday nights feature a decent happy hour 5:30–8:30 p.m., while on Thursday and Saturday nights, you can catch live cabaret performances. *Open daily 4 p.m.–1 a.m.*

Fallabella Bar

The Albion, 1650 James Ave. (Lincoln Rd.), South Beach, 305-913-1000
www.rubellhotels.com

Sleek, low-key, and smart with industrial-looking style, the tiny Fallabella Bar attracts the same kind of clientele that find their way to The Albion: fashion industry people, New Yorkers, and artsy hipsters who are over the see-and-be-seen hype. The vibe is quiet, and the ambience is sophisticated. Enjoy a glass of their signature champagne with passion fruit nectar. *Open Thurs.–Mon. 6:30 a.m.–2 a.m.*

Felt Billiards Club

1242 Washington Ave. (12th St.), South Beach, 305-531-2114

The pool table is an obligatory prop in many a South Beach bar, but at Felt, it's the main attraction—it's the only billiards hall in the town with official regulation-size tables. Friendly and absolutely lacking in attitude, Felt has a lounge scene where deejays spin and folks come to hang out and relax before or after clubbing. *Open daily 5 p.m.–5 a.m.* $

Grass Restaurant & Lounge

28 NE 40th St. (N. Miami Ave.), Design District, 305-573-3355
www.grasslounge.com

See Arty Party Restaurants, p. 112 for description.
Open Tues.–Thurs. 8 p.m.–3 a.m., Fri. 6 p.m.–4 a.m., Sat. 8 p.m.–4 a.m. $$$

Jade

1766 Bay Rd. (18th St.), South Beach, 305-695-0000
www.jadesobe.com
Best Gay Bars

Off the beaten South Beach path, this chic upscale lounge with a serene
Asian theme has multiple lounge areas and different theme nights to appeal
to a range of tastes: live jazz, deejays spinning R&B, hip-hop, old school,
merengue, salsa, and '80s music. Friday nights are the scene of one of the
Beach's most popular gay parties. The second-level art gallery sometimes
features open-mike poetry. *Open Wed.–Thurs. 9 p.m.–5 a.m., Fri. 7 p.m.–
5 a.m., Sat. 10 p.m.–5 a.m., Sun 9 p.m.–5 a.m.* $

Jazid

1342 Washington Ave. (13th St.), South Beach, 305-673-9372
www.jazid.net
Best Live Music Venues

One of the few clubs in Miami that promises live jazz every night of the
week, Jazid hosts local and occasionally international performers on its intimate downstairs stage, while the upstairs deejay lounge features cool blue
lighting, overstuffed couches, and a pool table. Expect R&B, Motown,
Brazilian beats, soul, and Latin sounds served up as they should be, in a
dark, sultry setting with absolutely no attitude. The eclectic crowd—young,
old, professional, Latin, black, Anglo—is here for the music. *Open nightly
9 p.m.–5 a.m.* $

Laundry Bar

721 N. Lincoln Lane (Meridian Ave.), South Beach, 305-531-7700
www.laundrybar.com
Best Theme Bars

Wash, dry, drink, fold, dance. With a slick stainless steel bar and front-
loading washing machines, high-tech sound system and dryers, the Laundry
Bar has transformed a chore into a party. It's gay oriented, but straights are
welcome. *Open daily 7 a.m.–5 a.m. Bar open noon–5 a.m.*

Mac's Club Deuce

222 14th St. (Collins Ave.), South Beach, 305-531-6200
Best Dive Bars

Wear your highest Blahniks and your winningest smile in hopes of getting
past the doorman here—oops, never mind, this is Club Deuce we're talking
about. Wear whatever you want and be whatever you want here: pimp, tattoo

artist, movie star, regular Joe, drag queen, seedy character, businessman, biker. Come late at night when there's rock playing on the jukebox and a pool game threatening to erupt into a brawl. You're just gonna nurse that Bud and mind your own beeswax. *Open daily 8 a.m.–5 a.m.* $

Metro Kitchen + Bar

Hotel Astor, 956 Washington Ave. (10th St.), South Beach, 305-672-7217

See Arty Party Restaurants, p. 113 for description.
Open for lunch Sat. 11:30 a.m.–2:30 p.m.; dinner Mon., Wed., Thurs. 7–11 p.m., Tues. 7 p.m.–12:30 a.m., Fri. 7 p.m.–midnight, Sat. 7 p.m.– 12:30 a.m., Sun. 7–10:30 p.m.; Sunday brunch noon–3 p.m. $$$

Pawn Shop Lounge

1222 NE 2nd Ave. (12th St.), Downtown Miami, 305-373-3511
www.thepawnshoplounge.com

Looking for street cred? Visit this monument to seediness, skankiness, and white trash cool, housed in a former 1930s pawn shop building in gritty downtown Miami where none other than the ubiquitous Paris Hilton kicked off the opening. Inside, there's an Airstream trailer refitted with garish vinyl seats, an old schoolbus-turned-lounge, seats swiped from a 727 airliner, original vaults that now serve as a wine cellar and coat check, plus an array of goofy stuff bound to resurrect all kinds of childhood memories, both pleasant and ugly. This modern-day speakeasy is attracting young scenesters who may not get the '60s and '70s references—or know much of anything about pawn shops—but they keep coming back for the novelty and the house music. Spring for the valet parking in this slightly dicey neighborhood. *Open Thurs.–Sat. 10 p.m.–5 a.m.* $

Playwright Irish Pub & Restaurant

1265 Washington Ave. (13th St.), South Beach, 305-534-0667
Best Theme Bars

Not a theme bar in the Disney sense of the word, this pub has a certain dingy appeal that seems authentic, perhaps because it attracts visitors from the U.K. who down pints of draft beer at the long wooden bar. Low-key entertainment consists of open-mike night, karaoke, and deejays on Friday and Saturday nights, but the real draw is European soccer on television. *Open daily 11 a.m.–5 a.m.*

Rooftop Lounge

TownHouse Hotel, 150 20th St. (Collins Ave.), South Beach, 305-534-3800
www.townhousehotel.com

So what if the TownHouse doesn't have a pool? They've got a cool rooftop lounge instead where they host their popular and trendy parties. Drink a saketini and lounge on the red waterbeds under red umbrellas, or chill in the glow-in-the-dark water tower and listen to surround sound. It's also the scene for popular weekly cocktail parties. Young metrosexuals make this fun hot spot their hangout. *Open Wed.–Sat. 8 p.m.– 2 a.m.* $

Rumi

330 Lincoln Rd. (Collins Ave.), South Beach, 305-672-4353
www.rumimiami.com
Best Restaurant/Lounges

See Arty Party Restaurants, p. 114 for description.
Open Tues.–Sat. 7 p.m.–5 a.m. $$$

Space

34 NE 11th St. (NE 1st Ave.), Downtown Miami, 305-375-0001
www.clubspace.com

The granddaddy of downtown Miami's many dance clubs, this warehouse has been transformed into a two-level, high-energy dance complex with top-flight sound and light systems, featuring both a main room with an oversize dance floor, and a second-floor rooftop where club kids can come to watch the sunrise (it's open till 10 a.m.). Note that superstar guest deejays like John Digweed and Paul Oakenfold can be found spinning here regularly. *Open Fri.–Sat 10 p.m.–10 a.m.* $

Sunday Soiree at the Raleigh

The Raleigh, 1775 Collins Ave. (18th St.), South Beach, 305-534-6300
www.raleighhotel.com
Best Sunday Parties

Spend Sunday afternoon by the Raleigh's stunning pool nursing a pomegranate margarita. It's one of the best pool parties in town, hosted by Ingrid Casares, Alan Roth, and Tommy Pooch, so you can count on enjoying mellow sounds in a gorgeous setting and possibly stumbling upon the likes of Uma Thurman and Ashton Kutcher. *Open Sundays noon–midnight.* $

Tantra Restaurant & Lounge

1445 Pennsylvania Ave. (Espanola Way), South Beach, 305-672-4765
www.tantrarestaurant.com

See Arty Party Restaurants, p. 116 for description.
Open nightly for dinner 7 p.m.–1 a.m. Lounge open till 5 a.m. $$$$

Taverna Opa

36–40 Ocean Dr. (1st St.), South Beach, 305-673-6730
www.tavernaoparestaurant.com

See Arty Party Restaurants, p. 116 for description.
Open daily 4 p.m.–3 a.m. $

Touch

910 Lincoln Rd. (Jefferson Ave.), South Beach, 305-532-8003
www.TouchRestaurant.com

See Arty Party Restaurants, p. 117 for description.
Open for dinner Sun.–Thurs. 7 p.m.–midnight, Fri.–Sat. 7 p.m.–1 a.m.
Lounge open Sun.–Thurs. till 1 a.m., Fri.–Sat. till 2 a.m. $$$

Upstairs at the Van Dyke Cafe

846 Lincoln Rd. (Jefferson Ave.), South Beach, 305-534-3600
Best Live Music Venues

This cozy second-story gem is one of South Florida's few live jazz clubs, delivering top-caliber performances from big names and regularly scheduled musicians nearly every night. The scene is dark and intimate, with loveseats and silently spinning ceiling fans, but you're not here for the ambience—it's all about the music. Jazz lovers, both locals and tourists, turn out for artists like Joe Williams, Freddy Cole, John Hicks, Mose Allison, and Mark Murphy, some of the luminaries who've performed here, along with local stars Nicole Henry and Rose Max. *Open daily 8 a.m.–2 a.m. Shows start Sun.–Thurs. 9 p.m., 10:30 p.m., midnight; Fri.–Sat. 10 p.m., 11:30 p.m., 1 a.m. $*

Zee Lounge

The National Hotel, 1677 Collins Ave. (17th St.), South Beach, 305-532-2311

Always stylishly tasteful, the National Hotel has created its own version of the beach party with Zee Lounge, a casually chic beachside space behind the stunning 205-foot infinity pool, with swinging hammocks and private cabana tents. The grill serves tasty tidbits to go with tropical cocktails. *Open daily 3:30 p.m.–midnight.*

Arty Party Miami:
The Attractions

ArtCenter/South Florida

800, 810, 924 Lincoln Rd. (Meridian Ave.), South Beach, 305-674-8278
www.artcentersf.org

When Lincoln Road started to undergo its renaissance 20 years ago, a group of local artists created a place where they could work, learn, and exhibit. The resulting ArtCenter is one of the Road's signature spaces—located in three historic buildings—where visitors can observe artists on the job. The campus includes more than 50 studios, exhibition galleries, art education classrooms, and offices. *Open daily 9 a.m.–11 p.m.*

Beach Scooter Rental

1341 Washington Ave. (13th St.), South Beach, 305-538-7878
www.beachscooter.com

Rent a zippy scooter so you can tool around South Beach with the wind in your hair and the sun on your face, to say nothing of eliminating parking hassles. If you've never driven a scooter before, they'll give you a free lesson and even pick you up from your hotel. Their Inventory includes current-year models from companies like Peugeot and Malaguti. *Open daily 10 a.m.–8 p.m.* $$$–$$$$

Britto Central

818 Lincoln Rd. (Meridian Ave.), South Beach, 305-531-8821
www.britto.com

You can't miss the colorful, playful works of Brazilian pop artist Romero Britto—they're everywhere. They're on billboards, vodka bottles, ceramics, aluminum outdoor sculpture, automobiles, canvas, and almost any other surface imaginable. Critics may pooh-pooh his exuberant stylized patterns, but Britto's managed to attract the attention of celeb collectors like Michael Jordan, Arnold Schwarzenegger, and Whitney Houston. *Open Mon.–Thurs 10 a.m.–11 p.m., Fri.–Sat. 10 a.m.–midnight, Sun. 10 a.m.–10 p.m.*

Design District

NE 40th St. and 2nd Ave., Design District

www.designmiami.com

This 18-square block area north of Downtown Miami has grown from a long-time headquarters for furniture and design showrooms to a hip community of design, surrounded by up-and-coming neighborhoods that are helping fuel its rebirth. No longer just for the trade, the home furnishings and interior design showrooms of stellar names like Holly Hunt, Ann Sacks, and Poltrona Frau are open to the public Monday through Saturday. The Design District is also home to prominent art galleries, including Bernice Steinbaum, Daniel Azoulay, and Adamar Fine Arts; fun restaurants; and even a velvet-rope late-night lounge. During the day, you can park on the streets or valet at NE 2nd and 39th St., and explore on foot—don't miss the whimsical open-air living room at the corner of NE 40th St. and N. Miami Ave. *Open Mon.–Sat.*

Don Shula's Golf Club

7601 Miami Lakes Dr. (NW 77th Ave.), Miami Lakes, 305-820-8088 / 800-247-4852

www.donshulahotel.com

Though he retired from coaching in 1995, former Miami Dolphins Head Coach Don Shula remains a household word, due in part to his upscale steakhouse chain (and perhaps because Dolphin fans can never forget his unduplicated perfect season). He's also got an eponymous hotel and golf club in the northwest suburb of Miami Lakes that's a favorite with visiting businesspeople. The newly redesigned Championship Course has a split personality—the front nine resembles a northern course, with long, narrow, tree-lined fairways; while the back nine showcases South Florida wildlife, with dense foliage, plenty of water, and marsh traps. There's also a lighted par-three 18-hole executive course open till 10 p.m. *Open 7 a.m.–5:30 p.m.; lighted course open till 10 p.m.* $$$$

Espanola Way

Between 14th and 15th Streets from Collins to Washington, South Beach

This romantic stretch got its start in 1925, when it was planned as a Spanish Village that would attract artists and art lovers, along the lines of Paris' Left Bank or New York's Greenwich Village. Well, this is Miami, a magnet for shady characters. So instead of bohemian types, they got bootleggers, bookies, and mobsters—rumor has it Al Capone even set up a gambling ring in the Clay Hotel while hiding from the cops. Later, in the same hotel, Cuban bandleader Desi Arnaz started the rumba craze in the 1930s. The little village languished until another kind of Miami vice—the television version—

revived interest here, and Espanola Way finally became the artsy side street its visionaries intended. The Clay Hotel is now a lovely hostel that attracts a young international crowd, and quaint sidewalk cafes are populated with intellectual artists. You'll also find offbeat boutiques, the Miami Beach Cinematheque, and a popular weekend market and jewelry bazaar.

Holocaust Memorial

1933–1945 Meridian Ave. (Dade Blvd.), South Beach, 305-538-1663
www.holocaustmmb.org

Sculptor Ken Triester's moving tribute to the 6 million Jewish victims of the Nazis during World War II, this dramatic monument depicts a huge bronze arm and hand stretching skyward, surrounded by a lily-filled reflection pond and photographic history of the infamous death camps. Note the significance of the numerical part of the address. *Open daily 9 a.m.–9 p.m.* Free.

Lincoln Road Mall

Lincoln Rd. between Alton Rd. and Washington Ave., South Beach

For the quintessential South Beach experience—sidewalk cafes, cool architecture, art galleries, people-watching, quirky shops, performance art, cultural venues, over-the-top clubs—spend the day at Lincoln Road. Once known as the Fifth Avenue of the South, this pedestrian street went through hard times before resurging in the 1990s as a vibrant destination. Although high rents have forced out some independent retailers, it hasn't totally sold out to chain stores. Two cultural venues—the Lincoln Theater and the Colony Theatre, now under renovation—are located here, as is the ArtCenter/South Florida. There's no better place for people-watching. Tourists, gay couples, elderly Beach residents, rollerbladers, models, drag queens, kids on skateboards, and others congregate here. There are antique and farmers' markets on Sundays; performance artists on weekends; and folks hanging out 24/7.

Lowe Art Museum

University of Miami, 1301 Stanford Dr., Coral Gables, 305-284-3536
www.lowemuseum.org

You'll see everything from modern Cuban paintings to rare Roman antiquities at the Lowe, one of South Florida's most wide-ranging art museums. Located at the Coral Gables campus of the University of Miami, the museum has a distinguished collection of Renaissance and Baroque art; Native American, Asian, and pre-Columbian objects; and contemporary works. *Open Tues., Wed., Fri., Sat. 10 a.m.–5 p.m., Thurs. noon–7 p.m., Sun. noon–5 p.m.* $

Margulies Collection

591 NW 27th St. (NW 5th Ave.), Downtown Miami, 305-576-1051
www.margulieswarehouse.com

Yet another glowing example of Miami's growing status as a major art city is
this collection of contemporary and vintage photography, video, sculpture,
and installation art from the holdings of Miami collector Martin Z. Margulies.
Housed in a newly converted warehouse near Downtown Miami, the collection includes works from Takashi Murakami, Gilles Barbier, Franz West,
Frank Stella, Anish Kapoor, Ulrich Ruckriem, Michael Heizer, and Tony
Cragg. The photography collection includes work from 1910 to the present,
tracing various major movements in 20th-century photographs. *Open
September–May, Fri.–Sat. 11 a.m.–4 p.m., Sun. noon–4 p.m.*

Miami Art Central

5960 57th Ave. (SW 60th St.), Coral Gables, 305-455-3333
www.miamiartcentral.com

Miami's newest venue for visual and performing arts, located near the
University of Miami campus in Coral Gables, aims to emphasize contemporary artists of Latin-American and Hispanic descent in changing exhibitions,
performances, and film and video screenings. *Open Tues.–Fri. 4–7 p.m.,
Sat.–Sun. 11 a.m.–6 p.m. and by appointment.*

Miami Beach Botanical Garden

2000 Convention Center Dr. (19th St.), South Beach, 305-673-7256
www.miamibeachbotanicalgarden.org

Peacefully tucked in the northwestern corner of the Miami Beach Convention
Center parking lot is the Miami Beach Botanical Garden, four and a half
acres of subtropical palms, orchids, bromeliads, flowering trees, and specialty gardens. Take the free daily tour from 11 a.m.–noon to learn more about
the collections, which include Japanese, herb, and butterfly gardens. *Open
Tues.–Sun. 9 a.m.–5 p.m.* Free.

Museum of Contemporary Art—MoCA

770 NE 125th St. (NE 8th Ave.), North Miami, 305-893-6211
www.mocanomi.org
Best Art Spaces

Many of the roots of Miami's rapidly expanding art scene are firmly anchored
in this dramatic Charles Gwathmey–designed structure. MoCA is widely
known for provocative and innovative exhibitions, showcasing such artists as
Roy Lichtenstein, Frank Stella, Keith Haring, and late designer Gianni

Versace. The permanent collection includes works from Louise Nevelson, Julian Schnabel, Nam June Paik, and José Badia. *Open Tues.–Sat. 11 a.m.–5 p.m., Sun. noon–5 p.m., last Fri. night of every month 7–10 p.m.* $

Rubell Collection

95 NW 29th St. (NW 1st Ave.), Downtown Miami, 305-573-6090
Best Art Spaces

The Rubell family, which has been acquiring contemporary art for decades, has opened its extraordinary collection to the public, and it's widely regarded as one of the most comprehensive in the country. Newly expanded and renovated, the space includes 29 galleries and a sculpture garden showcasing important works by such artists as Jeff Koons, Purvis Young, Keith Haring, Cindy Sherman, Rineke Dijkstra, and Peter Halley. It's open seasonally, with added hours during Art Basel in December (see p. 206). *Open Wed.–Sun 10 a.m.–6 p.m., second Saturdays 10 a.m.–10 p.m.* $

The Wolfsonian—FIU

1001 Washington Ave. (10th St.), South Beach, 305-531-1001
www.wolfsonian.org

You may never look at an old spatula quite the same way again after visiting this unusual museum. Housed in a beautifully restored fortress-like 1927 storage facility, the Wolfsonian preserves Mitchell Wolfson Jr.'s extraordinary collection of modern objects, focusing on how art and design shape and reflect the human experience. Those objects include propaganda posters, old radios, a London Underground sign, among many others—all from the Industrial Age, 1885–1945. You can expect to find special exhibitions, films, and lectures year-round. Don't miss the new store, cafe, and wine bar. *Open Mon.–Tues. 11 a.m.–6 p.m., Thurs. 11 a.m.–9 p.m., Fri.–Sat. 11 a.m.–6 p.m., Sun. noon–5 p.m.* $

ARTY PARTY

Outdoors Miami

Miami's great outdoors—balmy ocean breezes, warm ocean waters, subtropical wilderness, and plenty of sunny days—is one of the best reasons to come here, and with a full slate of activities available, you have the makings of a truly memorable vacation. If your idea of fun is getting wet on a jetski, exploring verdant flora and fauna, dining al fresco on the water, and spending every waking hour under the sun or stars, this itinerary is for you. You'll spend your days in greater Miami's favorite outdoor playground, Key Biscayne, and nearby Coconut Grove and Coral Gables.

Outdoors Miami:
The Itinerary

Our Hotel Choice: Grove Isle Hotel and Spa, because it's easy to make the most of the outdoors at this casually elegant hotel on a tropically landscaped private island overlooking Biscayne Bay.

Prime Time: Thurs.–Sat.

Day 1

Morning: Begin your morning with *a hearty breakfast* at the French bistro **Le Bouchon du Grove** in downtown Coconut Grove because you've got a full day ahead—the great subtropical outdoors is calling. Pack up your suit and towel, head to Hobie Beach on the Rickenbacker Causeway just east of the toll plaza, and select the adventure of your choice: go windsurfing or try out the latest extreme watersport—kiteboarding—at **Sailboards Miami**. Skim along Biscayne Bay on a catamaran from **Miami Catamarans**. Or get a pelican's-eye view of South Florida from an ultralight at **Ultralight Adventures**, north of the causeway just across the big bridge. If you want to explore the waters aboard *a waverunner* or ocean kayak, stay on the Rickenbacker onto Key Biscayne to **El Club**, where they'll fix you up with gear and tell you the best places to explore.

Lunch: Key Biscayne is all about casual waterfront restaurants, so take your pick. The **Bayside Seafood Restaurant** is known for delectable conch fritters and fried fish; the bayside **Sunday's on the Bay** next to Crandon Marina serves tasty seafood and *lethal frozen cocktails*.

Afternoon: If you're ready to relax after lunch, head back to the hotel for some pool time and perhaps an *in-room massage*. Another intriguing pool choice is Coral Gables' **Venetian Pool**, a rock quarry transformed into a Venice-inspired lagoon in 1924, and now a public swimming pool. While you're in the area, take the opportunity to take a drive around lush and beautiful **Coral Gables**. Or drive to **Fairchild Tropical Botanic Garden**, 83 acres of subtropical paradise best explored on the 45-minute tram ride. Cap off your afternoon with smoked fish and a cold beer at *local hideaway* **Jimbo's Place** on Virginia Key, a ramshackle conglomeration of buildings fronting the lagoon where the old *Flipper* TV series was filmed. All kinds of characters—from old salts to young models to high-profile locals—hang out here to watch the bocce ball tournaments.

Dinner: Your meals come with water tonight. Your first choice should be the **Cafe Sambal** at Mandarin Oriental, Miami, which provides an unusual west-facing view of the bay, the Miami skyline, and the beautiful *sunset* (and delicious Asian-inspired food, too). You'll be sharing the vista with hand-holding couples and business travelers looking to unwind. Or try **Big Fish**, with its stunning views of the Miami River, the rainbow neon art along the Metrorail track, and Downtown Miami. The *outdoor bar*—wrapped around an enormous banyan tree—is a good-natured after-work hangout for young professionals and local characters. You might prefer having a steak at **Smith & Wollensky**, South Beach's best place to watch your ship come in.

Nighttime: Finish off the evening at **Tobacco Road**, holder of the county's first liquor license. It ain't pretty, but the live music has kept patrons rocking for decades. Or go bar-hopping in downtown Coconut Grove at the rowdy bars best identified by the bodies spilling out into the streets. One of the loudest, **Mr. Moe's**, is best known for the novelty of its decor: South Florida ski lodge, with pine beams and a river rock fireplace. Or make your way through the crowded *singles scene* at the **Gordon Biersch Brewery Restaurant** for the beer called Dunkle. For a sophisticated South Beach loungey vibe with deejays, head to the **Oxygen Lounge.**

Day 2

Morning: If you spent the night partying in Coconut Grove, you will be amazed at the city's transformation in the morning: unlike you, it's fresh-faced, tranquil, and sublimely lush. Start your day with breakfast al fresco at the venerable Coconut Grove **Green Street Cafe** before heading to Key Biscayne to make the most of this *gorgeous island*. If tennis is your game, head to the **Tennis Center at Crandon Park**, home of the NASDAQ-100 Open. Golfers, your destination is the **Crandon Park Golf Course**, considered one of the most beautiful and difficult par-72 courses in Florida. And cyclists should rent a bike at **Mangrove Cycles**, where Bill will tell you the best way to explore the Key's 15 miles of bike trails.

Lunch: You'll want to have lunch overlooking one of Dr. Beach's *top ten beaches* in the U.S. That would be **Bill Baggs Cape Florida State Park**, where the open-air **Boater's Grill** overlooking scenic No-Name Harbor serves excellent seafood and *Cuban cuisine* to laid-back boaters and in-the-know beachgoers. Fresh-from-the-sea fare also tops the menu of the **Purple Dolphin**, the cheerful restaurant at the Sonesta Beach Resort, where you'll want to dine on the outdoor terrace for the best ocean view.

Afternoon: Take a stroll through the park, making sure to check out the historic lighthouse (tours leave at 1 p.m.) and the cluster of old houses called Stiltsville perched in the bay. A newfangled way for you to explore is on one of those Segway Human Transporters—the **Segway Excursion Center** at the Sonesta Beach Resort Key Biscayne will have you up and running after a 30-minute introduction. Or sneak off for a Key Lime Coconut Body Scrub and Soak at **The Spa at Ritz-Carlton, Key Biscayne**, or try a *Balinese synchronized massage* at **The Spa at Mandarin Oriental**.

Dinner: South Florida sunsets—magenta and blaze orange–streaked skies with violet edges—can make you gasp. One prime vantage point for this spectacular backdrop to *the Miami skyline* is the **Rusty Pelican** on Virginia Key, also the perfect spot for before-dinner cocktails. Then head to Coral Gables, well known for its many top-flight restaurants and a burgeoning pedestrian nightlife scene. Choose between two outstanding steakhouses: **Christy's** or **The Palm**, both old-school clubby restaurants where politicians and power brokers wheel and deal over prime ribs. Or perhaps you prefer the quietly chic **Carmen the Restaurant**, featuring *dazzlingly imaginative* Latin dishes, located in the David William Hotel.

Nighttime: Gear up for some strenuous bar-hopping (all of these places are within walking distance of each other). **The Globe Cafe and Bar** and **Houston's** are singles' magnets—just look for the droves of urbanites clutching *martinis* on the sidewalks. At **Fritz & Franz Bierhaus**, St. Pauli girl look-alikes deliver one-liter draft beers with Bavarian *gemütlichkeit*, and there's a good chance you'll hear *live blues* on weekends. **JohnMartin's Restaurant and Irish Pub** is one of Miami's few authentic Irish pubs, with live music on weekends. And at **The Bar** at Ponce and Giralda, the brew is tasty, the live rock rockin', and the scene loud and friendly.

Day 3

Morning: A quaint but tasty breakfast spot in Key Biscayne is the tiny **Donut Gallery**, one of those chatty neighborhood cafes that serves up satisfying breakfasts (but not donuts). After fortifying yourself, select from one of the following options (they all start from the north end of Miami Beach). Go *wreck diving* with **H20 Scuba** in Sunny Isles Beach or go out on the **Deep Sea Sport Fishing Boat** *Therapy IV*. Try your hand at kayaking at **Oleta River State Park**, Florida's largest urban park (which has ten miles of mountain bike trails). Or head to **Haulover Beach Park** where you can tackle the nine-hole golf course or catch some rays. Consider ordering a box lunch if you plan to be out all day. (Half-day options are available as well.)

Lunch: If you chose a half-day activity, it's time for a casual lunch. **Roger's Restaurant and Bar** in North Bay Village will welcome you with genuine Southern hospitality to an idyllic *waterfront dining patio* and giant tiki hut, and offers tasty Dixie-tinged cuisine. In Coconut Grove, **Scotty's Landing** is a well-kept secret where locals bring their dogs and tuck into seafood and cold beer.

Afternoon: After lunch, take a walk along Main Highway in **Downtown Coconut Grove**. Look for the concealed sign leading to **Barnacle Historic State Park**, a pristine sliver of bayfront land that's home to the 1891 bunga-low of yacht builder Ralph Munroe. If you love subtropical flora, you'll want to drive five minutes south on Douglas Road to **The Kampong**, the only National Tropical Botanical Garden located in the continental U.S. Tours are given by appointment only, so make arrangements before you arrive. You might have time for a *frozen margarita* at one of the Grove's many sidewalk cafes before heading back to your hotel for a shower.

Dinner: You've played hard. Now it's time for a sophisticated meal. **Baleen** fits the bill and then some, with a waterfront setting, whimsically elegant décor, and some of the *finest seafood* in town (you may see starry-eyed couples here; it's a choice site for proposals). Or make your way to **Azul** at Mandarin Oriental, Miami, Miami's only AAA Five Diamond restaurant. Or try the Biltmore Hotel's elegant signature restaurant, the **Palme d'Or**.

Nighttime: Have a nightcap at the sophisticated **M-Bar** at Mandarin Oriental, Miami, overlooking the skyline, *a dreamy place* to plan your next Miami adventure.

The Day After: Cap off your visit with the over-the-top Sunday Champagne brunch at the Biltmore Hotel's **1200 Restaurant & Courtyard**, famous for its sumptuous setting and outstanding selection of meat and seafood.

Outdoors Miami:
The Hotels

The Biltmore Hotel

1200 Anastasia Ave. (Granada Blvd.), Coral Gables, 305-445-1926 /
800-727-1926
www.biltmorehotel.com
Best Hotel Pools

Host to kings and presidents, Coral Gables' Biltmore Hotel is a truly grand hotel with an illustrious past. When it debuted in 1926 with hand-painted frescos on barrel-vaulted ceilings, carved mahogany furnishings, and lush gardens under a soaring Giralda tower, this Mediterranean fantasy quickly became one of the most fashionable resorts in the country, attracting European and Hollywood royalty like the Duke and Duchess of Windsor, Ginger Rogers, and Judy Garland. Even Al Capone stayed here. As the Jazz Age flourished, so did this dazzling property, hosting aquatic shows in the massive pool, fashion shows, gala balls, and world-class golf tournaments. With the onset of World War II, the Biltmore was converted into a huge hos-pital, and remained one until 1968. The hotel was boarded until it was acquired by the city, and reopened in 1987 following a massive restoration effort. Today, this gracious National Historic Landmark welcomes past and present luminaries (Bill Clinton is a favored guest) through its marble columned lobby. It's hard not to be awed by the spectacular pool (the largest in the continental U.S.) surrounded by tropical landscaping. There are 280 guest rooms with comfy feather beds, signature robes and slippers, and panoramic views of the city and the 18-hole, par-71 golf course. Its location in Coral Gables gives the visitor easy access to the myriad outdoor attrac-tions in nearby Coconut Grove and Key Biscayne. The elegant Palme d'Or (see p.144) overlooks the pool, while the 1200 Restaurant & Courtyard's lav-ish Sunday Champagne brunch (see p.139) in the rustic courtyard is one of the most extravagant in town. $$$

Fisher Island Club

One Fisher Island Dr., Fisher Island, 305-535-6076 / 800-537-3708
www.fisherisland.com

Once the winter retreat of William K. Vanderbilt, exclusive Fisher Island— 216 acres just south of Miami Beach—is now a luxurious residential com-munity and private club accessible only by ferry (allow 30 minutes to get off the island) or helicopter. Billionaires and superstar residents like Oprah

Winfrey, Boris Becker, and Anne Bancroft and Mel Brooks have homes here.
It is private, quiet, and old world, but the real draw is its diversions: the
championship P.B. Dye–designed golf course, 18 lighted tennis courts, the
20,000-square-foot Spa Internazionale, a mile-long stretch of beach, and
waterfront dining. The facilities may persuade you to spend your whole vacation onsite. Unless you like condominiums, hotel guests can stay in one of
the very few restored one- and two-bedroom Vanderbilt Cottages, or the
three-bedroom Rosemary's Cottage. All registered guests have free use of
golf carts during their stay. $$$$

Grove Isle Hotel and Spa

Four Grove Isle Dr. (S. Bayshore Dr.), Coconut Grove, 305-858-8300 /
800-884-7683
www.groveisle.com

Hidden on a quiet private island off Coconut Grove, this boutique hotel
overlooking the bay falls into that best-kept-secret category. Part of the
Noble House chain, Grove Isle is both elegant and casual, with a goofy
monkey and palm tree motif throughout. Each of the spacious 47 guest
rooms has a private terrace overlooking the marina or Biscayne Bay (and if
you book a corner suite, you'll enjoy especially impressive panoramic views
of the bay and skyline). The Colonial décor is comfortable, with tropical flo-
ral prints, blond mahogany furnishings, terra-cotta tile floors, and island
touches like ceiling fans and mosquito netting on beds. Amenities are all
first class: Frette linens, Bose CD players, and televisions in the bathrooms.
The brand new SpaTerre is a two-story spa with seven treatment rooms, couples massage room, Watsu pool with waterfall, yoga platform, and outdoor
massage areas on the bay. Although it's only a few minutes away from the
mainland, Grove Isle has enough activities to keep you busy for a long weekend: 12 Har-Tru clay tennis courts lit for night play; a heated pool and
hydro-massage whirlpool overlooking the bay; a 111-slip marina with char-
ters for fishing, sailing, cruising, and watersports (the dockmaster can
arrange excursions); and the incomparable waterfront Baleen (see p. 140),
one of Miami's finest seafood restaurants. $$$

The Ritz-Carlton, Coconut Grove

3300 SW 27th Ave. (Tigertail Ave.), Coconut Grove, 305-644-4680
www.ritzcarlton.com

The most formal-looking of the three Ritz-Carltons in South Florida, the
115-room Coconut Grove property owes its design inspiration to the Italian
Renaissance–style Vizcaya Museum. Yet this enclave is located in mellow
Coconut Grove, overlooking the marina and verdant surroundings, and con-

venient to all kinds of outdoor pursuits. You'll come upon arched hallways and ceilings, hand-wrought Italian lanterns, Venetian glass, and more than half a million dollars in original oil paintings. The spacious guest rooms, all with floor-to-ceiling windows and balconies, have British Colonial mahogany furnishings and warm island prints. Be sure to ask for a bay view room when you call to reserve. Amenities are particularly friendly for business travelers: multi-line phone, a large desk with high-speed Internet access, and a 24-hour technology butler on staff. The 6,000-square-foot spa and fitness center has six treatment rooms and European Vichy shower therapy. While the AAA Five Diamond–rated hotel is not waterfront (it's two blocks from the marina), the elevated pool does offer fine views of Coconut Grove. Bizcaya (see p. 141), their award-winning restaurant, serves classic Continental cuisine, freshly updated, in a luxurious setting of Biedermeier furnishings and silk damask draping. $$$$

The Ritz-Carlton, Key Biscayne

455 Grand Bay Dr. (Crandon Blvd.), Key Biscayne, 305-365-4500
www.ritzcarlton.com
Best Spas

This 402-room resort brings the Ritz-Carlton's comfortable elegance to carefree Key Biscayne. Best of all, it's ideally located on this picturesque island: right on the beach, and within walking, biking, or skating distance of Bill Baggs State Park. Floor-to-ceiling lobby windows display the magnificent tropical foliage, while the West Indies Colonial decor is elegantly understated. Guest rooms and suites have featherbeds and down comforters, Frette linens, and the pillows of your dreams, ordered from their pillow menu. When you book your room, keep in mind that the unencumbered views from the oceanfront rooms are particularly gorgeous. Sunbathing at one of the resort's two pools—an oceanfront zero-entry pool with a whirlpool, and a spa pool—is an almost painfully elegant experience, with staff offering Evian water mists, sunglass cleaning, chilled sunscreen, and cold scented hand towels, and a pool concierge on call to track down a best-selling novel or favorite CD. The 20,000-square-foot Spa at Ritz-Carlton, Key Biscayne (see p. 156), has 21 treatment rooms, while the Wellness Center takes advantage of the beachfront locale by offering beach fitness camps and aquatic kickboxing. Eleven tennis courts, all lit at night, include one hard court and ten soft-clay Hydro courts. The resort's signature restaurant, Aria (see p. 139), is arguably the Key's best fine-dining choice, while the beachfront Sandbar Grill (see p. 146) takes raw bar and casual seafood dining to a newly luxuriant level. $$$$

Sonesta Beach Resort Key Biscayne

350 Ocean Dr. (Crandon Blvd.), Key Biscayne, 305-361-2021 /
800-766-3782
www.sonesta.com

This longtime resort happily blends a casual, laid-back island vibe with some sophisticated surprises: an impressive collection of contemporary art from emerging and established artists; and a sunny spa that includes Kur Therapy and mineral-based European cleansing rituals. Of course, there are also simple pleasures like hammocks strung between coconut palms overlooking the wide white-sand beach. The eight-story modern structure, vaguely resembling a Maya temple, has 300 guest rooms with island or ocean views, and some have private balconies. (Note that the northeast corner rooms on the upper floors feature views of both the Atlantic and the bay.) Rooms are cheerfully modern. Because it's on recreational paradise Key Biscayne, expect to spend lots of time outdoors here: there's a heated Olympic-style pool and two whirlpool spas; a great beach with chaise lounges and cabanas; and kayaks, aqua bikes, catamarans, waverunners, sailboards, and other water toys available for rental. You can also rent a Segway for terrestrial exploration (see p. 155). There are seven Laykold tennis courts, three lit for night play; the popular Crandon Park Golf Course (see p. 152) is two miles away. $$$

Outdoors Miami:
The Restaurants

1200 Restaurant & Courtyard

The Biltmore Hotel, 1200 Anastasia Ave., Coral Gables, 305-445-1926

Best Sunday Brunches

Known for its spectacular Sunday brunches, this courtyard restaurant specializes in grilled meat and fish dishes, and spotlights Mediterranean appetizers and pastas. But it's the setting that makes this casual dining spot sparkle: old stone and tiles, a rustic fountain, and old French doors and windows are the framework for a delightfully romantic setting. If you're not a hotel guest, reservations for the Sunday brunch are a must. *Open daily 6:30 a.m.–10:30 p.m.; Sunday brunch 10:30 a.m.–2:30 p.m.* $$$

Aria

The Ritz-Carlton, Key Biscayne, 455 Grand Bay Dr. (Crandon Blvd.),
Key Biscayne, 305-365-4500
www.ritzcarlton.com

The Ritz-Carlton's award-winning hotel restaurant, Aria, serves fine Mediterranean cuisine that's been tricked out to wonderful effect. Entrées include grilled tuna loin prepared with a white bean and truffle purée, and *zarzuela*, a Spanish saffron seafood stew. Desserts are equally inventive, like the tiramisu prepared with coffee gelato and chocolate tagliatelle. After dinner, retire to the Library Lounge, a clubby enclave that's all leather and books, for a nightcap—and not a martini, please; they're known for their outstanding selection of more than 100 varieties of aged rums, vintage ports, malt whiskies, and Madeiras. *Open for breakfast daily 7–11 a.m.; brunch Sun. 11:30 a.m.–3 p.m.; lunch daily 11:30 a.m.–3 p.m.; dinner Sun.–Thurs. 6–10 p.m., Fri.–Sat. 6–11 p.m.* $$$$

Azul

Mandarin Oriental, Miami, 500 Brickell Key Dr. (Brickell Ave.),
Downtown Miami, 305-913-8254

Best Fine Dining

Fabulous innovative international cuisine, coupled with flawless service, make this a dining experience to savor. The space at the Mandarin Oriental's signature restaurant is unobtrusive, save for some stunning views of the skyline. Although Azul's longtime acclaimed chef Michelle Bernstein has gone on to other projects, the cuisine remains the same, blending Latin flavors with Asian, new Caribbean, and classic French influences. The results are dishes like lobster cappuccino with lemongrass froth, or Caribbean bouillabaisse. Desserts include vanilla passion fruit crème brûlée and warm chocolate lavender cake. Skip the pricey after-dinner coffee, and take your nightcap in the tranquil lobby lounge, watching the twinkling lights of the city. *Open for lunch Mon.–Fri. noon–3 p.m.; dinner Mon.–Sat. 7–11 p.m.* $$$$

Baleen

Grove Isle Hotel and Spa, Four Grove Isle Dr. (S. Bayshore Dr.), Coconut Grove, 305-858-8300
www.groveisle.com
Best Outdoor Dining

Stylish and romantic, Baleen occupies a quiet part of Grove Isle, a private island in Coconut Grove, and serves creative seafood dishes against a backdrop of lapping waves and—if the time is right—the magnificent moon over Miami. The interior space is luxurious, with oak-paneled walls and cozy booths, while outside tables on waterfront terraces are favorites with couples in love. The cuisine is simple and smart, with Asian and Caribbean accents in dishes like Chinese snapper with coconut rice, Asian slaw, and black bean sauce. *Open daily for breakfast 8–11 a.m.; lunch 11 a.m.–2 p.m.; dinner Sun.–Thurs. 7–10 p.m., Fri.–Sat. 7–11 p.m.* $$$

Bayside Seafood Restaurant

3501 Rickenbacker Causeway, Key Biscayne, 305-361-0808

Steer clear of the touristy Rusty Pelican for dinner and head instead to its hidden neighbor for a casual seafood dinner. Dubbed "The Hut" by locals, this out-of-the-way eatery on Virginia Key does a fine job with fresh seafood—sadly, not such an easy task even in Miami. Conch fritters are tasty and not overly greasy, broiled fish really is fresh from the docks, and the shrimp is sweet and delicious. It's all served on paper plates, and the rustic tiki hut setting is exactly what a seafood shack should be. Go on a Saturday night and you may catch live music. *Open daily noon–10 p.m.* $

Big Fish

55 SW Miami Avenue Rd. (SW 5th St.), Downtown Miami, 305-373-1770
www.thebigfishmiami.com
Best Views of Miami

Big Fish gives you a front-row seat to the busy Miami River against a dazzling backdrop of Downtown's brightest skyscraper, the Bank of America building, and the rainbow neon of the Metrorail overpass. Fresh seafood is handled with Italian skill, as are pastas and risotti. Most nights an eclectic crowd of after-work execs, youngish locals, and assorted oddballs gather at the patio bar wrapped around a giant banyan tree to share a friendly, casual vibe. *Open for lunch Mon.–Fri. noon–3:30 p.m.; dinner Mon.–Fri. 6 p.m.– midnight; Sat.–Sun. noon–1 a.m.* $$

Bizcaya

The Ritz-Carlton, Coconut Grove, 3300 SW 27th Ave. (Tigertail Ave.), Coconut Grove, 305-644-4675
www.ritzcarlton.com

The setting is Ritz-Carlton elegant—rich wood, Italian marble, Biedermeier furnishings, and silk damask draping—but the menu offers updated classics with delightful panache. Traditional onion soup is served with gruyère and black truffle; Florida yellowtail snapper comes with bouillabaisse broth and braised fennel; and duck à l'orange becomes blood orange glazed leg confit with crispy skin maigret breast and Grand Marnier duck liver mousse. The lavish and sophisticated Sunday brunch menu changes monthly, and is served both inside and outside overlooking the waterfall. It's one of the few fine dining locations in the Grove, and diners tend to be businesspeople and locals on a night out. *Open for breakfast daily 7–11 a.m.; brunch Sun. 11:30 a.m.–3 p.m.; lunch 11:30 a.m.–2:30 p.m.; dinner 6:30–11 p.m.* $$$

Boater's Grill

Bill Baggs Cape Florida State Park, 1200 S. Crandon Blvd., Key Biscayne, 305-361-0080
Best Outdoor Dining

Idyllically located at No Name Harbor in Cape Florida State Park, this uncrowded casual restaurant serves in-the-know locals and boaters (natch) outstanding seafood with Latin flavors: ceviche, lobster, paella, whole fried fish, all perfectly fresh, and served with beautiful views of the bay and down-town. There's also a top-rate selection of Spanish, Chilean, and Italian wines. Nothing fancy, and nothing better. *Open daily 9 a.m.–9 p.m.* $

Cafe Sambal

Mandarin Oriental, Miami, 500 Brickell Key Dr. (Brickell Ave.), Downtown Miami, 305-913-8251

Although casual all-day hotel restaurants abound, the Mandarin Oriental's is altogether different. Choose from gourmet bars featuring Vosges Haut-Chocolat in the morning pastry display case, Oriental-style bento boxes for lunch, and an extensive sake menu. The Asian-inspired menu is full of delights: turkey hash served with poached egg, Asian pesto, and hollandaise sauce on the breakfast menu; small plates with dishes like dumplings and crab cakes; noodle dishes and sushi, and large plate dishes that include Korean-barbecued New York steak. Lunch includes a healthy spa cuisine menu that's also available poolside. Get an outdoor table, order their signature lychee saketini, and take in the dramatic skyline views. *Open for breakfast daily 6:30 a.m.–noon; lunch noon–5:30 p.m.; dinner 5:30–11 p.m.* $$$

Carmen the Restaurant

David William Hotel, 700 Biltmore Way (Segovia Ave.), Coral Gables, 305-913-1944
www.carmentherestaurant.com

While the surroundings are a bit bland, Puerto Rican chef Carmen Gonzalez' bold take on Floribbean cuisine is anything but. Traditional dishes are stylized and infused with flavor and originality. Menu highlights include crunchy *aranitas*, delectable fried plantain fritters; wild Alaskan salmon with sweet *malanga*; and Florida lobster served with avocado terrine and key lime mayonnaise. Finish your meal with richly satisfying mango strudel and *dulce de leche* ice cream. A tasting menu allows you to sample a variety of dishes, or follow the lead of the locals who have discovered this little jewel and order wine and bites from the sophisticated bar. *Open for lunch Tues.–Fri. noon– 2 p.m.; dinner Tues.–Fri. 6–9:30 p.m., Sat.–Sun. 6–10 p.m.* $$$

Christy's

3101 Ponce de Leon Blvd. (Malaga Ave.), Coral Gables, 305-446-1400
www.christysrestaurant.com
Best Steakhouses

No need to reinvent the classic steakhouse here—Christy's follows the model to a T, and does it impeccably. All the details are correct: wood-paneled walls, crisp white tablecloths, formally dressed waiters, and sedate artwork. Then there's the corn-fed Midwestern beef, aged four to six weeks. Christy's signature Caesar salad comes with all entrées, and desserts include a spectacular baked Alaska. The other diners are likely the movers and shakers of the city quietly doing their job. *Open for lunch Mon.–Fri. 11:30 a.m.–4 p.m.; dinner seating Sun.–Thurs. till 10 p.m., Fri.–Sat. till 11 p.m.* $$$$

Donut Gallery

83 Harbor Dr. (Crandon Blvd.), Key Biscayne, 305-361-9985

No, they don't serve donuts here. But this tiny Key Biscayne counter is a breakfast institution nonetheless, dishing out eggs, toast, sausages, and heavy doses of local color with friendly efficiency. By the time you leave, you'll be up to date on all the gossip, and you'll have some new best friends, too. *Open daily Mon.–Sun 5:30 a.m.–1:30 p.m.* $

Green Street Cafe

3110 Commodore Plaza (Main Highway), Coconut Grove, 305-444-0244
www.greenstreetcafe.net

Snag an outdoor table under an awning, order a cappuccino and banana pancakes or baguette French toast, and watch the morning unfold before your eyes: early-morning cyclists whizzing down Main Highway; colorful Groveites having conversations with, well, themselves; and squawking blue-and-gold macaws competing with fuchsia bougainvillea in sheer color intensity. The lunch menu features fresh pasta, sandwiches on croissants, and baguettes, burgers, salads, and soups; for dinner, you'll find decent steaks and seafood, all served with casual friendliness. On weekends, this is primo people-watching real estate, so stake out your table early or be prepared to wait. *Open Sun.–Thurs. 7:30 a.m.–10:45 p.m., Fri.–Sat. 7:30 a.m.–11:45 p.m.; open Thurs.–Sat. till 2:30 a.m. for drinks.* $

Jimbo's Place

Duck Lake Rd. (Rickenbacker Causeway), Virginia Key, 305-361-7026
www.jimbosplace.com
Best Dive Bars

Since 1954, Jimbo Luznar has been selling shrimp, beer, and smoked fish in this out-of-the-way spot on Virginia Key. You might recognize some of the shacks from music videos or fashion shoots; Jimbo has hosted everyone from celebrities and politicians to good friends and neighbors here. Aside from drinking, you can practice the fine art of bocce ball. It's not easy to find. Take the Rickenbacker Causeway to Virginia Key, turn left after the light at MAST Academy, then follow the road, staying to the right at the first fork. When you come to the end of the road, stay to the left. You'll see the water treatment plant. Make a right and look for the driveway ahead on the right—cars will be parked along the road. *Open daily 6 a.m.–6:30 p.m.* $

Le Bouchon du Grove

3430 Main Highway (Grand Ave.), Coconut Grove, 305-448-6060

For that French sidewalk cafe experience South Florida–style, Le Bouchon du Grove is de rigueur. The bistro menu includes classic French onion soup, homemade pâté, and splendid tarte Tatin. The chatty waitstaff mingles with the Grovey bohemian crowd. So authentic, you'll find yourself engaged with your seatmate in a spirited discussion about Sartre and existentialism. *Open Mon.–Fri. 9:30 a.m.–3 p.m., Sat.–Sun. 8 a.m.–3 p.m.; Sun.–Thurs. 5–11 p.m., Fri.–Sat. 5 p.m.–midnight.* $

Monty's Raw Bar and Outdoors Restaurant

2550 S. Bayshore Dr. (Aviation Ave.), Coconut Grove, 305-856-3992
www.montysstonecrab.com
Best Waterfront Joints for a Cold Beer

When the reggae band is playing, as it does most nights and weekends, you'll catch that island vibe at Monty's, a longtime raw bar and seafood restaurant next to the water and marina in Coconut Grove (there's another Monty's at the Miami Beach Marina). Enjoy the fresh seafood and stone crabs, conch fritters, grouper, and other local favorites washed down with a pitcher of cold beer—no worries, mon. *Open Mon.–Thurs. 11:30 a.m.–11:30 p.m.; Fri. 11:30 a.m.–1:30 a.m.; Sat.–Sun. noon–1:30 a.m.* $$

The Palm

Village of Merrick Park, 4425 Ponce de Leon Blvd. (San Lorenzo Ave.),
Coral Gables, 786-552-7256
www.thepalm.com
Best Power Lunches

Movers and shakers meet at this New York steakhouse chain to talk deals over juicy 28-ounce prime aged porterhouse steaks and three-pound Nova Scotia lobsters. It may not help anyone's cholesterol levels, but business is evidently booming, judging by the crowds at this young restaurant in Coral Gables' Village of Merrick Park. *Open for lunch Mon.–Fri. 11:30 a.m.–3p.m.; dinner Mon.–Fri. 3–10:30 p.m.; Sat.–Sun. 5–10:30 p.m.* $$$$

Palme d'Or

The Biltmore Hotel, 1200 Anastasia Ave. (Granada Blvd.), Coral Gables,
305-913-3201
Best Fine Dining

The elegant signature restaurant of the grand Biltmore Hotel, the Palme d'Or is sporting a new look and a new approach to its classic French cuisine—and the makeover is getting rave reviews. The traditional interior has been modernized, with sleek leather upholstery and vintage photography, while the menu focuses on letting diners create their own custom-designed tasting dishes. Chef Philippe Ruiz' objective is to seduce your palate, with choices like Maine lobster and crème fraîche cappuccino, sevruga caviar spoons with potato mousseline, green asparagus beignets, and roasted rabbit saddle. *Open Tues.–Thurs. 6–10:30 p.m., Fri.–Sat. 6–11:30 p.m.* $$$$

Pascal's Restaurant and Bar

2611 Ponce de Leon Blvd. (Valencia Ave.), Coral Gables, 305-444-2024
www.pascalmiami.com

Chef Pascal Oudin, who trained under luminaries Alain Ducasse and Roger Vergé, has created an elegant, unpretentious little jewel of a French restaurant, a cozy place with pots of fresh herbs on the tables. Pascal's specializes in a light, fresh cuisine using French technique and fresh foods and products from the Americas. Start with his brandy-flavored lobster bisque, add a sautéed yellowfin tuna au poivre, and wrap it up with a red and blackberry mille-feuille with vanilla cream and passion fruit aspic, and you'll join other savvy locals and Oudin followers in a keen appreciation for his special magic. *Open for lunch Mon.–Fri. 11:30 a.m.–2:30 p.m.; dinner Mon.–Thurs. 6–10:30 p.m., Fri.–Sat. 6–11 p.m.* $$$

Purple Dolphin

Sonesta Beach Resort Key Biscayne, 350 Ocean Dr. (Crandon Blvd.),
Key Biscayne, 305-361-2021 / 800-766-3782
www.sonesta.com

One of South Florida's coveted oceanview restaurants, the Purple Dolphin takes casual seafood fare a creative step further. The fresh dolphin (mahi mahi) sandwich has a tamarind rum barbecue glaze, and the crispy rare yellowfin tuna is served with a mango edamame salad with a citrus ponzu dipping sauce. And the Florida lobster bisque is a delight. *Open daily for breakfast 7–11 a.m.; lunch noon–3 p.m.; dinner 6–10:30 p.m.* $$

Restaurant St. Michel

Hotel Place St. Michel, 162 Alcazar Ave. (Ponce de Leon Blvd.),
Coral Gables, 305-444-1666
www.hotelplacestmichel.com
Best Romantic Dining

Greater Miami does not have much in the way of quaint vine-covered European-style inns, which is one of many reasons the Restaurant and Hotel Place St. Michel is such a standout. Located in a charmingly restored 1926 hotel, the dining room has warm wood floors, giant windows with lace curtain silhouettes, and soft romantic lighting. The French-laced New American cuisine focuses on fresh local fish, prime-aged meats, wild game, and homemade desserts. After dinner, the intimate mahogany-paneled piano bar is a popular place for a nightcap. *Open for breakfast Mon.–Fri. 7–9:30 a.m.; lunch and dinner Sun.–Thurs. 11 a.m.–10:30 p.m., Fri–Sat. 11 a.m.–11:30 p.m.; Sunday brunch 11 a.m.–2:30 p.m.* $$$

Roger's Restaurant and Bar
1601 79th St. Causeway, North Bay Village, 305-866-7111

Even though Miami Beach is a beach destination, waterfront restaurants are a rare commodity. Although it's not clear why that's the case, it certainly makes one appreciate the ones there are. The latest entry, Roger's Restaurant and Bar, is a friendly and unpretentious place in North Bay Village, just west of Miami Beach. Floor-to-ceiling windows and an outdoor tiki bar give diners swell views of the water while they dine on creative American cuisine ranging from pan-seared mahi mahi with lobster mashed potatoes to classic burgers, freshly ground. *Open Sun.–Thurs. 11:45 a.m.–10:45 p.m.; Fri.–Sat. 11:45 a.m.–11:45 p.m.* $

Rusty Pelican
3201 Rickenbacker Causeway, Key Biscayne, 305-361-3818
Best Views of Miami

Location, location, location: that's what makes this touristy seafood house such a perennially popular destination. From its vantage point off the Rickenbacker Causeway, you'll see the glittering Brickell Avenue condos, the illuminated Downtown skyline, the glowing cobalt bridge to the Port of Miami, the calm bay waters, and—if the timing is right—a gorgeous sunset and luminous moonrise (even if you've seen it a million times, it's still breathtaking). *Open Mon.–Thurs., Sun. 5–11 p.m., Fri.–Sat. 5 p.m.–midnight. Bar open until 1 a.m. daily.* $$

Sandbar Grill
The Ritz-Carlton, Key Biscayne, 455 Grand Bay Dr. (Crandon Blvd.),
Key Biscayne, 305-365-4500
www.ritzcarlton.com

Leave it to Ritz-Carlton to kick the waterfront casual dining concept up a notch at the Sandbar Grill, where instead of the usual fried seafood, you can feast on banana leaf grilled mahi mahi or *churrasco*. Stake out your seat under the chickee hut, order a frozen bananas Foster cocktail, gaze out over the quiet Biscayne Bay waters, and savor a perfect slice of blissful relaxation. *Open Sun.–Mon. 11 a.m.–6 p.m., Tues.–Sat. 11 a.m.–9 p.m.* $$

Scotty's Landing
3381 Pan American Dr. (S. Bayshore Dr.), Coconut Grove, 305-854-2626
Best Waterfront Joints for a Cold Beer

Locals would just as soon keep this little gem to themselves, since it fills up pretty quickly on sultry evenings when the sky turns magenta and lavender.

Tucked behind a marina on a quiet part of the bay, Scotty's Landing is an unassuming beer and wine joint with decent seafood and live music. Being a best-kept secret and all, it's a little tricky to find: turn onto Pan American Drive past the Coconut Grove Convention Center and drive past the divider with the trees on your left. The parking lot for Scotty's Landing and the Grove Key Marina are on the left. *Open Mon.–Thurs. 11 a.m.–10 p.m., Fri.–Sat. 11 a.m.–11 p.m., Sun. 11 a.m.–10 p.m.* $

Smith & Wollensky

One Washington Ave. (1st St.), South Beach, 305-673-2800
www.smithandwollensky.com
Best Views of Miami

This branch of the popular New York steakhouse chain has one of the best locations in town: at the southernmost end of South Beach, where you can see magnificent ocean views, the Downtown skyline, and cruise ships en route to the Port of Miami. Traditional steakhouse fare—dry-aged beef, sides like creamed spinach and onion rings, cheesecake and carrot cakes—is on the menu, along with Florida stone crab claws in season. There's also a note-worthy compilation of more than 650 American wines that include classics, cult wines, and a collection of little-known exceptional wines rarely found on other wine lists. *Open Mon.–Sat. noon–2 a.m., Sun. 11:30 a.m.–2 a.m.* $$$

Sunday's on the Bay

5420 Crandon Blvd., Key Biscayne, 305-361-6777
Best Waterfront Joints for a Cold Beer

This is the kind of place that might tempt you to sell the house, move to Florida, and buy a boat. Sunday's on the Bay is next to the Crandon Park Marina, where some quite impressive yachts are docked. Order a Heineken, some conch fritters, and fried squid; put your feet up; and ponder the tech-nicolor sunset and the 36-foot *Contender* docked across the way. After a few more brews, you'll be working out the details of your escape. *Open Mon.–Thurs. 11 a.m.–10 p.m., Fri.–Sun. 11 a.m.–11:30 p.m.* $$

Outdoors Miami:
The Nightlife

The Bar
172 Giralda Ave. (Ponce de Leon Blvd.), Coral Gables, 305-442-2730

You certainly won't find $15 guava martinis, trance music, or sheer curtains to hide behind at The Bar. Instead, you'll find an impressive selection of imported beers, including the aromatic and potent Belgian Trappist Ten; old-fashioned board games like Parcheesi; sports television; buffalo wings and dolphin fingers; and kick-ass live rock'n'roll on weekends. Any questions? *Open Mon.–Fri. 11:30 a.m.–2 a.m., Sat. 5 p.m.–2 a.m., Sun. 5 p.m.–2 a.m.*

Fritz & Franz Bierhaus
60 Merrick Way (Aragon Ave.), Coral Gables, 305-774-1883
www.bierhaus.cc

A Bavarian beer garden in steamy South Florida? *Ja!* The beer steins, vintage tubas, and Austrian artifacts are authentic, and so is the menu, with German draft beer served in one-liter glasses by friendly *fräulein*. Convivial German-Austrian restaurateur Harald Neuweg flies in Bavarian musicians for his annual Oktoberfest, which draws professional thirty- and forty-somethings. He also has a weakness for the blues, so there's a good chance you'll be treated to live blues on a weekend night. *Open daily 11 a.m.–1 a.m.* $

The Globe Cafe and Bar
377 Alhambra Circle (LeJeune Rd.), Coral Gables, 305-445-3555
Best Meet Markets

On weeknights, this bar can't come close to containing the crowds of young professionals thirsty for martinis and mingling, so they spill out onto the sidewalks—and darned if there isn't a mobile bar right there. On weekends, the mob is smaller and quieter, the better to relax with live jazz and a baked brie. *Open Mon.–Thurs. 11:30 a.m.–midnight, Fri.–Sat. 11:30 a.m.–2 a.m.*

Gordon Biersch Brewery Restaurant
1201 Brickell Ave. (SE 12th St.), Downtown Miami, 786-425-1130
www.gordonbiersch.com
Best Meet Markets

What's brewing? Good lager beers and plenty of variety: blond bock, Märzen, Dunkles, and seasonal specialties, all brewed behind glass walls. This welcome addition to the Financial District after-hours scene attracts swarms of urbanites who work and live nearby. Be forewarned: after work and on weekends, you'll find one rowdy singles scene here. *Open Mon.–Thurs. 11:30 a.m.–10:30 p.m., Fri.–Sat. 11:30 a.m.–midnight, Sun. 11 a.m.–midnight.*

Houston's

201 Miracle Mile (Ponce de Leon Blvd.), Coral Gables, 305-529-0141
www.houstons.com
Best Meet Markets

This handsome chain restaurant became a popular singles hangout from the moment it opened. Whether it's an answer to pent-up demand, or simply the right place at the right time, the enormous free-standing bar is constantly packed with young to middle-aged well-dressed urbanites hitting the martinis. Their Racquet Club Sandwich is a standout among more substantial dishes like steaks and seafood. *Open Sun.–Mon. 11:30 a.m.–10 p.m., Tues.–Thurs. 11 a.m.–11 p.m., Fri.–Sat. 11:30 a.m.–midnight.* $

JohnMartin's Restaurant and Irish Pub

253 Miracle Mile (Ponce de Leon Blvd.), Coral Gables, 305-445-3777
www.johnmartins.com

This convivial pub has been proudly keeping folks in Guinness and Harp since the 1980s. On weekends, there's live rock, blues, or jazz, and sometimes Irish cabaret. In addition to a fine drink menu that includes a long list of single-malt and blended Scotch whiskeys, JohnMartin's serves classic pub fare with some hearty Irish specialties like corned beef and cabbage, and homemade potato soup. *Open Mon.–Thurs. 11:30 a.m.–midnight, Fri.–Sat. 11:30 a.m.–1 a.m., Sun. 11:30 a.m.–10:30 p.m.* $

M-Bar

Mandarin Oriental, Miami, 500 Brickell Key Dr. (Brickell Ave.), Downtown Miami, 305-913-8288
www.mandarinoriental.com
Best Classic Hotel Bars

If they were to make a new James Bond movie in Miami, he'd be nursing his shaken-not-stirred martini here. It's small, discreet, and stylish, mildly suggestive of international intrigue. There are lovely views of downtown—and a lavish menu of 250 martinis to choose from, plus any other libation you can dream up. *Open Mon.–Thurs. 5 p.m.–midnight, Fri.–Sat. 5 p.m.–1 a.m.*

Mr. Moe's

3131 Commodore Plaza (Main Highway), Coconut Grove, 305-442-1114

You've gotta love a joint that bucks the Art Deco trend and instead resembles a log cabin with a river rock fireplace blazing when it's 90 degrees out. Nor is it one of the trendy loungey bars. No, think karaoke, ladies' nights, mechanical bull-riding, and televisions tuned to sports events. Rowdy, boozy fun and decent food served till 5 a.m. *Open daily 11 a.m.–5 a.m.* $

Orchid Lounge

Mayfair House, 3000 Florida Ave. (Virginia St.), Coconut Grove, 305-441-0000
www.mayfairhousehotel.com

Located in the architecturally distinctive Mayfair House Hotel, the Orchid Lounge is an intimate bar with curvy Art Nouveau–accented nooks and alcoves that lend themselves nicely to romantic trysts. Order a flute of champagne to sip while admiring the stained glass, orchids, and unusual antiques that are part of the eccentric design. The clientele includes businesspeople, hotel guests, and well-dressed older couples. *Open daily 5–11 p.m.*

Oxygen Lounge

Streets of Mayfair, 2911 Grand Ave. (Virginia St.), Coconut Grove, 305-476-0202
www.oxygenlounge.biz

The Grove's answer to a South Beach–style lounge, Oxygen is a club and sushi bar with a sophisticated vibe located in the Streets of Mayfair center. Deejays spin different tunes on theme nights: Latin rock, funk, and disco; international beats; hip-hop and electronic fare. It's a refreshing alternative to the beer-guzzling frat boy scene that typifies most of the Grove nightspots. *Open daily 8 p.m.–5 a.m.* $

Tobacco Road

626 S. Miami Ave. (SW 7th St.), Downtown Miami, 305-374-1198
www.tobacco-road.com
Best Dive Bars

Since it opened in 1912, the Road has managed to survive Prohibition, hurricanes, the Depression, the revocation of its liquor license, and attempts by the city of Miami to have it legally shut down on charges of "lewd, wanton, and lascivious" behavior. Patrons reward this feisty bar by turning out to hear live rock, blues, jazz, and indie music; to drink; and to eat decent bar food. *Open Mon.–Fri. 11:30 a.m.–5 a.m., Sat.–Sun. noon–5 a.m.* $

Outdoors Miami:
The Attractions

Barnacle Historic State Park

3485 Main Highway (Commodore Plaza), Coconut Grove, 305-442-6866
www.floridastateparks.org

Take a few steps off busy Main Highway into the Barnacle, and you'll feel like you've set the Way-Back Machine to 1851, when pioneer Ralph Middleton Munroe built his bungalow atop a limestone ridge overlooking Biscayne Bay. The oldest home in the county that's in its original location, the Barnacle provides a glimpse into Munroe's life, and also a rare unencumbered view of the bay—as long as you don't use your peripheral vision to see the luxury housing unfortunately flanking this slice of pristine paradise. *Open Fri.–Mon. 9 a.m.–4 p.m.* $

Bill Baggs Cape Florida State Park

1200 S. Crandon Blvd., Key Biscayne, 305-361-5811
www.floridastateparks.org/capeflorida
Best Beaches

Part of South Florida's barrier island ecosystem, Cape Florida is the opposite of the beach scene on Miami Beach. Here, the beach is pristine and peaceful, guarded by a historic lighthouse, South Florida's oldest structure, which you can tour with a guide. From the southern end, you can see standing in the ocean the last few houses that make up Stiltsville. The Boater's Grill (see p. 141) overlooking No Name Harbor serves fresh seafood and Cuban cuisine. *Open daily 8 a.m.–sundown.* $

Coral Gables

LeJeune Rd. and Miracle Mile, Coral Gables

You can spot this suburb from the plane—a dense patch of green impaled by the burnt-orange tower of the Biltmore. Lush foliage and distinctive Mediterranean-style architecture are both hallmarks of the City Beautiful, one of the country's first planned communities, developed in the 1920s by George Merrick. Today, the Gables is one of Miami's best preserved cities, headquarters for thriving multinational companies. Tour the city's interesting landmarks on a self-guided driving tour. Pick up a free map at City Hall at LeJeune Road and Coral Way, and follow the marked attractions. Among them: the Venetian Pool (see p. 157), a rock quarry transformed into an exotic pool in 1924; the stately Biltmore Hotel (see p. 135), a National

Landmark; theme residential villages such as the Dutch South African and French Normandy villages; and Miracle Mile, a pedestrian-friendly street of shops and restaurants that's undergone a major renaissance in recent years.

Crandon Park Golf Course

6700 Crandon Blvd., Key Biscayne, 305-361-9129

Best Golf Courses

Not only is this championship 18-hole golf course on Key Biscayne one of the prettiest courses in the state—with saltwater lakes, mangrove thickets, and bayfront holes—it's also one of the most challenging. From the first hole—a dogleg par-five requiring a drive over water and mangroves—to the last—another par-five with water on both sides of the fairway—Crandon consistently makes top course lists in golf magazines. There's a fully stocked pro shop, cart and equipment rentals, pro lessons, a lighted driving range, and practice chipping and putting greens. All carts use ParView, a golf distancing and communications system. *Open daily 7 a.m.–7 p.m.* $$$$

Deep Sea Sport Fishing Boat *Therapy IV*

Haulover Dock, 10800 Collins Ave., Miami Beach, 305-945-1578
www.therapy4.com

Indulge your Hemingway-esque fantasies of battling that leaping marlin. Spend the morning on the 58-foot fishing yacht *Therapy IV*. Captain Stan Saffan will take you and up to five others out in the Atlantic in search of shark, sailfish, and marlin. The vessel is air-conditioned, and all tackle is furnished, so all you have to bring is a camera for the impressive look-what-I-caught photo. *Open daily 8 a.m.–5 p.m.* $$$$

Downtown Coconut Grove

Main Highway and Grand Ave., Coconut Grove
www.coconutgrove.com

Before it gained a reputation as Miami's bohemian artist colony, Coconut Grove was an early village settled by Bahamian shipbuilders. While a few remnants of its past remain—such as the preserved pioneer home The Barnacle—today the Grove downtown is a pedestrian-friendly conglomeration of shops, cafes, restaurants, galleries, and nightspots set against a lush tropical backdrop. Always a cultural center, it's home to the venerable Coconut Grove Playhouse, where Beckett's *Waiting for Godot* premiered in 1956, and site of the long-running Coconut Grove Arts Festival every February. Though the village's quirky character is slowly becoming more mainstream as pricey real estate projects and shopping centers like the Cocowalk take over, it's still a popular place to wander around by day and night, and its sidewalk cafes are some of the best people-watching vantage points in town. Mornings here are a quiet pleasure, while weekend evenings tend to be packed with roving crowds in the streets.

El Club

425 Grand Bay Dr. (Crandon Blvd.), Key Biscayne, 305-361-9191
www.elclub.us
Best Watersports

Whatever watersport you're eager to try, El Club can set you up: waverunners, sailboats, catamarans, kayaks, paddleboats, and other toys. Located in Key Biscayne on the beach between the Sonesta Beach Resort and the Ritz-Carlton, this full-service facility provides training along with rentals, and also offers one-hour guided waverunner tours and snorkeling trips. *Open daily 10 a.m.–6 p.m.* $$

Fairchild Tropical Botanic Garden

10901 Old Cutler Rd., Coral Gables, 305-667-1651
www.fairchildgarden.org

You could easily spend the whole day at this gorgeous 83-acre botanic garden that shows off South Florida's subtropical splendor in all its lush abundance. There's a two-acre rainforest complete with a waterfall and stream, huge vine pergola, a rare plant conservatory, and collections of palms and cycads. Take the narrated tram ride, held hourly 10 a.m.–3 p.m. (till 4 p.m. on weekends), then explore on your own. On Saturday mornings, you can taste rare fruits at the tropical fruit pavilion. The Garden also hosts events throughout the year, including the Ramble in November, the International Mango Festival in July, and major shows featuring orchids, palms and cycads, and flowering trees. Their sophisticated shop stocks great gifts and a library of gardening books and periodicals. *Open daily 9:30 a.m.–4:30 p.m.* $

H2O Scuba

160 Sunny Isles Blvd. (Collins Ave.), Miami Beach, 305-956-3483 /
888-389-3483
www.h2oscuba.com

Whether you're a first-timer or a longtime diver, H2O Scuba can take care of you. They'll equip you and train you, then take you out to some of Miami's more than 50 divable wreck sites where you can see a kaleidoscope of colorful fish, sponges, and hard and soft corals. The dive charter boat leaves from the dock behind their Sunny Isles shop. *Open Tues.–Fri. 9 a.m.–6 p.m., Sat. 8 a.m.–5 p.m., Sun. 8 a.m.–4 p.m.* $$$$

Haulover Beach Park

10800 Collins Ave., Miami Beach, 305-944-3040
Best Beaches

Everything you want in a beach is right here at this county park: a mile and a half of clean white beaches with lifeguards, sand dunes, waves for swimming and surfing, picnic areas, a marina, restaurant, and even kite shops. Not only does Haulover attract a diverse blend of beachgoers—French Canadian snowbirds from Hallandale, European tourists, South American visitors—but it has a nude beach, a gay beach, and other specialized areas. There are six lighted tennis courts and the bayfront nine-hole Haulover Golf Course. *Open daily sunrise–sunset. $*

The Kampong

4013 Douglas Rd. (El Prado Blvd.), Coconut Grove, 305-445-8076
www.ntbg.org/kampong.html

Listed on the National Register of Historic Places, this National Tropical Botanical Garden was the home and garden of plant explorer David Fairchild. The splendid flowering trees, vines, and tropical fruit cultivars, along with the Indonesian-inspired main house of The Kampong, reflect many of the discoveries of Fairchild's travels. The serene bayfront view is breathtaking. Tours are sometimes available by appointment, so call well in advance to book a tour of this botanical treasure. *Open by appointment. $*

Mangrove Cycles

260 Crandon Blvd. (East Dr.), Key Biscayne, 305-361-5555

Whether you need a basic beach cruiser or a multi-speed specialty bicycle, Mangrove Cycles will set you up. They rent bikes by the hour, day, or week, and offer a full range of accessories, including helmets and locks. Best of all, they have detailed maps and are glad to point out the best bike trails on Key Biscayne. *Open Tues.–Sun. 9 a.m.–6 p.m. $*

Miami Catamarans

Rickenbacker Causeway, Key Biscayne, 305-345-4104
www.miamicatamarans.com
Best Watersports

Join all those folks having fun on the bay on those cool catamarans. Located on Hobie Beach where the seas are protected from high waves, Miami Catamarans gives instruction at various levels and rents Hobie Cats, Trifoilers, and other catamarans if you're experienced. They're on the Rickenbacker Causeway just past the tollbooth. *Open daily 10 a.m.–6 p.m. $$$$*

Oleta River State Park

3400 NE 163rd St. (NE 34th Ave.), North Miami, 305-919-1846
www.floridastateparks.org/oletariver

The largest urban park in the state, Oleta is an amazingly pristine 1,000-acre patch of paradise sandwiched between tracts of dense, relentless development. Named for the Oleta River, the park's mangrove-lined shoreline provides a sheltered habitat for waterbirds. Endangered West Indian manatees are sometimes spotted here. Kayaking, canoeing, bicycling, and inline skating are popular, and the park has more than ten miles of challenging intermediate mountain bike trails. The concession that rents canoes, kayaks, and bicycles is open from 9 a.m. to an hour and a half before closing. *Open 8 a.m.–sundown.* $

Sailboards Miami

Rickenbacker Causeway, Key Biscayne, 305-361-7245
www.windsurfingmiami.com
Best Watersports

If you can ride a bicycle, you can windsurf. Or so they say at Sailboards Miami, where they've been teaching folks how to capture the wind and sail across the warm bay waters for the past 20 years. Located on the south side of the Rickenbacker Causeway after the tollbooth, they have instruction and rental equipment for beginners through advanced levels. If it's a light wind day, go for one of the kayaks. They also teach the latest extreme watersport, kiteboarding. Whatever you choose, bring water and non-oily sunscreen. *Open Thurs.–Tues. 10 a.m.–6 p.m.* $$$$

Segway Excursion Center

Sonesta Beach Resort Key Biscayne, 350 Ocean Dr. (Crandon Blvd.),
Key Biscayne, 305-365-4087

Here's your chance to try out those odd-looking Segway Human Transporters. The world's first excursion center offers a variety of tours on these new self-balancing, electric-powered transportation devices. You can opt to take a spin on a brief 45-minute grounds jaunt, or be more ambitious and head out for a two-and-a-half-hour safari to Bill Baggs State Park that includes a ranger-guided tour along oceanside nature trails, a stop at the historic lighthouse, and lunch at the Boater's Grill. *Open daily 9 a.m.–6 p.m.* $$$$

The Spa at Mandarin Oriental

500 Brickell Key Dr. (Brickell Ave.), Downtown Miami, 305-913-8288 /
866-888-6780
www.mandarinoriental.com
Best Spas

Exotic treatments and harmonious design characterize the deluxe three-level
waterfront spa at the Mandarin Oriental, which draws on Ayurvedic, Chinese,
European, Balinese, and Thai cultures for its treatments. For extreme pampering, the luxurious 15,000-square-foot spa even offers six top-floor spa
suites custom-designed for special treatments. Their treatment menu
includes Ayurvedic holistic body massages, Balinese synchronized massage,
Mandarin hot stone therapy, and jet lag reviver aromatherapy. Whatever you
choose, be sure to book well in advance, as weekends fill up quickly. *Open
daily 9:30 a.m.–9:30 p.m.* $$$$

The Spa at Ritz-Carlton, Key Biscayne

455 Grand Bay Dr. (Crandon Blvd.), Key Biscayne, 305-365-4500
www.ritzcarlton.com
Best Spas

This top-rated spa emphasizes natural therapies using familiar Florida botanical products: coconut, mango, lime, honey, and other tropical flavors make
up many of their treatments, such as the Key Lime Coconut Body Scrub and
Soak treatment or the Everglades Grass Body Wrap. Of course, they're not
immune to catering to desperate folks who need a quick fix; their Red Carpet
Makeover package comes in a one-week emergency version where spa professionals buff, polish, and transform you into a knockout fit for any red carpet
event. Whatever you choose, book in advance over weekends and holidays.
Open daily 9 a.m.–8 p.m. $$$$

Tennis Center at Crandon Park

7300 Crandon Blvd., Key Biscayne, 305-365-2300
www.co.miami-dade.fl.us/parks/Parks/crandon_tennis

Sweat on the same courts as the William sisters and other stars at this lush
Key Biscayne facility. Home to the NASDAQ-100 Open, now one of the
largest international tennis tournaments, the tennis center has 17 Laykold
cushioned hard courts, six of which are lighted for evening play; eight state-
of-the-art clay courts, four with red European clay and four with green
American clay; and two grass courts. It's located next to the Crandon Park
Golf Course, and right across the street from the Crandon Park Beach. *Open
daily 8 a.m.–10 p.m.* $

Ultralight Adventures

3401 Rickenbacker Causeway, Key Biscayne, 305-361-3909
www.ultralightadventures.com

You got a good, if fleeting, look at Miami's skyscrapers, hotels, and beaches when you flew in, right? Now get an even closer view from an ultralight aircraft. Choose from one or more routes that take you over the port and Star Island, South Beach, Key Biscayne, Coconut Grove, and Downtown. Flights take off and land from the water, can fly at heights ranging from a few feet above the water to 2,000 feet up, and include instruction if you want to learn about flying. *Open Tues.–Fri. 10 a.m.–sunset.* $$$$

Venetian Pool

2701 De Soto Blvd. (Toledo St.), Coral Gables, 305-460-5356
www.venetianpool.com

Resort hotels may be going all out with their extravagant swimming pools, but few capture the charm of the Venetian Pool. In 1924, this former rock quarry was transformed into what was billed as the world's most beautiful swimming hole, with limestone rock outcroppings and caves, an island, and vine-covered porticos. In its early days, gondolas floated alongside Venetian street lamps, orator William Jennings Bryan held lectures, and orchestras serenaded poolside dancers. Nowadays, it's a popular spot for local residents and visitors. In the summer, the pool's 800,000 gallons of water is replenished each day from the subterranean aquifer that flows beneath it. *Open Tues.–Sun. 10 a.m.–4:30 p.m. (Nov. 1–Mar. 31); Tues.–Fri. 11 a.m.–5:30 pm., Sat.–Sun. 10 a.m.–4:30 p.m. (Apr. 1–May 29); Mon.–Fri. 11 a.m.–7:30 p.m., Sat.–Sun. 10 a.m.–4:30 p.m. (May 30–Sept. 5); Tues.–Fri. 11 a.m.–5:30 p.m., Sat.–Sun. 10 a.m.–4:30 p.m. (Sept. 6–Oct. 31).* $

Clásico Miami

Greater Miami started hosting sun-seeking visitors as soon as Henry Flagler got an intoxicating whiff of orange blossom and opened a hotel here, and the town's been selling souvenir alligators and pink flamingos ever since. Your grandparents may have stayed at these Art Deco hotels and swinging '60s resorts, and your parents may have taken you to these places when you were a kid. Just like you, they've all grown up, but they remain a central part of the classic Miami experience and are ready for another look. We've thrown in some of the best Latin-flavored hot spots and restaurants, so get ready to rumba. *¡Bienvenidos a Miami!*

Clásico Miami:
The Itinerary

Our Hotel Choice: Fontainebleau Hilton Resort, because this big, brash Morris Lapidus spot is the same, fabulous, gaudy resort it was in the '60s and is the ultimate symbol of Miami's early heyday.

Prime Time: Thurs.–Sat.

Day 1

Morning: It wouldn't be a classic Florida experience without fresh orange juice on the beach. There are lots of Ocean Drive cafes, most of them cheesy tourist traps; to avoid that scene, head to the **Front Porch Cafe** in the Penguin Hotel for healthy *fresh breakfast fare*. Make sure you don your Brazilian flip-flops and cool shades—you'll be out and about on foot today. After breakfast, get some perspective on the Art Deco Historical District's distinctive architecture by signing up for an hour-and-a-half guided tour, or a self-guided hour-long audio tour, from the district's **Art Deco Welcome Center** at Ocean Drive and 10th Street.

Lunch: Now that you can tell Streamline Moderne from *Tropical Art Deco*, reward yourself with lunch in architecturally intriguing surroundings. Go straight to to the delightful Deco building that's home to the enormous **Jerry's Famous Deli** and order up some pastrami and rye and a Dr. Brown's. For lighter fare, grab an outdoor table and snack on Spanish tidbits and some Rioja wine at **Tapas y Tintos** on charming tree-lined Espanola Way.

Afternoon: After lunch you should have time to *catch some rays* at **Lummus Park Beach**. Or find yourself something dressy at the shops on **Collins and Washington Avenues**.

Dinner: Select your dinner destination among the following: the colorful Haitian restaurant **Tap Tap**; the boisterous **Macarena Tavern and Restaurant**, with Spanish cuisine followed by *flamenco dancing* and occasionally live music from up-and-coming Latin artists; or **Escopazzo**, a loud, tiny treasure trove for fine Northern Italian cuisine.

Nighttime: Check out **Mango's Tropical Cafe** on Ocean Drive, where *sexy Latina dancers* and live music keep things *muy caliente* all night long. or check out the raucous crowd on the aquarium dance floor at **Club Deep**. If you're looking for even faster action, drive out to **Miami Jai-Alai** to bet on players of what's billed as the world's fastest game. *Late night*, make your way to **Big Pink**, where they dish out heaping helpings of good old American comfort food 24/7.

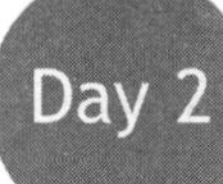

Day 2

Morning: First, pop into the oceanfront **Les Deux Fontaines Lobster Cafe and Bar** at the Hotel Ocean for a chocolate croissant and *cappuccino*. Your next stop is Downtown Miami—where you'll find the usual chaotic big-city mélange of foreign languages, odd characters, and unusual aromas. Though generally not much of a tourist destination, Downtown is home to the Philip Johnson–designed Miami-Dade Cultural Center, a Mediterranean-style fortress housing the **Historical Museum of Southern Florida**, the **Miami Art Museum**, and the Miami-Dade Public Library, all definitely worth the trip. Both museums give intriguing insights into South Florida—the historical museum reaches back to the area's Native American roots, and presents the culturally diverse present; and the art museum showcases Miami-based artists in an international context. (If you like Floridiana, the historical museum's gift shop has a wonderful collection of stylish souvenirs.)

Lunch: It's time for the quintessential *Cuban dining experience*. Drive west to 35th Avenue and SW 8th Street for lunch at **Versailles**, whose name, green-and-white awnings, and gaudily mirrored, chandeliered interior are a designer's low-budget vision of the French palace. Or head two blocks west to **La Carreta**, where an enormous wagon wheel and sugarcane plants in front announce its more rustic fare. Either way, you can't go wrong—both places serve food that's as Cuban as Ricky Ricardo.

Afternoon: Head over to the working-class part of town called **Little Havana**. Park off SW 8th Street around 12th Avenue. Keep in mind that this is a neighborhood, not a tourist attraction, so don't expect any animated characters to show you around. Head first to Domino Park at 15th Avenue to watch the *spirited domino games* (and to admire the backdrop, a mural of world leaders painted by schoolchildren after 1994's Summit of the Americas); continue to Memorial Boulevard, which is lined by memorials to Cuban patriots. Then stop in any of the *botánicas* selling candles and oils; the **El Credito Cigar Factory**; and the handy souvenir shop called **Little**

Havana to Go. On your way back to your hotel, drive down royal palm-lined Biscayne Boulevard, Miami's Champs-Elysées. In recent years colorful Orange Bowl floats and bands marched down this street, as did deafening Grand Prix racecars. On the east side is Bayfront Park, home to a memorial honoring the *Challenger* astronauts and the Freedom Torch erected to honor JFK; the touristy Bayside Marketplace; and the high-tech AmericanAirlines Arena. Across the Boulevard is the 1925 Freedom Tower, patterned after the Giralda Tower in Sevilla, Spain; Cuban refugees arriving to Miami were processed in the Freedom Tower in the 1960s and 1970s. The massive building just north of the I-195 overpass is the Performing Arts Center, a new Cesar Pelli–designed structure that will straddle Biscayne Boulevard. Then head to *the beach* or your hotel pool to catch some late-afternoon sun, or a catnap before your *Latin night* on the town. Don't forget to polish those dancing shoes.

Dinner: Tonight's dining choices include Latin-Caribbean cuisine interpreted by some of Miami's best-known and most imaginative chefs. In Coral Gables, Cindy Hutson's cheerfully tropical **Ortanique on the Mile** serves *wicked mojitos*, memorable ceviches, and Jamaican-influenced dishes to a noisy crowd of young urbanites every night. In Miami's up-and coming East Side, Douglas Rodriguez' **OLA Restaurant**—Of Latin America—does Nuevo Cuban proud. Another outstanding choice is **Norman's** in Coral Gables, where New World Cuisine devotees flock to taste the latest from Norman Van Aken.

Nighttime: Finish off the evening getting sauced with some salsa and *merengue*. Head over to **Bongos Cuban Cafe**, Gloria and Emilio Estefan's touristy club next to the AmericanAirlines Arena, or the grittier Little Havana hole-in-the-wall called **Hoy Como Ayer**, where you'll get to dance to real Cuban *ritmo*.

Day 3

Morning: Fortify yourself for the day ahead with a little something Italian-Mediterranean for breakfast at the **Pelican Cafe** in the cool Diesel Jeans–owned Pelican Hotel. For a sightseeing tour with the consummate Miami expert, find out which *historical tour* **Dr. Paul George's Tours** has planned for today (check the Historical Museum of Southern Florida website in advance for details). If you're here for the golf or are in the mood to indulge in any of a range of **spa treatments**, head directly to the renowned **Doral Golf Resort & Spa** (where you should book your tee times well in advance of your vacation).

Lunch: Pick up some *tasty crustaceans* from the take-out division of the legendary **Joe's Stone Crab Restaurant** for a picnic at nearby South Pointe Park, where cruise ships and seagulls offer ample entertainment as you ease into the day. Otherwise, grab a casual bite at the cafe affiliated with the afternoon activity of your choice.

Afternoon: Make like a tourist by visiting one of Miami's longtime attractions: the opulent Italian Renaissance–style bayfront **Vizcaya Museum and Gardens** in Coconut Grove; the newly relocated **Parrot Jungle Island** on Watson Island on the MacArthur Causeway; or the **Miami Seaquarium**, *Lolita the killer whale's hangout* on the way to Key Biscayne. It will take an afternoon to explore each of these popular sites.

Dinner: For dinner, consider **Yuca**, Lincoln Road's upscale Cuban eatery, popular with well-dressed young Latinos; or **Novecento Miami**, where pan-Latin bistro cuisine is served in a setting that recalls turn-of-the-century Argentina. Or visit an *opulent Beach classic*, **The Forge**, which serves dry-aged steaks, game, and seafood to a jet-setting clientele.

Nighttime: After dinner, have a Cohiba and listen to Latin music *en vivo* at Lincoln Road's lively **Tropical Cigars**. For all-night dancing, join the international set at **Bash Club and Lounge**. If you dined at the Forge, just walk next door to the *wild nightclub* **Jimmy'Z**, where you'll party the night away with models, entertainers, local trendsetters, Fortune 500 businessmen, and celebs. **Señor Frog's**, another popular destination, holds fiestas every Saturday night.

The Day After: Before brunch, drag your bleary-eyed self over to the lobby of the Eden Roc hotel for a gander at the swell Morris Lapidus–designed lobby that recalls the glamour days of Sinatra and his Rat Pack. Playful curvy MiMo (Miami Modern) designs are also part of the Fontainebleau Hilton lobby, where you can chow down at the lavish brunch in the **Bleau View**, a classic buffet with carving tables, dramatic seafood layouts, and chefs awaiting your order.

Clásico Miami:
The Hotels

Fontainebleau Hilton Resort

4441 Collins Ave. (44th St.), Mid-Beach, 305-538-2000 /
800-548-8886
www.fontainebleau.hilton.com
Best Hotel Pools

When it opened in 1954, the Fontainebleau Hilton became the most talked-about resort in the country. Its sweeping curves, crystal chandeliers, and staircases to nowhere—all signatures of architect Morris Lapidus—attracted presidents, jet-setters, and movie stars. Elvis Presley, Frank Sinatra, Ann-Margret, and Liberace all performed in the famous La Ronde Room, now known as Tropigala. Classic films like *Goldfinger*, Jerry Lewis' *The Bellboy*, and Al Pacino's *Scarface* were filmed here. Today, the hotel still dazzles because of its scale and glitz: 900-plus rooms, 20 lushly landscaped beach-front acres, a magnificent half-acre rock grotto pool with cascading water-falls, Latin-flavored Las Vegas–style revues at Tropigala (see p. 178). Most of the guest rooms have undergone complete renovations, and the 40,000-square-foot full-service beachside spa offers a full range of services. Guests include honeymooners, conventioneers, European and Latin-American tourists, and occasionally celebs and their entourages (Jennifer Lopez, Plácido Domingo, and former New York Mayor Rudy Giuliani have stayed here). Ask for a room in the recently renovated Chateau Tower. $$$

Hotel Impala

1228 Collins Ave. (12th St.), South Beach, 305-673-2021 /
800-646-7252
www.hotelimpalamiamibeach.com

One of those happy discoveries tucked behind a charming courtyard, the tiny Hotel Impala is a Mediterranean Revival treasure only steps from the hubbub of Collins Avenue. It's like a small Tuscan villa—there are only 14 rooms and three suites, but each is comfortably outfitted with wooden armoires, sleigh beds, imported cotton linens, and wrought iron fixtures. All your entertain-ment needs (TV, CD, VCR) are here; movies and music are available from the friendly staff. A favorite at this boutique hotel is the Grand Suite, which has a private balcony. Although the hotel doesn't have a pool, it's not far from the beach. Hotel guests enjoy free Continental breakfast at Spiga downstairs, a dandy little Northern Italian restaurant that is a well-kept secret. $$

Hotel Nash

1120 Collins Ave. (11th St.), South Beach, 305-674-7800 /
800-403-6274
www.hotelnash.com

This handsome 52-room restored 1935 Art Deco hotel appeals to guests who value relaxation and personal service. The three soothing plunge pools—mineral water, saltwater, and freshwater—are surrounded by fragrant jasmine bushes which provide some natural aromatherapy. All the guest rooms are tasteful havens of sage green and ivory, and are custom furnished with bleached-wood shield-shaped armoires. The spacious green-tiled bathrooms are equipped with rainforest showerheads. The Art Deco lobby has the original terrazzo floors and a museum-style concierge desk that stocks an extensive library of classic and unusual videos. For all its low-key elegance, the Nash has a high-profile chef, Mark Militello, at its lobby-level restaurant, Mark's South Beach (see p. 84). When you call to reserve, ask for a room on the third floor overlooking the pool, as these are considered the most desirable and are the most requested. $$$

Hotel Ocean

1230 Ocean Dr. (13th St.), South Beach, 305-672-2579
www.hotelocean.com

If you prefer homey antiques to the cold, hard lines of Streamline Moderne, this is the place for you. The Hotel Ocean is more Mediterranean than Art Deco, and has a charming courtyard fountain, a popular seafood cafe, and friendly European service. The 27 rooms are comfortably decorated with French and English furnishings, and all the bathrooms have cheerful colored tilework, fine French toiletries, and monogrammed bathrobes. All guests receive complimentary breakfast; VIP passes to Crunch (see p. 97), the designer gym; and a cookie with milk at turndown. Try to reserve one of the oceanview suites, as you'll then get to savor the gorgeous views from the privacy and comfort of your own room; if you feel like a splurge, note that their penthouse suite, accessed by a private elevator, has its own lovely terrace overlooking the beach. $$

Lido Spa Hotel/The Standard

40 Island Ave., South Beach, 305-673-1717 / 800-327-8363
www.lidospa.com

The hip Standard Hotels' entry into the Miami marketplace is a complete renovation of the old Lido Spa Hotel, where retirees and value-seekers came during the season for a traditional spa vacation with hot tubs, massages, and three meals a day. The Standard has updated the rooms and properties to reflect casual, fresh Florida style—think polished terrazzo, private verandas, outdoor tubs, and cool, light décor—that includes a wide range of modern spa features: a hammam, steam room, cedar sauna, Roman waterfall hot tub, arctic plunge pool, clothing-optional clay baths, waterfront yoga, in-room spa services, an outdoor sound pool with underwater music, and various custom-blended organic amenities. One of the hotel's biggest assets is its tranquil location on Belle Isle, a residential island on the Venetian Causeway just off 17th St., with serene and unencumbered north-facing views of the bay. Relax—you're five minutes from South Beach action. $$

Clásico Miami:
The Restaurants

Big Pink
157 Collins Ave. (2nd St.), South Beach, 305-532-4700
www.bigpinkrestaurant.com
Best Late-Night Eats

This is diner food, all duded up in a fun and funky industrial setting. Take the TV dinner, a stainless steel six-compartment tray heaped with fried chicken, mashed potatoes and gravy, salad, veggies, and dessert. But there's no way you'll mistake this for Swanson's. The owner of the place is the same person behind top-notch eateries Nemo and Shoji Sushi, and every dish here reveals the same careful attention to taste, without the stellar price tag. Breakfasts are bountiful, and include hot malted waffles, French toast made from homemade brioche, and corned beef hash cooked from scratch. Sandwiches, burgers, pizza, and wraps round out the menu. Save room for home-baked desserts, like their signature four-layer red velvet cake. Everyone from families with kids, to models, to hungry locals turns up here. *Open Sun.–Thurs. 9 a.m.–1 a.m., Fri.–Sat. 9 a.m.–2 a.m.* $

Bleau View
Fontainebleau Hilton Resort, 4441 Collins Ave. (44th St.), Mid-Beach, 305-674-4670
www.fontainebleau.hilton.com
Best Sunday Brunches

Located in the sprawling Fontainebleau Hilton, this hotel restaurant serving Mediterranean and classic cuisine might go unnoticed were it not for its wildly extravagant Sunday brunch. Seafood, caviar, sushi, carving stations, pasta, salads, and elaborate desserts are laid out for your gorging pleasure. *Open daily 6:30 a.m.–midnight; Sunday brunch 10 a.m.–3 p.m.* $$$$

Capital Grille
444 Brickell Ave. (SE 4th St.), Downtown Miami, 305-374-4500
www.thecapitalgrille.com
Best Power Lunches

Bankers, international financiers, low-key entertainers, and politicians like local-girl-made-good Janet Reno are clients of this elegant Financial District chain steakhouse on the Miami River. Dry-aged, hand-cut in-house steaks like the 24-ounce porterhouse are the prime attraction for dinner, while the lunch crowd loves their signature cheeseburger, a huge sirloin burger topped with smoked bacon, Havarti cheese, and jalapeño onion marmalade. The wine list—and service—are impressive. *Open for lunch Mon.–Fri. 11:30 a.m.–3 p.m.; dinner Mon.–Thurs. 5–10:30 p.m., Fri. 5–11 p.m., Sat. 6–11 p.m., Sun. 5–10 p.m.* $$$

Chispa
225 Altara Ave. (Ponce de Leon Blvd.), Coral Gables, 305-648-2600
www.chisparestaurant.com
Best Tapas Bars

Chispa means "spark" in Spanish, and it's a theme renowned chef Robbin Haas has thoroughly plumbed in this contemporary Latin restaurant. Dramatic lighting fixtures heat up the environs, an open kitchen generates excitement, and creative takes on traditional Hispanic cuisine (by a gringo chef, no less) inflame passion: shrimp and black-eyed pea *croquetas, lechón asado risotto,* even *humble arroz con pollo.* Chispa also does a blazing bar business as a Coral Gables hot spot for twenty-to forty-something profession-als. *Open for lunch Mon.–Sat. 11:30 a.m.–3:30 p.m., Sun. noon–3:30 p.m.; dinner Sun.–Thurs. 5:30–10:30 p.m., Fri.–Sat. 5:30 p.m.–12:30 a.m.* $$

Escopazzo
1311 Washington Ave. (13th St.), South Beach, 305-674-9450
www.escopazzo.com

Locals and celebs like Patti LaBelle, Harrison Ford, and Michelle Pfeiffer have gone crazy for the fine Northern Italian food and wine at Escopazzo, where Roman-born chef Pino Bodoni and his wife Giancarla oversee the kitchen in this small, elegant restaurant. You'll savor earthy dishes like grilled radicchio filled with smoked scamorza and prosciutto with fig and balsamic confiture, pumpkin ravioli with truffle-infused cream sauce, and other housemade risotti and pastas. The wine cellar houses 170 cases of wines and champagnes from Italy. Look for monthly events featuring regional Italian dishes and wines. *Open Tues.–Sun. 6 p.m.–midnight.* $$$

The Forge
432 41st St. (Royal Palm Ave.), Mid-Beach, 305-538-8533
www.theforge.com
Best Always-Trendy Tables

The Forge stands alone among Miami Beach restaurants, a monument to lux-ury and excess in décor, cuisine, and entertainment. It's where golden girls, playboys, conventioneers, locals, celebrities, and anyone looking for high-class fun will most certainly find it. It's hard to describe all its attributes without using the word "decadent." Five dining rooms, featuring over-the-top décor in the form of 20-foot ceilings, a massive chandelier, gilded paintings, ornate stained glass. A collection of more than 300,000 bottles of wine that includes an 1822 Chateau Lafite Rothschild. National recognition for slow-grilled dry-aged steaks. Clients like Robert De Niro, Madonna, Michael Jordan, and Muhammad Ali, among many, many others. And, of course, wild parties that include girls dancing on the tables. Do you need to experience these excesses? Of course you do. *Open Mon., Tues., Thurs., Sun. 6–11 p.m., Wed., Fri., Sat. 6 p.m.–midnight.* $$$$

Front Porch Cafe

Penguin Hotel, 1418 Ocean Dr. (14th St.), South Beach, 305-531-8300

Better known for undistinguished joints with waitstaff relentlessly badgering the steady stream of tourists, Ocean Drive has a gem of a little cafe at the Art Deco Penguin Hotel. The fare here is several cuts above the ho-hum cuisine of its neighbors, especially its breakfasts: omelettes and breakfast burritos, biscuits, granola pancakes, French toast with orange zest and cinnamon, and fresh squeezed juice. Pizza, salads, vegetarian dishes, sandwiches, pasta, fish, steaks, and chicken are served for lunch and dinner, and there's a full liquor menu. *Open daily 8 a.m.–10 p.m.* $

Jerry's Famous Deli

1450 Collins Ave. (Espanola Way), South Beach, 305-532-8030
www.jerrysfamousdeli.com

Hey, this is Miami Beach... you gotta have deli, and Jerry's Famous is where you get it. Just ask the hordes of late night club kids here at 4 a.m., or celebs like Shaquille O'Neal and Jerry Seinfeld. Housed in an old Art Deco ballroom, this huge, noisy restaurant, bar, deli, bakery, and takeout establishment is open round the clock. The menu is enormous, and so are the portions. Expect all the deli classics: knishes, gefilte fish, chicken soup with matzo ball, chopped chicken liver, tongue, whitefish salad, pastrami on rye, Brooklyn egg creams, and Dr. Brown's. You'll also find steaks, seafood, pasta, hamburgers, hot dogs, pizza, and a full bar. *Open daily 24 hours.* $

Joe's Stone Crab Restaurant

11 Washington Ave. (Biscayne St.), South Beach, 305-673-0365 /
take away 305-673-4611
www.joesstonecrab.com

Stone crab claws—sweet, meaty, flamingo-pink-and-black crustacean appendages served cold with melted butter or mustard sauce—are one of South Florida's true seasonal treats, and the trend started here at Joe's.

Back in the 1920s, Joe Weiss figured out that these local crabs were in fact edible. He started serving them cracked with potatoes, cole slaw, and mayonnaise, and an institution was born. Will Rogers, Amelia Earhart, and Damon Runyon were early customers, and over the years, this South Beach institution weathered all kinds of changes: boom to bust and back to boom again. Today, this noisy restaurant is jammed with locals and tourists during stone crab season (mid-October through mid-May), requiring long waits (they don't take reservations), which makes their take-out service a smart choice. All the popular items from the restaurant menu are available: stone crabs with mustard sauce or melted butter, hash brown potatoes or cottage-fried sweets, creamed spinach, coleslaw, key lime and apple pies. The claws cost a pretty penny more than the 75 cents for four or five they cost in 1921, but it's a splurge no one regrets. *Open Oct. 15–May 15: lunch Tues.–Sat. 11:30 a.m.–2 p.m.; dinner Sun.–Thurs. 5–10 p.m., Fri.–Sat. 5–11 p.m.* $$$$

La Carreta

3632 SW 8th St. (36th Ave.), Little Havana, 305-444-7501
Best Cuban Food

Owned by the same folks as Versailles up the street, La Carreta serves Cuban food, country-style. At least, the wagon wheel, sugarcane, and rustic facade out front make it look that way. You'll find locals—Anglos and Cubans alike—feasting on good solid staples like *lechón asado* (roast pork), rice and beans, *croquetas,* yuca, and plantains. Order the *clásico,* a sampler of all the basic taste treats. There are other locations throughout Miami, and if you happen to miss this dining experience in Little Havana during your stay, you can make it up at Miami International Airport, where there's a La Carreta on Concourse D. *Open Mon.–Thurs. 6 a.m.–2 a.m., Fri.–Sun. 24 hours.* $

Les Deux Fontaines Lobster Cafe and Bar

Hotel Ocean, 1230 Ocean Dr. (13th St.), South Beach, 305-672-7878
www.lesdeuxfontaines.com

This charming little French restaurant in the Mediterranean-style Hotel Ocean is a refreshing antidote to the touristy vibe that blankets much of Ocean Drive. The breakfast menu features chocolate croissants and Belgian waffles, among heartier American choices; lunch dishes are seafood-intensive; and the dinner menu is a lobster lovefest, offering multiple variations featuring the succulent crustacean. Enjoy it steamed, broiled, grilled, oven-roasted, or in a seafood stew. Evenings feature live jazz, swing, and Dixieland music for an eclectic grown-up crowd. *Open daily 7:30–11 p.m.; live entertainment nightly.* $$

Macarena Tavern and Restaurant

1334 Washington Ave. (13th St.), South Beach, 305-531-3440

First, disregard the silly dance-craze name of this Spanish restaurant, night-club, and live music venue. Second, order traditional Spanish cuisine here—tapas, paella, *crema catalana,* perhaps accompanied by a fine Spanish wine. The proprietors are from Madrid, so they know their stuff. Third, sit back and watch as the restaurant turns into a stage for passionate flamenco shows and salsa dancing all night long. Macarena also draws Latin crowds for concerts from new and recognized Latin artists from time to time. *Open Mon.–Tues. 7 p.m.–midnight, Wed.–Thurs. 7–11:30 p.m., Fri.–Sat. 7 p.m.–5 a.m.* $$

Mosaico

1000 S. Miami Ave. (SW 10th St.), Downtown Miami, 305-371-3473
www.mosaicorestaurant.com

Everyone's loco for Spanish cuisine and its casual form—tapas—these days. Barcelona native Jordi Valles takes the trend huge leaps forward with his contemporary Spanish dishes at Mosaico, and the buzz is deafening. Located upstairs in a historic firehouse building in the Brickell Village area of Downtown Miami, this handsome space with a balmy terrace is attracting serious foodies and downtown sophisticates for openers like lobster with avo-cado sorbet, tomato consommé and olive powder, and potato and bacalao cannelloni; and moves on to entrées like braised beef cheeks and pork roast-ed for seven hours. Pair his adventurous cuisine with excellent Spanish wines for the total experience. *Open for lunch Mon.–Fri. noon–3 p.m.; dinner Mon.–Thurs. 6:30–10:30 p.m., Fri. 6:30–11 p.m., Sat. 7–11 p.m.; happy hour Fri. 5–8 p.m., Sat. 6:30–11:30 p.m.* $$

Norman's

21 Almeria Ave. (SW 37th Ave.), Coral Gables, 305-446-6767
www.normans.com
Best Fine Dining

Norman Van Aken can tell you all about New World cooking—after all, he did write the book on it—but why not treat yourself to a dinner at his eponymous restaurant in Coral Gables and experience it for yourself? In his warm, Caribbean-homey restaurant, you can order favorites like peeky toe crab cakes with mojo verde, or Cuban-style roast pork tenderloin with black bean salsa. Or try his signature tasting menu, which includes some of his all-time favorites, ending with his banana split with rum-flamed bananas and macadamia nut brittle ice cream, and you'll be a New World convert too. *Open Mon.–Thurs. 6–10 p.m., Fri.–Sat. 6–10:30 p.m.* $$$$

Novecento Miami

1080 Alton Rd. (11th St.), South Beach, 305-531-0900
www.bistronovecento.com

Dubbed Nuevo Bistro, the cuisine at Novecento draws on Argentinian, Mediterranean, and Pan-Latin cuisines. This means you'll find menu items like empanadas, quesadillas, risotto, grilled steaks and seafood, and desserts that make use of signature South Florida ingredients like passion fruit and banana. Old refurbished cafe chairs, rustic wood flooring, and vintage photography recall turn-of-the-century Argentina, while world music and Brazilian jazz add a modern lounge touch. Argentinians and Europeans, as well as savvy locals, have discovered this convivial bistro, which is only a short walk from busier Lincoln Road. *Open daily 6 p.m.–midnight, Sunday brunch 11 a.m.–4 p.m.* $$

OLA Restaurant

5061 Biscayne Blvd. (NE 50th St.), East Side Miami, 305-758-9195
www.olarestaurant.com
Best Mojitos

The name is an acronym for Of Latin America, and hot chef Douglas Rodriguez raids much of the Western Hemisphere for inspiration: caviar arepa, a Colombian-style yellow corn cake with quail egg, osetra caviar, and crème fraîche; plantain-crusted mahi-mahi; and baby sweet conch with coconut water, Thai basil, ginger, and coconut gelée. Sweets are equally fresh, like the chocolate cigar made of mousse and peanut nougat. Order the tasting menu so you can try a sampling of dishes and ceviches. The huge windowless building is divided into dynamic spaces: a ceviche room, a buzzy bar, a community table, and an enormous kitchen. OLA has endeared itself to Rodriguez' aficionados and local hipsters in this up-and-coming East Side 'hood by hosting free roast-pig barbecues, half-price mojitos, and live Latin music on Thursday nights. *Open for lunch Mon.–Fri. 11 a.m.–3 p.m.; dinner Mon.–Thurs. 6–11 p.m., Fri.–Sat. 6 p.m.–midnight, Sun. 6–10:30 p.m.* $$$

Ortanique on the Mile

278 Miracle Mile (Ponce de Leon Blvd.), Coral Gables, 305-446-7710
Best Mojitos

Caribbean in décor and cuisine, this delightful little restaurant—named after a Jamaican fruit—showcases Cindy Hutson's Cuisine of the Sun. Tropical-inspired dishes include ceviches, island salads using tropical mango or spicy fried calamari, and sumptuous main dishes like Caribbean bouillabaisse and jerk double pork chops with guava glaze. Be sure to finish off the evening with Blue Mountain coffee ice cream with banana fritters. The bar is always at least two deep with hip young Coral Gables professionals. The delectable food and happy island vibe have been such a hit that other Ortaniques have opened in Las Vegas and Washington, D.C. *Open for lunch Mon.–Fri. 11:30 a.m.–2:30 p.m.; dinner Wed.–Thurs. 6–10:30 p.m., Fri.–Sat., 6–11 p.m., Sun. 5:30–9:30 p.m.* $$$

Pelican Cafe
826 Ocean Dr. (8th St.), South Beach, 305-673-3373

Load up on excellent Mediterranean-Italian cuisine at the Ocean Drive cafe of the whimsical Diesel Jeans–owned Pelican Hotel. Open for breakfast, lunch, and dinner, the Pelican serve inspired snacks like guacamole crostini, carpaccio with arugula and parmigiano reggiano, and a variety of panini. Don't miss their rustic ciabatta bread—it's homemade and a real treat. *Open daily 7:30 a.m.–midnight.* $

Piola
1625 Alton Rd. (Lincoln Rd.), South Beach, 305-674-1660
www.piola.it

You'd swear you were in Milan, not South Beach, at Piola, where a noisy, good-looking crowd turns out to watch hunky Italian pizza-makers slide rounds of dough into the oven all night. You'll even find very Italian topping choices on the extensive menu: potatoes, fried eggs, and tuna, to name a few. Carpaccio, salads, and pastas are also on the menu, but it's the thin-crusted, slightly charred, flavorful crusts with the bubbly toppings that take top billing. *Open daily 6 p.m.–1 a.m.* $

The River Oyster Bar
650 S. Miami Ave. (SE 6th St.), Downtown Miami, 305-530-1915
www.therivermiami.com

Popular with downtown business types and locals, this relaxed Brickell Village restaurant is one of Miami's very few oyster bars. Selections from the Pacific Northwest—Fanny Bay, Emerald Cove, and Penn Cove Select, among others—are on the menu, along with lobster and Florida stone crabs in season. Even if oysters aren't really your thing, you can enjoy the stylish setting and an array of light bites. Note that the happy hour here is particularly, uh, happy. *Open Mon.–Thurs. 11:30 a.m.–10:30 p.m., Fri. 11:30 a.m.–11:30 p.m., Sat. 6–11:30 p.m.* $$

Tap Tap
819 5th St. (Meridian Ave.), South Beach, 305-672-2898

It's better to experience Haitian cuisine at this colorful little South Beach restaurant than in dicey Little Haiti: the food is good and there's always a carefree party vibe here, with occasional live Caribbean music and island drumming. Start with a soleil, their potent signature drink made of rum, passion fruit juice, and Triple Sec. Then go on to try some of their dishes and stews, which feature fish, lamb, goat, and conch. Service might be a bit leisurely, but it's always friendly. *Open Mon.–Thurs. 5–11 p.m., Fri.–Sat. 5 p.m.–midnight, Sun. 5–10 p.m.* $

Tapas y Tintos
448 Espanola Way (Pennsylvania Ave.), South Beach, 305-538-8272
www.tapasytintos.com
Best Tapas Bars

This rustic tapas bar at the end of bohemian Espanola Way is as authentic as anything in old Madrid: crude barrel tabletops, mismatched chairs, artsy young types downing red wine and reading foreign newspapers. The tapas are also the real deal: Manchego cheese, seafood salad, cured meats, chorizo, and Spanish tortilla. You can also order seafood paella here. Finish with a *crema catalana*—custard with caramel sugar. Live entertainment ranges from tango classes to salsa and flamenco; Sundays are all about paella and televised soccer. *Open Mon.–Thurs. 4 p.m.–midnight, Fri.–Sun. noon–2 a.m.* $

Versailles
3555 SW 8th St. (SW 35th Ave.), Little Havana, 305-444-0240
Best Cuban Food

In Little Havana, there are scores of Cuban restaurants where the *croquetas* melt in your mouth, the *arroz con pollo* is savory, and the Elena Ruz sandwich oozes with carb-y goodness. Versailles (pronounced the Spanish way, vair-SAH-yes) delivers all that and more, in a faux palace of garish mirrors and gaudy décor. The menu includes every Cuban dish that exists, and you'll see all facets of the community, from Latinas having a girls' night out to extended families celebrating a sweet 15 party. *Open Sun.–Thurs. 9 a.m.– 1 a.m., Fri.–Sat. 9 a.m.–3:30 a.m.* $

CLASICO

Yuca

501 Lincoln Rd. (Drexel Ave.), South Beach, 305-532-9822
www.yuca.com
Best Cuban Food

At Yuca—an acronym for Young Urban Cuban American—delectable Cuban cuisine is all tricked out in its finest guayabera and elevated to Nuevo Latino. Popular Latin-American and Caribbean ingredients like guava and chayote turn up in sophisticated presentations, like spicy guava baby-back ribs, sugarcane skewered and seared jumbo shrimp with a guava-chili glaze, and chayote coleslaw. Even humble black bean soup gets designer treatment, served with a hot rice pancake, sour cream, and scallions. Look for hot Latin entertainment upstairs. *Open daily noon–11:30 p.m.* $$

Clásico Miami:
The Nightlife

Bash Club and Lounge

655 Washington Ave. (6th St.), South Beach, 305-538-2274
www.bashsobe.com

One of South Beach's original hot spots in 1993 when it was owned by actor
Sean Penn and Mick Hucknall of Red, Bash has changed owners, but not its
energy. Party people are lured to the spacious main dance floor and the
Enchanted Garden, an outdoor patio area, for cutting-edge house and heavily
Latin international music. Adding to the fun are creative theme nights like
Carnaval Bash, designer fashion shows, jungle bash, and movie parties. It's a
favorite with hip twenty-something Latinos. *Open Fri.–Sat. 11 p.m.–5 a.m.*

Bongos Cuban Cafe

AmericanAirlines Arena, 601 Biscayne Blvd. (NE 6th St.), Downtown Miami,
786-777-2100
www.bongoscubancafe.com
Best Latin Night Out

Local heroes Gloria and Emilio Estefan have created a gaudy restaurant-
disco that's their technicolor vision of 1950s Havana. Located at the downtown Miami AmericanAirlines Arena, the tropical Deco-designed space serves
typical Cuban dishes like *papa rellena* (breaded potato stuffed with ground
beef) and *croquetas de jamon* (ham croquettes), then turns into a wild nightclub with Latin dance music on Friday and Saturday nights. *Restaurant open
for lunch Friday–Sun. 11:30 a.m.–5 p.m.; dinner Wed.–Sun. 5–11 p.m.; night-
club open Fri.–Sat. 11 p.m.–4 a.m.* $$

Clevelander

1020 Ocean Dr. (10th St.), South Beach, 305-531-3485
www.clevelander.com

This is the quintessential South Beach collage: rowdy shirtless frat boys,
screaming fuchsia neon, comely college freshmen ingesting vast quantities
of martinis, dirty dancing, copious cleavage, and the promise of hazy hang-
overs the next morning. With five bars, a big screen for special sports events,
live entertainment, and some shallow pools to stumble into, this Ocean Drive
landmark is headquarters for collegians. If you just wanna party, this is your
place; if you've already marked your territory here during some long-ago
Spring Break, visit for old times' sake. *Open daily 11 a.m.–5 a.m.*

Club Deep

621 Washington Ave. (6th St.), South Beach, 305-532-1509
www.clubdeep.com

If you're not impressed by austere Zen lounges playing incoherent lounge tunes and prefer your clubs high energy and heavy on the hip-hop, Club Deep is the place for you. The dance floor sits on top of a 2,000-gallon aquarium, while a thunderous sound system and dazzling light show assault the senses. It's a big favorite with hip-hop stars like Trick Daddy, Pit Bull, and Ja Rule, and pro athletes like Dennis Rodman and Vince Carter. *Open Wed.–Sun. 10 p.m.–5 a.m. $*

Hoy Como Ayer

2212 SW 8th St. (SW 22nd Ave.), Little Havana, 305-541-2631
www.hoycomoayer.net
Best Latin Night Out

This isn't the sanitized-for-your-protection themed version of a Cuban nightspot, but the real deal, a dark Little Havana club that pays well-deserved homage to artists like Benny More and Celia Cruz. At Hoy Como Ayer (which translates as "today is just like yesterday" in Spanish), Cubans find plenty of nostalgia-inducing rhythms: Latin percussion, funky beats, cool vocals from the likes of Albita Rodriguez, Malena Burke, and Luis Bofill. Order a Cuba libre and a tamal platter, get a crash course in authentic musical forms like son and boleros, and settle in for the night. *Open Thurs.–Sun. 9 p.m.–3 a.m. $*

Jimmy'Z

432 41st St. (Royal Palm Ave.), Mid-Beach, 305-538-8533

Everyone from South Beach socialites to sugar daddies, hip-hop moguls to Michael Jackson and Madonna comes out to play at Jimmy'Z at The Forge. This former cigar lounge, transformed into a see-and-be-seen club with some help from nightlife impresario Regine, packs in the well-dressed, the well-connected, and the well-to-do. Theme nights include Brazilian Thursdays, Latin Fridays, and Saturday's St. Tropez night. If you dine at The Forge, you'll bee able to avoid the cover charge for dancing after dinner. *Open Wed.–Sat. 10 p.m.–5 a.m. $$$*

Macarena Tavern and Restaurant

1334 Washington Ave. (13th St.), South Beach, 305-531-3440

See Clásico Restaurants, p. 170 for description.
Open Mon.–Tues. 7 p.m.–midnight, Wed.–Thurs. 7–11:30 p.m., Fri.–Sat. 7 p.m.–5 a.m. $$

Mango's Tropical Cafe

900 Ocean Dr. (9th St.), South Beach, 305-673-4422
www.mangostropicalcafe.com

Feelin' hot-hot-hot? Head to Mango's Tropical Cafe for a Latin-Caribbean experience, with reggae music, salsa, and professional dancers and models showing a lot of rhythm and even more skin. It's like Brazilian Carnaval with wildly colored costumes, sexy dancing, and throbbing beats. After a couple of caipirinhas, you can be sure you'll be out there sweating with the best of them. *Open daily 11 a.m.–5 a.m.*

Miami Jai-Alai

3500 NW 37th Ave. (NW 34th St.), Airport, 305-633-6400
www.fla-gaming.com

Jai-alai (say HIGH-aligh) is billed as the fastest game on Earth, with players hurling a ball with blinding speed against a wall for opponents to return. Of course, the main objective of this Basque pari-mutuel is wagering. Miami Jai-Alai has matinees and evening games that start at 7 p.m. Note that you can wager on thoroughbred and harness racing simulcasts here, too. If you're feeling lucky, this is the place for you. *Open for matinees Mon., Wed.–Sat. noon, Sun. 1 p.m.; evenings Mon., Fri., Sat. 7 p.m. $*

Señor Frog's

616 Collins Ave. (6th St.), South Beach, 305-673-5262

When dinner's done, the fiesta begins every weekend at this popular Mexican restaurant. This rollicking nightspot has a main room and patio lounge with indie rock nights and parties like Surreal Fridays and the popular La Fiesta Caliente on Saturdays. There's no question it feels a little like spring break, but the Coronas are cold, the music is loud, and everybody's happy. *¡Andale! Open Tues.–Thurs., Sun. 11:30 a.m.–1 a.m., Fri. 11 a.m.–4 a.m., Sat. 11 a.m.–5 a.m., Mon. 11 a.m.–5 a.m. $*

Tropical Cigars

740 Lincoln Rd. (Meridian Ave.), South Beach, 305-673-3194

The cigar craze of recent years may have died down, but for some folks, the evening just isn't complete without a Macanudo and something to wet your whistle. For you, there's Tropical Cigars, a casual Lincoln Road hangout where the smoke is thick and the mojitos are strong. Cigar lovers relax under patio umbrellas listening to live Latin music, including rumba, merengue, vallenato, salsa, and sometimes Brazilian. *Open Mon.–Thurs. 11 a.m.–1 a.m., Fri.–Sun. 11 a.m.–2 a.m.* $

Tropigala

Fontainebleau Hilton Resort, 4441 Collins Ave. (44th St.), Mid-Beach, 305-672-7469

www.clubtropigala.com

Best Latin Night Out

Bejeweled, half-naked showgirls with feathered headdresses are alive and well and performing at Tropigala in the Fontainebleau Hilton Resort. Formerly the La Ronde Room where mink-wearing glamour pusses and their dapper hubbies watched Sinatra and Liberace, Tropigala now presents lavish shows that have entertained the likes of John Travolta, Rosie O'Donnell, and Matt Dillon. On weekends, you can see (for an extra charge) shows by Latin performers like Willy Chirino, Nelson Ned, and Braulio, and occasionally the Dominican impersonator Julio Sabala. Although you can opt to have a full dinner here—conventional fare like chicken breast or filet mignon—you're not really here for the food. Come for the late show and just order up some tapas and drinks. *Showtimes: Thurs. 8:30 p.m.; Fri.–Sat. 8 p.m., 10 p.m.; Sun. 8:30 p.m.* $$$$

Clásico Miami:
The Attractions

Art Deco Welcome Center
1001 Ocean Dr. (10th St.), South Beach, 305-531-3484
www.mdpl.org/tours.html
Best Guided Tours

You can't miss this former auditorium plunked right in the middle of Ocean Drive on the beach side—consider it your headquarters for all things Deco in this National Historic District. If you've got an hour and a half, sign up for the guided walking tours that start at 10:30 a.m. Otherwise, you can rent one of the self-guided audio tours. They'll give you your bearings not only for South Beach, but for the many unique and unusual design elements in some of the 800 buildings that still survive from the 1930s and '40s. *Open daily 10 a.m.–7:30 p.m.* $

Collins and Washington Avenues
Collins and Washington Aves., South Beach

While South Beach doesn't have any enclosed malls, scores of boutiques and shops line Collins and Washington between 5th and 12th Streets. Collins has any number of places where you can go to pretty yourself up for a night on the town: Intermix, Nicole Miller, and A/X Armani Exchange for a hot little black dress; Mac and Sephora for makeup; Kenneth Cole for shoes; and Urban Outfitters and Von Dutch for that trendy accessory. Washington Avenue, which is better known for its clubs than its shops, nonetheless is home to Versace Jeans Couture and Diesel, among others. While you're there, don't miss the funky grown-up toy store called Pop—it's overflowing with an eclectic array of essentials like Hello Kitty paraphernalia and Pee-wee Herman talking dolls.

Dr. Paul George's Tours
305-375-1621
www.historical-museum.org
Best Guided Tours

If you want the real skinny on Miami's colorful past, book a tour with Dr. Paul George, historian for the Historical Museum of Southern Florida. On most weekends from September through June, Dr. George leads tours on foot, bike, boat, and coach to some of Greater Miami's most intriguing destinations, including Stiltsville, a community of six houses on stilts in Biscayne

Bay, doomed to be washed away by the next hurricane; the Miami River, where ancient Tequesta Indians settled; and the Caribbean-flavored neighborhoods of Coconut Grove, Little Haiti, and Little Havana. Don't miss the Mystery and Mayhem: Crime Coach Tour if it coincides with your stay—you'll find out the real scoop on what inspired *Miami Vice* and *Scarface*. You'll find the complete and current schedule on the website. If the tour you want isn't taking place when you're there, keep in mind that private customized tours are also available. $$

Doral Golf Resort & Spa

4400 NW 87th Ave. (NW 44th St.), Doral, 305-592-2000
www.doralresort.com
Best Golf Courses

Doral has five 18-hole championship courses—Red, Gold, Silver, the Greg Norman–designed Great White, and the famous Blue Monster—all recently restored and renovated under the direction of championship winners like Ray Floyd, Greg Norman, and Jerry Pate. The Great White Course, the only desertscape course in the humid Southeast, has hundreds of palm trees, tightly packed coquina sand, and more than 200 pot bunkers. The Gold Course resembles a tropical island, with water accenting 16 of its 18 holes. And the legendary Blue Monster—home to the Ford Championship every spring—was lengthened by 166 yards, making it one of the longer Florida tournament stops. Remember to book tee times well in advance. *Open daily 6:30 a.m.–7 p.m.* $$$$

El Credito Cigar Factory

1106 SW 8th St. (SW 11th Ave.), Little Havana, 305-858-4162 / 877-523-9945

Watch workers turn giant tobacco leaves into handsome hand-rolled cigars, one by one. Among the cigars produced here are the highly regarded La Gloria Cubana brand. Of course, you can buy the closest thing to Cuban cigars here individually or by the bundle. So you should be sure to stock up while you have the chance. *Tours offered Mon.–Fri. 11 a.m.–4 p.m. Open Mon.–Fri. 9 a.m.–4 p.m.*

Historical Museum of Southern Florida

101 W. Flagler St. (NW 1st Ave.), Downtown Miami, 305-375-1492
www.historical-museum.org

If you've been out and about at all, you'll surely have noticed that Miami is one very diverse community. This compact museum does an outstanding job of making sense of multicultural South Florida by focusing on the steady arrival of people who came to stay, starting with the prehistoric Indians 10,000 years ago up to present-day immigrants from Cuba, Haiti, and other countries. Many of the collections relate to the history, folklife, and archaeology of South Florida and the Caribbean, with exhibitions that touch on such cultural phenomena as Cuban *quinces* (sweet 15 celebrations) or Bahamian Junkanoo costumes. The exquisite gift shop is a treasure trove of Floridiana. *Open Mon.–Sat. 10 a.m.–5 p.m., Sun. noon–5 p.m. Closed Thanksgiving, Christmas, and New Year's Day.* $

Little Havana

SW 8th St. between 12th and 17th Avenues, Little Havana

First things first: this is not a theme park. In order to best experience Little Havana's tastes, smells, and sounds, you'll want to explore on foot this culturally diverse working-class neighborhood made up of Cubans and other Hispanics. Calle Ocho (SW 8th St.) is one way eastbound after 22nd Ave., so head westbound on SW 7th St. When you get to SW 12th Ave., park wherever you find a space. Your first stop should be Memorial Blvd. (SW 13th Ave.), home to a number of Cuban monuments and an enormous ceiba tree, believed to be sacred by the followers of the Afro-Cuban Santería religion—look for offerings of chickens scattered around its roots. At SW 14th Ave. is Máximo Gómez Park, known locally as Domino Park, where old Cuban men argue about politics over spirited domino games. The stars on the sidewalks mark the Calle Ocho Hall of Fame, honoring local-girl-made-good Gloria Estefan and the late beloved singer Celia Cruz, among others. Back on Calle Ocho, your wanderings will take you past cigar factories; *botánicas* selling candles and oils to followers of Santería; fresh fruit stands where you can get fresh coconut water and sugarcane juice (*guarapo*); stores selling the cotton four-pocket shirts called *guayaberas*; and music stores blasting the latest salsa music. If you happen to be in town the last Friday of the month, stop by for the cultural block party called Viernes Culturales 7:30–11 p.m.

Little Havana To Go

1442 SW 8th St. (SW 14th Ave.), Little Havana, 305-857-9720 /
888-642-8262
www.littlehavanatogo.com

Savvy merchandisers have arrived in this neighborhood, and they are marketing Little Havana with true Disney-esque flair with their array of "official souvenirs." These would include T-shirts, Cuban CDs, dominoes, cigars, *guayaberas*, gifts, posters, and a whole range of oddities that include a replica of the 1958 Havana telephone directory. *Open Mon.–Sat. 10:30 a.m.–6 p.m., Sun. 11 a.m.–5 p.m.*

Lummus Park Beach

Ocean Dr. from 5th to 15th Streets, South Beach, 305-673-7714
Best Beaches

Lummus Park is the formal name given to the public beach that runs the length of most of South Beach. Folks know it better for its goofy colorful lifeguard stands, each one funkier than the last. You'll find a public boardwalk, beach volleyball courts, and vendors along the way. Note that you can sunbathe topless here, but not totally nude (for that, you have to make your way over to Haulover Beach). Expect to see anyone and everyone here, from resident retirees, to extended families, to tourists from all over the world. *Open daily sunrise to midnight.*

Miami Art Museum

101 W. Flagler St. (NW 1st Ave.), Downtown Miami, 305-375-3000
www.miamiartmuseum.org

Making up one third of the Downtown Miami-Dade Cultural Center (the Historical Museum of Southern Florida and public library fill out the bill), the ambitious Miami Art Museum specializes in international art that reflects greater Miami's cultural and cross-cultural traditions. Collections include works from Gabriel Orozco, Robert Rauschenberg, Marcel Duchamp, Teresita Fernandez, and Feliz Gonzalez-Torres. Top-quality traveling exhibitions frequently make their way here, so be sure to check the website for current information on what's on display. *Open Tues.–Fri. 10 a.m.–5 p.m., Sat.–Sun. noon–5 p.m., closed major holidays.* $

Miami Seaquarium

4400 Rickenbacker Causeway, Virginia Key, 305-361-5705
www.miamiseaquarium.com

Flipper is still alive and flipping at this old-timey marine attraction, along with Lolita the killer whale and Salty the sea lion. Frankly, modern marine theme parks like SeaWorld offer way cooler experiences, but the Seaquarium does have an attraction that's well worth splurging on: the WADE (Water and Dolphin Exploration) Program includes a swim-with-the-dolphins experience. You might even get to "ride" a dolphin across their lagoon. *Open daily 9:30 a.m.–6 p.m.* $$$

Parrot Jungle Island

1111 Parrot Jungle Trail (MacArthur Causeway), Downtown Miami, 305-258-6453
www.parrotjungle.com

This venerable tourist attraction has been around for ages, though it has moved from its suburban location to its new home on Watson Island on the MacArthur Causeway. It will take time for the lush landscaping to fill out, but in the meantime, the same rainbow-hued macaws and cockatoos are doing their shtick. Reptile shows, monkeys, tortoises, aviaries, and a maze of jungle trails round out the experience. (And yes, you can still visit the old Parrot Jungle site; it's now a gorgeous city-owned park called Pinecrest Gardens). *Open daily 10 a.m.–6 p.m.* $$

Vizcaya Museum and Gardens

3251 S. Miami Ave. (32nd Rd.), Coconut Grove, 305-250-9133
www.vizcayamuseum.com

Since it's unlikely you'll be visiting any of Miami's private bayfront mansions, the next best thing is a tour of Vizcaya Museum and Gardens for a good look at how the very wealthy lived during the Gilded Age. Industrialist James Deering started construction on this 34-room Italian Renaissance–style estate overlooking Biscayne Bay in 1914, later adding expansive gardens, fountains, and pools, and furnishing it with lavish European antiques. *Open daily 9:30 a.m.–4:30 p.m.; gardens till 5:30 p.m.* $

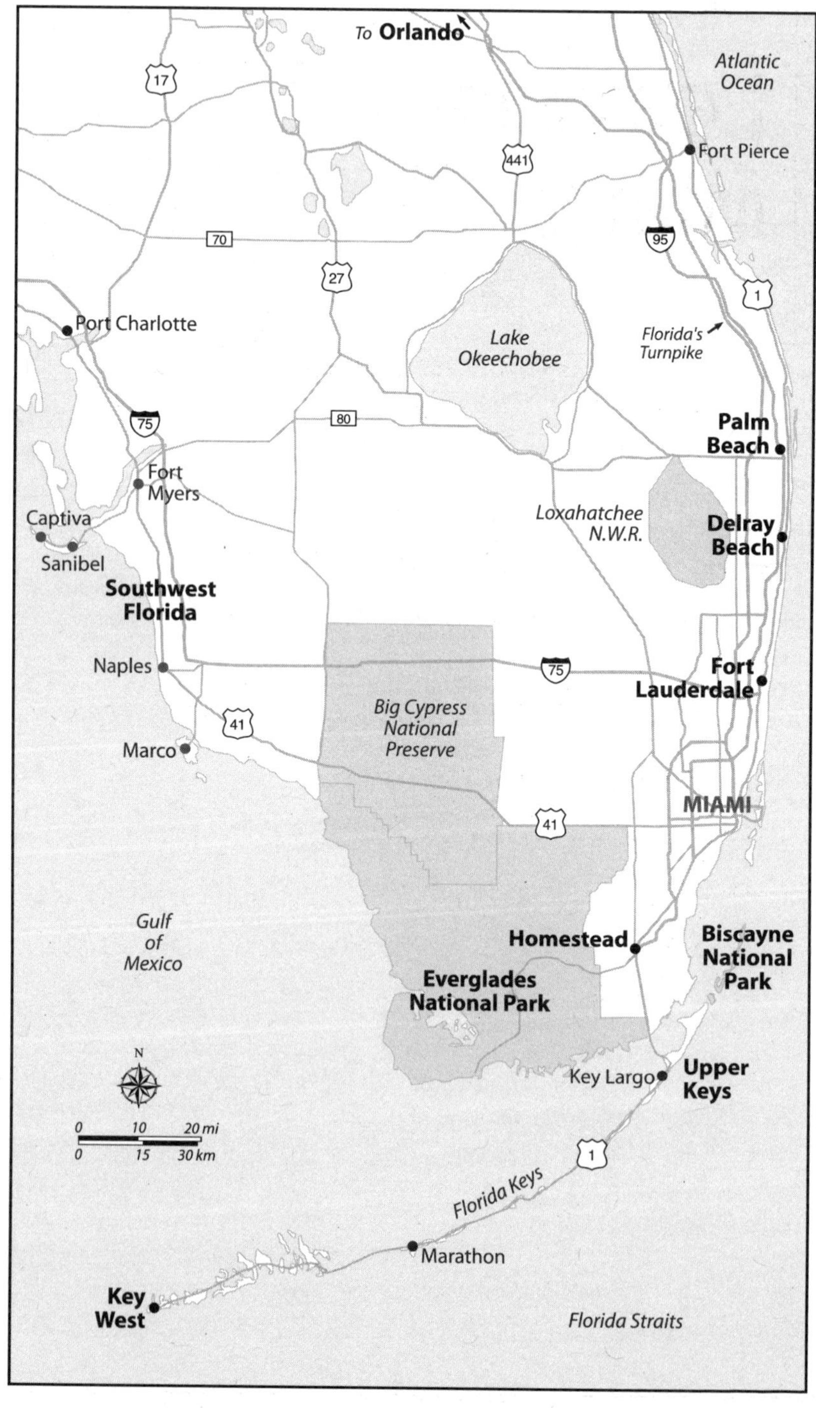

To Orlando
Atlantic Ocean
17
441
Fort Pierce
70
95
27
1
Port Charlotte
Lake Okeechobee
Florida's Turnpike
80
Palm Beach
75
Fort Myers
Loxahatchee N.W.R.
Captiva
Delray Beach
Sanibel
Southwest Florida
Naples
75
Fort Lauderdale
41
Big Cypress National Preserve
Marco
MIAMI
41
Gulf of Mexico
Homestead
Biscayne National Park
Everglades National Park
N
Key Largo
Upper Keys
0 10 20 mi
0 15 30 km
1
Florida Keys
Marathon
Key West
Florida Straits

Leaving Miami

When you've had your fill of urban fun, it's time to head out of town and discover what Florida has to offer beyond Miami. From party-ing in the Keys to lounging in luxurious Palm Beach, from swanky shopping in Fort Lauderdale to soaking up the natural beauty of Everglades National Park, you have a rich and diverse list of attractions to choose from. You'll find overnight destinations listed first, com-plete with hotel and nightlife recommenda-tions, followed by day-trip excursions.

Key West

Prime Time: February and March are high season, and the island is packed. Summer brings bargains and fewer crowds.

The Lowdown: Ninety miles from Cuba, this island paradise feels a lot more like the Caribbean than like Florida, with charming gingerbread architecture, tin-roofed conch houses, and brilliant bougainvillea climbing through lush tropical foliage. Key West has attracted all kinds over the years, from pirates, settlers, wreckers, and farmers; to luminaries like Ernest Hemingway, Thomas Edison, Harry Truman, and Tennessee Williams; to the present-day sophisticates, derelicts, and tourists by car, plane, and cruise ship. Never mind that the Old Town's quirky charm has been compromised by endless T-shirt shops, souvenir stands, and an icky touristy vibe—there are still enough genuine nuts and fruits populating the town to make it well worth your stay. Don't miss the Hemingway House, where those cats running around the grounds are supposedly descendants of the macho writer's six-toed felines. Watching the sunset at Mallory Square has become a tourist attraction of the first degree, with jugglers, mimes, and street performers on hand for your entertainment or annoyance. Other must-do activities in Key West include renting mopeds to get around, bar-hopping, and shopping at the many unique artisan boutiques and galleries. Whenever you decide to go, don't wait till last minute to book; rooms sell out quickly during holidays. Consider joining thousands of other revelers for the incredibly popular Fantasy Fest (see p. 205) in October, a week of parties, events, and costumed festivities—but book your lodging well ahead.

Best Attractions

Audubon House and Tropical Gardens 205 Whitehead St., Key West, 305-294-2116
Tour of lovely 1840s home and tropical garden of Captain Geiger.

Conch Tour Train 1805 Staples Ave., Key West, 305-294-5161, 800-868-7482
Amusing, informative narrated one-and-a-half-hour journey through city.

Dry Tortugas National Park Day Trip Elizabeth and Greene Streets, Key West, 305-296-5556
Catamaran trips to the islands and waters of Dry Tortugas National Park, 70 miles west of Key West.

Ernest Hemingway Home & Museum 907 Whitehead St., Key West, 305-294-1136, www.hemingwayhome.com
Tours of the house and gardens of the iconic American writer.

Key West Cemetery Margaret and Angela Streets, Key West
Colorful old graveyard reveals much of Key West history.

Best Hotels

Eden House 1015 Fleming St., Key West, 305-296-6868, www.edenhouse.com
Quiet inn off noisy Duval St. with pool, rooms with terraces.

Gardens Hotel 526 Angela St., Key West, 305-294-2661, www.gardenshotel.com
Luxurious guest suites amid one of Florida's oldest tropical gardens.

Marquesa Hotel 600 Fleming St., Key West, 305-292-1919, www.marquesa.com
Four exquisitely restored 1884 conch houses and an outstanding restaurant located right in the historic district.

Paradise Inn 819 Simonto St., Key West, 305-293-8007, www.theparadiseinn.com
Elegant cottages and suites on spacious and lush tropical grounds.

Sunset Key Guest Cottages at Hilton Key West Resort 245 Front St., Key West, 305-292-5300, www.hilton.com
37 deluxe and secluded guest cottages on Sunset Key, a boat ride from Key West.

Best Restaurants/Nightlife

Blue Heaven 729 Thomas St., Key West, 305-296-8666, blueheavenkw.com
Casual outdoor dining amid chickens in Bahama Village.

Café Marquesa 600 Fleming St., Key West, 305-292-1919
Award-winning contemporary American cuisine, theater kitchen.

Captain Tony's Saloon 428 Greene St., Key West, 305-294-1838
It's true that this colorful old bar is more touristy than gritty, but what the hey—it's Key West.

Green Parrot 601 Whitehead St., Key West, 305-294-6133
Dive bar that's popular with locals, known for good beer selection.

Jimmy Buffett's Margaritaville 424A Fleming St., Key West, 305-296-9089
Live music, burgers and seafood, and of course margaritas.

Kelly's Caribbean Bar, Grill & Brewery 301 Whitehead St., Key West, 305-293-8484
Casual eatery located in historic home of Pan American Airways.

Key West Contacts

The Florida Keys and Key West 800-352-5397, www.fla-keys.com

LEAVING

Getting There: Take Florida's Turnpike south to Florida City, and stay on U.S. 1—the Overseas Highway—to Key West. This is the only road into and out of the Keys, so accidents can cause lengthy delays. Barring problems, it should take you three and a half hours from Miami. Less than an hour away by air, Key West is served by Air Key West, American Eagle, Gulfstream International, and USAirways.

Orlando

Prime Time: Summer is hot, humid, and crowded. Winter is priciest and busy. The fall months are mild and pleasant.

The Lowdown: With nearly 100 attractions; 300 lakes, springs, and rivers; 114,000 rooms in resorts and hotels; 150 golf courses; and 4,500 restaurants, Orlando aims to keep you very, very busy. Its main attractions are Walt Disney World and Universal, each a destination unto itself, followed by marine theme parks SeaWorld and Discovery Cove, in addition to a variety of lesser attractions.

Although you can stay anywhere from $39-a-night generic hotels to $500 suites at luxury chains like the Ritz-Carlton, consider selecting a hotel where you'll enjoy recuperating from the parks' many activities. If your stay is short, your best bet is to spend one day at Epcot's World Showcase and the other at Universal. Unless you're here with kids, you'll want to make your way straight to Epcot, one of the most entertaining spots for grown-ups, where you can start with beer and tortilla chips at the Mexico pavilion and drink your way around the world. At night, head to Downtown Disney for more food and fun—there's a House of Blues, Wolfgang Puck Café, and Planet Hollywood, among other theme restaurants, and the avant-garde fantasy Cirque du Soleil *La Nouba*.

It's possible to spend half a day each at Universal Studios and Islands of Adventure, but you'll miss some of the greatest rides ever created. Both parks are geared toward older kids and adults, so expect heart-stopping special effects and hip jokes for those old enough to get them. If you're in town in October, come for Universal's Halloween Horror Nights when park lights are dimmed and chainsaw-wielding characters and muscled guys with flamethrowers sneak up on unsuspecting guests. Universal CityWalk, their nighttime dining and entertainment district, has theme restaurants and nightclubs with reggae, live jazz, dance music, karaoke, and Latin music. For up-close looks at marine mammals, head to SeaWorld for high-tech shows with Shamu the killer whale and exhibits like Wild Arctic, home to polar bears, walruses, beluga whales, and harbor seals. Discovery Cove—an Anheuser-Busch attraction, like SeaWorld—is a pricey marine attraction ($129-plus per person, which includes lunch and equipment) that lets you get downright intimate with the various sea creatures. Attendance is limited to 1,000 per day, so instead of facing long lines, you get to hang out in their coral reef, lagoon, and aviary, and do an optional swim with dolphins for an extra fee.

Best Attractions

Discovery Cove 877-434-7268, www.discoverycove.com
Exclusive marine park with coral reef and lagoon, one-on-one dolphin swims.

SeaWorld 800-327-2424, www.seaworld.com
Marine theme park with killer whale, dolphins, Arctic exhibits, rides.

Universal Studios, Universal Islands of Adventure 877-837-2273,
www.universalorlando.com
Two theme parks, each filled with state-of-the-art rides and attractions, more geared toward grown-ups.

Walt Disney World Resort 800-327-2996, disneyworld.disney.go.com
Four separate theme parks plus hotels, shopping and entertainment districts, restaurants.

Best Hotels

Disney's Grand Floridian Resort & Spa 800-647-7900
This huge Victorian-themed property is one of Disney's finest onsite hotels, and is home to the award-winning Victoria & Albert restaurant.

The Ritz-Carlton Orlando, Grande Lakes 407-206-2400
It includes a spa, an 18-hole championship golf course, and six dining options, and is located near the area's famous attractions and premier shopping areas.

Royal Pacific Resort 888-273-1311
This Loews hotel is Balinese-themed, with lush landscaping and Indonesian furniture and art. Also here you'll find Emeril's Tchoup-Chop Restaurant.

Best Restaurants/Nightlife

Downtown Disney 407-828-3800
Top restaurants include House of Blues, Wolfgang Puck Café, and Bongos Cuban Cafe; Pleasure Island has nightclubs for all tastes.

Universal CityWalk 407-224-2691, www.citywalk.com
It's home to Emeril's Restaurant Orlando, Hard Rock Cafe Orlando, Pat O'Brien's Orlando, Jimmy Buffett's Margaritaville, and assorted nightclubs.

Orlando Contacts

Orlando/Orange County Convention & Visitors Bureau 407-363-5872,
www.orlandoinfo.com

Getting There: The most direct (but boring) route is via Florida's Turnpike. Go north for three and a half hours to Kissimmee, then follow the signs to the parks. Or you can save the tolls and take I-95 north to the Beeline Expressway (528), then head west to Orlando. Orlando is about an hour away from Miami by air, with flights several times daily on Gulfstream, American Airlines, and Delta.

Southwest Florida

Prime Time: November through April are the best months, when the weather is milder and the mosquitoes aren't so plentiful (but bring repellent whenever you go).

The Lowdown: The tranquil Gulf Coast is a world apart from fast-paced Greater Miami. Much of this area is bounded by wilderness: the maze of uninhabited mangrove patches making up the Ten Thousand Islands; the sawgrass marsh of the Everglades; and the pines, hardwoods, and prairies of Big Cypress National Preserve, a habitat for deer, bear, and the endangered Florida panther. Start out on the Tamiami Trail, the southernmost east-west route across the Everglades. The Miccosukee Village is a traditional village with a variety of attractions. About 35 miles west of Miami is the gallery of nature photographer Clyde Butcher. The terrain changes from flat sawgrass to stands of cypress at Big Cypress National Preserve. Visit the Gulf Coast Visitors Center of Everglades National Park to see bottle-nosed dolphin, manatees, sea otters, alligators, and crocodiles. Or head to Marco Island, an outdoor playground with clean white beaches and good shelling. Nearby Naples is a pedestrian-friendly town with historic shopping districts, waterfront plazas, and countless galleries. It's said more millionaires per capita live here than in any other Florida city.

The next day, continue north to the beautiful barrier islands of Sanibel and Captiva. While Hurricane Charley in 2004 took a major toll on Captiva's lush green canopy, Sanibel fared better and remains one of the world's top shelling destinations. Sanibel is home to the 6,000-acre J.N. "Ding" Darling National Wildlife Refuge, with fine birding, footpaths, winding canoe trails, and a four-mile scenic drive. Nearby Fort Myers is a pretty town so beloved by inventor Thomas Edison that he built his winter house here. Inside Edison's home, laboratory, and gardens are rare antique cars and phonographs. Next door, in the home of his buddy Henry Ford, a 1914 Model T and 1929 Model A are among the cars on display. For a different perspective on the river of grass, take I-75 (Alligator Alley) back to Miami.

Best Attractions

Big Cypress National Preserve Tamiami Trail, halfway between Naples and Miami, 239-695-1201, www.nps.gov/bicy
Visitor center has a wildlife exhibit, movie, details on self-guided tours and trails.

Clyde Butcher 52388 Tamiami Trail, Ochopee, 239-695-2428, clydebutcher.com
Nature photographer known for stunning black-and-white Everglades landscapes.

Edison and Ford Winter Estates 2350 McGregor Blvd., Fort Myers, 239-334-7419, www.edison-ford-estate.com
Edison's house and laboratory, plus Ford's home, are surrounded by lush gardens.

Everglades National Park Gulf Coast Visitor Center, Route 29, Everglades City, 239-695-3311, www.nps.gov/ever
Interpretive natural history exhibits and displays at the visitor center. The marina has naturalist-led boat trips, kayak and canoe rentals.

J.N. "Ding" Darling National Wildlife Refuge 1 Wildlife Dr., Sanibel, 239-472-1100, dingdarling.fws.gov
Explore this 6,300-acre area on foot, bicycle, canoe, kayak, and via open-air tram.

Miccosukee Indian Village Tamiami Trail 25 miles west of Florida's Turnpike, 305-223-8380, www.miccosukee.com
Village displays crafts, foods, and lifestyle. Airboat rides into the Everglades.

Best Hotels

Bellaserra Hotel 221 Ninth St. S., Naples, 239-280-1790
Small luxury resort near downtown shopping and dining district.

The Inn on Fifth 699 5th Ave. S., Naples, 866-301-8777, www.naplesinn.com/fifth/
Elegant boutique hotel in a former bank building in the trendy 5th Avenue S. area.

The Inn at Pelican Bay 800 Vanderbilt Beach Rd., Naples, 239-597-8777, www.naplesinn.com/pelicanbay/
Intimate lakefront inn a short stroll to the Gulf of Mexico.

The Naples Beach Hotel & Golf Club 851 Gulf Shore Blvd. N., Naples, 800-455-1546, www.naplesbeachhotel.com
Friendly beach resort has onsite championship golf, tennis, and a full-service spa.

The Ritz-Carlton Golf Resort, Naples 2600 Tiburon Dr., Naples, 239-593-2000, www.ritzcarlton.com
Luxury resort overlooking Greg Norman–designed Tiburon golf course.

Best Restaurants/Nightlife

McCabe's Irish Pub & Grill 699 5th Ave. S., Naples, 239-403-7170
Traditional Irish pub fare and live entertainment.

Rod and Gun Club 200 Riverside Dr., Everglades City, 239-695-2101
Restaurant serving fresh seafood, stone crab claws in historic building.

Tin City U.S. 41 E. at Goodlette Rd., Naples, 239-649-5858
1920s clam-shelling plant and is now a waterfront dining and shopping center.

Southwest Florida Contacts

Beaches of Fort Myers and Sanibel 800-237-6444, www.fortmyers-sanibel.com

Greater Naples, Marco Island, Everglades Convention & Visitors Bureau 800-688-3600, www.paradisecoast.com

Getting There: Take the Tamiami Trail (SW 8th St./U.S. 41) west to the Gulf coast, then north to Fort Myers. On the return trip, you can avoid backtracking by taking I-75 (Alligator Alley) east to Fort Lauderdale, where it connects with I-95, then head south to Miami. American Eagle flies nonstop from Miami into Southwest Florida International Airport.

Biscayne National Park

Prime Time: Come on a calm, sunny day between November and April and be sure to bring a picnic lunch.

The Lowdown: From aboveground, this 173,000-acre national park looks pretty much all alike: wet. But underwater, it's a world of wonders: a pristine reef teeming with sea turtles, dolphins, brilliant tropical fish, manatees, and corals. The largest marine park in the national park system, Biscayne is 95 percent underwater. Start at the Dante Fascell Visitor Center for an overview of the park ecosystem and its history. Rangers give short walks and porch talks about topics like mangroves, manatees, pirates, and pioneers. The easiest way to observe the reef is aboard three-hour glass-bottom boat tours that leave at 10 a.m. Snorkeling trips set off at 1:15 p.m. daily and include all equipment and a brief orientation from a park ranger. If you're a certified diver, reserve ahead for scuba-diving outings—two-tank dives are offered on weekend mornings. You can also rent kayaks and canoes for exploring the mangrove shorelines. If you really want to rough it, go camping on one of the park's two barrier islands: Elliott Key, where there are picnic tables, grills, cold freshwater showers, and restrooms; or Boca Chita Key, with designated sites, a saltwater restroom, but no sinks or showers, so you'll have to bring in your own cooking and drinking water. Fishing is allowed in certain areas of both islands. Come prepared—you'll find mosquitoes, raccoons, and rodents in abundance here.

Biscayne National Park Contacts

Biscayne National Park 305-230-7275, www.nps.gov/bisc
Largest marine park in the national park system.

Concessionaire 305-230-1100
Choose from glass-bottom boat tours, snorkel and scuba trips, night dives, canoe and kayak rentals.

Getting There: Take Florida's Turnpike south to Exit 6 (Speedway Blvd.). Turn left from the exit ramp and continue south to SW 328th Street (North Canal Drive). Turn left and continue about five miles to the end of the road. The entrance is on the left.

Delray Beach

Prime Time: It's fun to visit year-round, but come on a weekend for the festivals, craft shows, concerts, and greenmarkets.

The Lowdown: If you're looking for a charming little beach town without tall condos casting shadows across the beach or other rampant development, take a drive up to Delray Beach. With balmy beaches, a lively historic cultural center, and a downtown shopping district with sophisticated cafes and restaurants, Delray Beach does a good job of keeping it real. Start at Delray Beach's epicenter, Atlantic Avenue, to pick up a map of the 1.3-mile Cultural Loop walking trail that links key historic sites and cultural museums such as the Old School Square Cultural Arts Center, a National Historic site housing the Cornell Museum of Art and History and other buildings. Atlantic Avenue is home to 150 boutiques, galleries, and restaurants. Ten minutes from downtown Delray is the Morikami Museum and Japanese Gardens, a center for Japanese arts and culture in South Florida, including an exhibit chronicling the history of the Japanese farming colony that lived in South Florida 100 years ago.

Best Attractions

Morikami Museum and Japanese Gardens 4000 Morikami Park Rd., Delray Beach, 561-495-0233, www.morikami.org
Serene garden and museum chronicling Japanese arts and culture in South Florida.

Best Restaurants

Blue Anchor 804 E. Atlantic Ave., Delray Beach, 561-272-7272, www.theblueanchor.com
Reconstructed 19th-century British pub serving authentic fare.

De La Tierra/Sundy House 106 S. Swinton Ave., Delray Beach, 877-439-9601, www.sundyhouse.com
Historic restaurant and inn with gorgeous tropical gardens.

Delray Beach Contacts

Downtown Delray www.downtowndelraybeach.com

Getting There: Head north on I-95 to Atlantic Avenue east, then drive east to the Intracoastal Waterway Bridge.

Everglades National Park

Prime Time: From November through April, temperatures are cooler, humidity is lower, and the mosquitoes are bearable.

The Lowdown: The Everglades—that vast flat river of grass championed by conservationist Marjory Stoneman Douglas for its uniqueness and diversity—makes up much of the South Florida peninsula. A million and a half acres in size, Everglades National Park is the only subtropical preserve in North America and is a World Heritage Site. Set aside your notions of seeing a park with grand vistas; this park rewards observers of details, connoisseurs of wide spaces, and lovers of wildlife. The only place in the world where alligators and crocodiles exist side by side, this fragile ecosystem is home to roseate spoonbills, great blue herons, and egrets. There are two southeastern Florida park entrances. Shark Valley, an hour west of Miami Beach, offers two-hour tram rides into the sawgrass marsh and bicycle rentals so you can dodge gators on the the 15-mile tram road on your own. An hour southwest of Miami Beach, the Ernest F. Coe Visitor Center offers displays, films, and activity information. Four miles west is the Royal Palm Visitor Center, where the self-guided Anhinga Trail, a half-mile boardwalk through a sawgrass marsh, starts. You can continue 38 miles to Flamingo on Florida Bay.

Best Attractions

Everglades Alligator Farm 40351 SW 192nd Ave., Florida City, 305-247-2628, www.everglades.com
Thousands of gators, reptile shows, and airboat rides.

Best Restaurants

Robert Is Here 19200 SW 344th St., Homestead, 305-246-1592
Scrumptious fruit milkshakes, fresh produce and honey, and a big tortoise display.

Rosita's Mexican Restaurant 199 W. Palm Ave., Florida City, 305-246-3114
Tasty, authentic Mexican food in a casual setting.

Everglades National Park Contacts

Everglades National Park 305-242-7700, www.nps.gov/ever

Flamingo Lodge and Marina 239-695-3101, www.flamingolodge.com

Getting There: To get to Shark Valley, take SW 8th St. (also known as U.S. 41 and the Tamiami Trail) west—it's 25 miles after Florida's Turnpike. To reach the Homestead entrance, take Florida's Turnpike south till it ends at Florida City, and follow the signs west to the park entrance.

Fort Lauderdale

Prime Time: Anytime is a good time to visit here, with the busiest tourist months between Christmas and Easter.

The Lowdown: Fort Lauderdale ditched its spring break image long ago. This yachting capital is now sporting a sophisticated look, going after grown-up fun with stylish shopping streets, cultural attractions, over 23 miles of beaches, and 300 miles of waterways. Water taxis, riverboats, and catamarans are ready to whisk you away. The landscaped beachfront promenade has a breezy white-wave wall and brick-paved path, with places to dine and shop across the street. The waterways lead to some spectacular mansions, which you can see from any of the tour boats. Fort Lauderdale's shopping district, Las Olas Boulevard, features fun boutiques, designer stores, and some excellent restaurants and cafes. Nearby Riverwalk is a promenade showcasing cultural attractions along the New River. The wildly popular shopping destination, Sawgrass Mills, is 20 minutes west of downtown.

Best Attractions

Jungle Queen Riverboat 2455 E. Sunrise Blvd., Fort Lauderdale, 954 566-5533, www.junglequeen.com
Sightseeing and dinner cruises along Fort Lauderdale's waterways.

Riverwalk Fort Lauderdale New River Downtown, Fort Lauderdale, 954-468 1541, www.goriverwalk.com
Winding riverside walkway includes museums, cultural centers, shopping, and dining.

Sawgrass Mills 12801 W. Sunrise Blvd., Sunrise, 800-356-4557, www.sawgrassmillsmall.com
Mega designer outlet, with 270-plus brand-name and designer outlets.

Best Restaurants

Himmarshee Bar & Grille/Side Bar 210 S.W. 2nd St., Fort Lauderdale, 954-524-1818
Eclectic and creative cuisine, great wines, noisy fun in lively Himmarshee district.

Mark's Las Olas 1032 E. Las Olas Blvd., Fort Lauderdale, 954-463-1000
Sleek spot with open kitchen, cozy booths, and exceptional Florida cuisine.

Fort Lauderdale Contacts

Greater Fort Lauderdale Convention & Visitors Bureau 800-227-8669, www.sunny.org

Getting There: Take I-95 north to Sunrise Blvd., then head east till you reach Fort Lauderdale Beach. From there, head south on A-1-A to get to Las Olas Boulevard. Sawgrass Mills is located in west Broward County, off I-595 in Sunrise.

Homestead

Prime Time: November to March is the winter growing season, so look for ripe tomatoes and juicy strawberries in early spring.

The Lowdown: In the mood to get away from the well-worn tourist path? Only an hour south but light-years away from the glitz and glam of South Beach is the friendly rural town of Homestead, incorporated in 1913, with a main street as cozy as any you'd find in the Midwest. This is the heart of South Florida's agricultural industry, surrounded by fields of strawberries, pole beans, tomatoes, and squash, and ornamental nurseries. You'll find excellent Mexican restaurants, roadside produce stands and U-Pic fields, and quaint antique stores. Downtown Homestead's main drag is Krome Ave. Pick up a walking-tour map at Old City Hall at 43 N. Krome Ave. to lead you to the properties listed on the National Register of Historic Places.

Best Attractions

Coral Castle 28655 S. Dixie Hwy., Miami, 305-248-6345 www.coralcastle.com
Weird coral rock castle hand-built by one man as a monument to the girlfriend who jilted him. How did he move 1,000-plus tons of rock? No one knows.

Fruit and Spice Park 24801 SW 187th Ave., Homestead, 305-247-5727
Charming garden park known for fruit, nut, spice, and herb trees and shrubs, many available to sample.

Knaus Berry Farm 15980 SW 248th St., Miami, 305-247-0668
Open late Nov.–April (closed Sun.), this farm stand run by German Baptists sells cinnamon rolls, pastries, fruit milkshakes, fresh produce.

Seminole Theatre 18 N. Krome Ave., Homestead, 305-242-9320, www.seminoletheatre.com
The city's only Art Deco structure, undergoing renovation for use as a concert venue.

Best Restaurants

Main Street Café 128 N. Krome Ave., Homestead, 305-245-7575, www.mainstreetcafe.net
Tasty diner fare, warm service, and one of South Florida's few folk-music destinations.

Homestead Contacts

Tropical Everglades Visitor Association 305-247-9180, www.tropicaleverglades.com

Getting There: Take Florida's Turnpike south to the U.S. 1 north exit (Exit 1). Turn right on South Dixie Highway and head north half a mile to SW 6th St. Turn left and continue to Krome Avenue. Make another left and you're in downtown Homestead.

Palm Beach

Prime Time: The weather is best from November to April, which is high season, when rates are higher and lines longer.

The Lowdown: Palm Beach conjures up visions of extravagant parties, fabulous mansions, a playground for the really, really rich. You only get a vague sense of the city's tremendous wealth, as grand residences are concealed behind tall ficus hedges, and legendary Worth Avenue looks unremarkable from the street. But prepare to gawk: start at Mar-a-Lago at 1100 S. Ocean Blvd. Once heiress Marjorie Merriweather Post's 118-room mansion, it's now Donald Trump's private club. Head north along the beach to view more splendid residences, then turn east at Worth Avenue, lined with designer boutiques like Chanel and Hermès. Stop at the Flagler Museum, described as the world's most magnificent private dwelling. Off-island, West Palm Beach has a trendy shopping district, Clematis Street, and CityPlace. Don't miss the Norton Museum of Art, Florida's largest art museum. Consider coming in May for SunFest (see p. 204) in West Palm Beach, Florida's largest art, music, and waterfront festival.

Best Attractions

CityPlace 700 S. Rosemary Ave., W. Palm Beach, 561-366-1000, www.cityplace.com
Lively if predictable mix of retailers, restaurants, and a 20-screen movie theater.

Flagler Museum Coconut Row and Whitehall Way, Palm Beach, 561-655-2833
National Historic Landmark with original furnishings, art, and his own railroad car.

Norton Museum of Art 1451 S. Olive Ave., W. Palm Beach, 561-832-5196,
www.norton.org
The Norton is known for masterpieces by Matisse, Monet, Picasso, and O'Keeffe.

Best Restaurants

Cafe Boulud at the Brazilian Court 301 Australian Ave., Palm Beach, 561-655-6060
Illustrious chef Daniel Boulud's French-American cuisine, courtyard garden.

Cafe l'Europe 331 S. County Rd., Palm Beach, 561-655-4020
Known for its excellent cuisine, its outstanding service, and its caviar bar.

Leopard Lounge and Restaurant 363 Cocoanut Row, Palm Beach, 561-659-5800
Eclectic New American cuisine, afternoon tea, hot bar, and nightspot.

Ta-Boo 221 Worth Ave., Palm Beach, 561-835-3500
Order a Bloody Mary with lunch at this landmark. Expect a hot nightly bar scene.

Palm Beach Contacts

Palm Beach Convention & Visitors Bureau 800-554-7256, www.palmbeachfl.com

Getting There: Take I-95 north to Southern Blvd., then east to A-1-A.

Upper Keys

Prime Time: A popular weekend getaway year-round. Winter months are high season, summer and fall are value months.

The Lowdown: Only an hour from Miami, the northernmost islands of the Florida Keys chain give a satisfying taste of this laid-back recreational destination. This is an easy day trip, but casual motels and resort hotels abound if you want to stay longer. Linked together by U.S. Highway 1—the Overseas Highway—the Upper Keys begin at Key Largo, which consists of cheesy shops and fast-food joints but also harbors the stunning, mostly underwater John Pennekamp Coral Reef State Park, a favorite for snorkelers and divers. As you continue, you'll see less land and more water as you pass through Tavernier, with quaint preserved buildings, and on to Islamorada, which claims to be the Sportfishing Capital of the World. Be sure to visit the Holiday Isle Resort for the requisite frozen Rumrunner at the Tiki Bar. No directions needed—just look for the vehicles lined up along the highway.

Best Attractions

Holiday Isle Resorts and Marina 84001 Overseas Hwy., Islamorada, 800-327-7070, 305-664-2321, www.holidayisle.com
Beach resort complex best known for its Tiki Bar, but you can also set off on watersports and fishing adventures from here.

John Pennekamp Coral Reef State Park Mile Marker 102.5, Key Largo, 305-451-1202, www.floridastateparks.org/pennekamp/
Sign up for glass-bottom boat tours, snorkel outings, or scuba-diving trips. The visitor center's 30,000-gallon aquarium gives you a sneak preview of area marine life.

Best Restaurants

Islamorada Fish Company 81532 Overseas Hwy., Islamorada, 800-258-2559, www.IFCStonecrab.com
Fresh seafood and stone crabs in season served al fresco, with great sunsets.

Upper Keys Contacts

The Florida Keys and Key West: www.fla-keys.com

Getting There: Take Florida's Turnpike south to Florida City, and stay on U.S. 1 as long as you please—it ends at Key West. Consider taking Card Sound Road at Florida City, a scenic toll road. U.S. 1 is the only road into and out of the Keys, and accidents can cause major delays.

The Miami Calendar

With our month-by-month calendar of events, there's no excuse to miss out on any of Miami's events. We tell you when to be here and why, so you can be sure to be where the action is at the right time. With Miami's international reputation as a fabulous destination, it's no surprise that some of the world's greatest events—highlighting world-class sports, arts, and food, among many others—take place right here. But don't miss out on some of Miami's smaller neighborhood festivals when the real local flavor shines through in all its quirky glory.

The Miami Calendar

January**

FedEx Orange Bowl
Football Game

February**

Art Deco Weekend
Coconut Grove
  Arts Festival*
Miami Int'l Boat Show*
Miami Int'l Film Festival
South Beach Wine
  and Food Festival

March**

Carnaval Miami/Calle
  Ocho Festival*
Ford Champion
  at Doral
NASDAQ-100 Open
Winter Music Conference
Winter Party Festival

April**

Billboard Latin
  Music Conference
  and Awards

May

West Palm Beach
SunFest

June

Miami-Bahamas
  Goombay Festival

July

America's Birthday
  Bash at Bayfront Park
Int'l Mango Festival

August

September

Festival Miami

October

Key West Fantasy Fest*

November

Miami Book Fair Int'l

December**

Art Basel Miami Beach*
Bayfront Park's
  New Year's Eve
King Mango Strut

* The Fun Seeker's Top Five Events
**High Season is from late December through early April

January

FedEx Orange Bowl Football Game

Pro Player Stadium, Northwest Miami, 305-623-6100, www.orangebowl.org

When: One day during first week of the New Year.

The Lowdown: Although it's no longer played at the creaky Orange Bowl stadium, this annual sporting event is one of the granddaddies of college football, having been around since 1935. The Orange Bowl has also served as college football's national title game more than any other bowl. Another tradition is a big-bucks halftime show, with dazzling special effects and big names like Jessica Simpson and Chante Moore.

February

Art Deco Weekend

South Beach, 305-672-2014, www.artdecoweekend.com

When: Fri.–Sun., third weekend in February.

The Lowdown: Immerse yourself in South Beach's trademark architectural style—or just hang around for the fun—during this stylish event celebrating the arts and culture of the Art Deco era, from 1925 to 1945. Every year revolves around a particular theme such as the WPA—giving a sophisticated focus for the lectures, exhibits, entertainment, and even the street festival. Take advantage of the walking, bicycle, and trolley tours to see this historic district in fascinating detail.

Coconut Grove Arts Festival*

Downtown Coconut Grove, 305-447-0401, www.coconutgroveartsfest.com

When: Sat.–Mon., including Presidents' Day (third Monday in February).

The Lowdown: Free-spirited Coconut Grove gets back to its inner artist every year when three-quarters of a million people converge on Bayshore Drive for this enormous arts festival. More than 300 international artists and craftspeople show off their works for art (and beer) lovers who shuffle along in the sunshine. While the caliber of its art may not be stellar, the festival is a Grove classic—you'll find great street food, free concerts, and convivial crowds. The parking situation for this festival is an ordeal; your best bet is taking the shuttle service from the Coconut Grove Metrorail station.

Miami International Boat Show*

Miami Beach Convention Center and other venues, 954-441-3220, www.discoverboating.com/miami

When: Thurs.–Mon., mid-February.

The Lowdown: You're standing behind the wheel of your 43-foot Chris-Craft Roamer with the maple-and-cherrywood details, guiding it skillfully down the Intracoastal Waterway, while bystanders gaze on in admiration. Bring that testosterone-fueled fantasy closer to reality at one of the largest new-boat shows in the world. Lissome beauties help showcase the latest in powerboats, sailboats, engines, electronics, and accessories. The show is so big it takes place in three locations, but a free shuttle bus takes you from one to the other.

Miami International Film Festival

Downtown Miami, 305-237-3456, www.miamifilmfestival.com

When: Ten days, Fri.–Mon, in early February.

The Lowdown: Over the last 20 years, this festival has gained respect as a major regional festival, launching such filmmakers as Pedro Almodóvar, Lasse Hallström, Fernando Trueba, and Atom Egoyan. In addition to showcasing acclaimed films from a variety of genres and countries, the festival zooms in on Ibero-American cinema. It takes place over ten days during the busy winter tourist season, and there are plenty of special parties and events, many open to the public. It's worth attending to visit the splendid Downtown Gusman Center for the Performing Arts.

South Beach Wine and Food Festival

Multiple venues, 866-333-7623, www.sobewineandfoodfest.com

When: Fri.–Sun., last weekend in February.

The Lowdown: The crème de la crème of celebrity chefs and personalities—Mario Batali, Daniel Boulud, Anthony Bourdain, Nigella Lawson, Nobu Matsuhisa, and Charlie Trotter, among many others—turn out for this two-day celebration of food, wine, and spirits. Depending on how much you want to shell out, you can golf with celeb chefs at the Biltmore, learn about bubbly and fine wines, and hobnob with foodies. The signature event is the Grand Tasting on Ocean Drive, with culinary demonstrations, food from fabulous restaurants, and wines and spirits served up against a backdrop of sand and surf.

March

Carnaval Miami/Calle Ocho Festival*

Multiple locations in Little Havana, 305-644-8888, www.carnavalmiami.com

When: Nine days ending the second Sunday in March. Primetime: the final Sunday Calle Ocho Festival on SW 8th St.

The Lowdown: Get your dance on as culturally diverse Miami celebrates its Hispanic community with ten days of beauty pageants, domino tournaments, cooking contests, and music. The grand finale, known as the Calle Ocho Festival, is billed as the world's largest street party. The day-long event is spread over 23 city blocks of musical stages featuring live merengue, salsa, pop, and Caribbean music; folkloric presentations; dances; and all the fried snacks and rum cocktails you can scarf.

Ford Championship at Doral

Doral (west of Miami International Airport), 305-477-4653, www.fordchampionship.com

When: Wed.–Sun., first weekend in March.

The Lowdown: Golfing greats like Nicklaus, Els, Palmer, Faldo, and Floyd have competed in this tournament, the longest continuously running PGA Tour event in Florida. Held at the legendary Blue Monster course at the Doral, the event has far more than just golf for spectators—there's a Salsa on the Green concert and an evening of symphonic music and fireworks under the stars on the 18th green.

NASDAQ-100 Open

Key Biscayne, 305-446-2200, www.nasdaq-100open.com

When: Late March to early April.

The Lowdown: Gawk as the elite names in tennis—Roddick, Sampras, Agassi, the Williams sisters—deliver their breathtaking serves at the largest tournament in the world with title sponsorship. The 12-day Open features the world's top-ranked pros in singles and doubles competition. About a quarter of a million people show up for this prestigious event, so don't wait too long to buy tickets; packages go on sale at the end of August, and single-session tickets the first of the year.

Winter Music Conference

Various venues, 954-563-9444, www.wmcon.com

When: Five days in March, usually beginning on a Saturday.

The Lowdown: Thousands of music industry professionals from more than 60 countries gather in Miami Beach for dance music's major networking event. What this means for dance music lovers is plenty of opportunities to hear famous international deejays performing at top music venues throughout South Beach, along with a fair number of recording artists, plus parties, parties, parties—many of which are open to the public. Wherever you end up this week, the music will be awesome.

Winter Party Festival

Various venues, South Beach, www.thetaskforce.org

When: Wed.–Mon., beginning the first Wednesday in March.

The Lowdown: Everybody to the beach! One of the biggest gay party fundraisers, Winter Party Week encompasses five days of events culminating in a wild dance party on the beach along Ocean Drive and 14th St. About 10,000 visitors from around the world turn out for special events involving theater, music, art, food, wine, and scenic tours, plus nightclub and hotel parties with celebrity deejays throughout South Beach. The celebration benefits the lesbian, gay, bisexual, and transgender community.

April

Billboard Latin Music Conference and Awards

Various venues, www.billboardevents.com

When: Mon.–Thurs., beginning the last Monday in April.

The Lowdown: Latin music superstars Ricky Martin, Luis Miguel, and Ednita Nazario take center stage, and romantic ballads, salsa, and Spanish-language pop nudge out the usual hip-hop every April when the Billboard Latin Music Conference comes to Miami Beach. Capping the event is the awards show honoring the most popular Latin music and performers—it's open to the public and broadcast live on Telemundo. Not all industry parties are open to outsiders, but plenty of visiting performers and fresh talent make appearances at local nightclubs during the conference.

May

West Palm Beach SunFest

West Palm Beach, 800-786-3378, www.sunfest.com

When: Wed.–Sun., ending the first Sunday in May.

The Lowdown: Although SunFest doesn't take place in Miami proper, it's a fabulous party that every fun seeker visiting the area should know about. Florida's largest music, art, and waterfront festival, SunFest attracts more than 300,000 people over five days for crafts, food, and concerts from headliners like Santana, Lenny Kravitz, Sheryl Crow, Shaggy, and Bonnie Raitt. The downtown West Palm Beach setting overlooking the Intracoastal Waterway couldn't be more scenic, and the festival includes fireworks, arts and crafts, and plenty of interactive fun.

June

Miami/Bahamas Goombay Festival

Downtown Coconut Grove, 305-567-1399, www.goombayfestival.com

When: Sat.–Sun., first full weekend in June.

The Lowdown: Coconut Grove revisits its Bahamian roots every year at this raucous party weekend, one of the largest Black heritage festivals in the United States. Dazzling costumed junkanoos with cowbells and whistles strut to Caribbean rhythms, while the Royal Bahamian Police Marching Band performs with military precision. Expect plenty of arts and crafts, a straw market, and tasty island food.

July

America's Birthday Bash at Bayfront Park

Downtown Miami, 305-358-7550, www.bayfrontparkmiami.com

When: The Fourth of July.

The Lowdown: If you're in town for the Fourth, catch the best fireworks display in town at this party at Bayfront Park. Before the show lights up the bay, you can listen to live American music, Miami-style—that is, a little of everything, including Latin, hip-hop, country, and rock—and sample street foods and check out arts and crafts in the park.

International Mango Festival

Fairchild Tropical Botanic Garden, Coral Gables, 305-667-1651, www.fairchildgarden.org

When: Sat.–Sun., second weekend in July.

The Lowdown: Miamians take their mangos seriously. Well, in serious fun at this unique two-day celebration of the luscious tropical fruit at Fairchild Tropical Botanic Garden. There are tastings, lectures, kids' activities, music, cook-offs, and plenty of mango smoothies, chutneys, and ice creams. At the Sunday brunch, the menu starts with mango Bellinis and just gets better as top Miami chefs present their specialties (advance reservations are essential). The festival ends with the entertaining Mango Auction, where bidders pay up to $100 for a plate of their favorite cultivar.

September

Festival Miami

University of Miami and other locations, Coral Gables, 305-284-4940, www.music.miami.edu

When: The end of September and throughout October.

The Lowdown: For five weeks every fall, music lovers pore through the bountiful offerings of this international festival sponsored by the University of Miami. What started two decades ago as a classical music festival has expanded its repertoire to include jazz, cabaret, folk music, flamenco, klezmer, and Latin music.

October

Key West Fantasy Fest *

Key West, 305-296-1817, www.fantasyfest.net

When: Nine days ending Sunday after the last Saturday in October. Primetime: Thurs.–Sat. before final Sunday.

The Lowdown: Fantasy Fest takes place in Key West, not Miami, but fun seekers definitely need to be tuned into this world-class event extraordinaire. Only in Key West could such debauchery go on for ten crazed days of outlandish costumes, dizzying parties, and bizarre pageants, all culminating in a fantastic parade attracting 70,000 revelers. This normally abnormal island town showcases its staggering swagger down Duval Street every year: painted bodies, elaborate floats, beads, bands, and balls, and everyone in splendid masquerade. Officials point out that nudity is illegal, but the line is quite blurry indeed—or perhaps that's the tequila talking. Anyway, reserve hotel rooms well in advance for this popular event.

November

Miami Book Fair International

Miami Dade College, Downtown Miami, 305-237-3258, www.miamibookfair.com

When: Sun.–Sun., beginning the first or second Sunday in November.

The Lowdown: Miami ain't no cultural backwater—this fair at the Downtown campus of Miami Dade College is one of the year's biggest events, attracting more than half a million book lovers every year. More than 250 authors, including top names like Pat Conroy, Susan Isaacs, Dave Barry, Carl Hiaasen, Tom Wolfe, and James Ellroy, read from their works, chat with their fans, and answer questions face-to-face. More than a million books are for sale, and an Antiquarian Annex features collectible items like historic handmade volumes, signed first editions, circus posters, sheet music, old maps, and vintage postcards.

December

Art Basel Miami Beach*

Miami Beach Convention Center and other venues, 305-674-1292, www.artbasel.com

When: Thurs.–Sun., first weekend in December.

The Lowdown: The American sister event of the prestigious Art Basel in Switzerland thrust Miami into the hip international world of extreme art, attracting visitors from all over the world to the Miami Beach Convention Center. The show includes all forms of visual art—paintings, drawings, sculpture, installations, photographs, performances, digital, and video art—with sale prices ranging from a few hundred dollars into the millions for museum-quality masterpieces. This mega-event takes place throughout Greater Miami, with visits to public and private art collections, exclusive receptions, and wild parties on the agenda, and local museums staging top-flight exhibitions to coincide with the show.

Bayfront Park's New Year's Eve

Downtown Miami, 305-358-7550, www.bayfrontparkmiami.com

When: December 31.

The Lowdown: You can spend a gazillion bucks to jam into some happening South Beach club on New Year's Eve. Or you can spend next to nothing and join the crowds to watch the neon Big Orange—Miami's version of the Big Apple—ascend to the top of the InterContinental Miami from Bayfront Park. Name entertainment, lots of ethnic foods, a laser show, a huge Christmas tree, ice skating, and tens of thousands of revelers make this a party to remember. Happy New Year!

King Mango Strut

Downtown Coconut Grove, 305-401-1171, www.kingmangostrut.org

When: One afternoon between Christmas and New Year's.

The Lowdown: Witness the hilarious vestiges of Coconut Grove's eccentric nature in this spoof on the late Orange Bowl Parade. Topical, risqué, and way too clever for its own good, this self-described weirdest parade in the universe has featured participants like Cuban Eye for the Gringo Guy (giving Miami makeovers to the crowd) and the red neckerchief–clad Running of the Bullshitters, and perennial favorites the Marching Freds (all named Fred), and beaming Little Miss Mangos (they're all crowned winners, boys and girls). All musical entries finish up with a concert at Peacock Park. There's no funnier way to end the year.

The Miami Black Book

Where was that hot new jazz club I was just reading about? Or the little Cuban joint I heard about? No one should have to get along without a little black book that contains all the important names and phone numbers at their fingertips. Ours is packed with helpful information, so you can choose your venue by theme, location, or price. It's the best of the city condensed into a few invaluable pages. Don't leave home without it.

The Fun Seeker's Miami Black Book

Hotels

NAME WEBSITE	ADDRESS (CROSS STREET) PRICE DESCRIPTION	AREA*	PHONE 800 NUMBER	EXPERIENCE PERFECT	PAGE** PAGE
The Albion www.rubellhotels.com	1650 James Ave. (Lincoln Rd.) $$ Hip Art Deco hotel, New York vibe.	SB	305-913-1000 877-782-3557	Arty Party	105
The Biltmore Hotel www.biltmorehotel.com	1200 Anastasia Ave. (Granada Blvd.) $$$ Classic grand hotel, dazzling pool.	GA	305-445-1926 800-727-1926	Outdoors Hotel Pools	135 47
Delano www.morganshotelgroup.com	1685 Collins Ave. (17th St.) $$$$ Trendy boutique hotel.	SB	305-672-2000 800-606-6090	Hot & Cool	75
Fisher Island Club www.fisherisland.com	One Fisher Island Dr. $$$$ Ultra-luxe resort on private island.	FI	305-535-6076 800-537-3708	Outdoors	135
Fontainebleau Hilton Resort www.fontainebleau.hilton.com	4441 Collins Ave. (44th St.) $$$ Glamorous beachfront resort.	MB	305-538-2000 800-548-8886	Clásico Hotel Pools	*159*, 163 47
Four Seasons Hotel Miami www.fourseasons.com	1435 Brickell Ave. (SE 14th St.) $$$$ Luxury hotel, dramatic art; 3 pools.	DM	305-358-3535 800-332-3442	Hot & Cool Hotel Pools	75 47
Grove Isle Hotel and Spa www.groveisle.com	Four Grove Isle Dr. (S. Bayshore Dr.) $$$ Waterfront hotel on secluded island.	CG	305-858-8300 800-884-7683	Outdoors	*131*, 136
The Hotel www.thehotelofsouthbeach.com	801 Collins Ave. (8th St.) $$$ Whimsical Todd Oldham design.	SB	305-531-2222 877-843-4683	Hot & Cool	76
Hotel Astor www.hotelastor.com	956 Washington Ave. (10th St.) $$ Minimalist Art Deco hotel.	SB	305-531-8081 800-270-4981	Arty Party	105
Hotel Impala www.hotelimpalamiamibeach.com	1228 Collins Ave. (12th St.) $$ Chic, tiny Mediterranean Revival.	SB	305-673-2021 800-646-7252	Clásico	163
Hotel Nash www.hotelnash.com	1120 Collins Ave. (11th St.) $$$ Handsome, low-key 1935 Art Deco.	SB	305-674-7800 800-403-6274	Clásico	164
Hotel Ocean www.hotelocean.com	1230 Ocean Dr. (13th St.) $$ Charming European boutique hotel.	SB	305-672-2579 800-783-1725	Clásico	164
Hotel Victor www.hotelvictorsouthbeach.com	1144 Ocean Dr. (11th St.) $$$ Latest luxurious boutique hotel.	SB	305-428-1234	Hot & Cool	76
Lido Spa Hotel/The Standard www.lidospa.com	40 Island Ave. $$ Revival of old Deco spa hotel.	SB	305-673-1717 800-327-8363	Clásico	165
Mandarin Oriental, Miami www.mandarinoriental.com	500 Brickell Key (Brickell Ave.) $$$$ Five-star luxury island resort.	DM	305-913-8288 866-888-6780	Hot & Cool	77
The Marlin www.marlinhotel.com	1200 Collins Ave. (12th St.) $$ Tiny rock-and-roll hotel/studio.	SB	305-604-3595	Arty Party	106
The National Hotel www.nationalhotel.com	1677 Collins Ave. (17th St.) $$$$ Stunning Art Deco restoration.	SB	305-532-2311 800-327-8370	Arty Party	*101*, 106
The Raleigh www.raleighhotel.com	1775 Collins Ave. (18th St.) $$$ Buzzy Art Deco hotel, pool parties.	SB	305-534-6300 800-848-1775	Arty Party	107
The Ritz-Carlton, Coconut Grove www.ritzcarlton.com	3300 SW 27th Ave. (Tigertail Ave.) $$$$ Elegant Italian Renaissance decor.	CG	305-644-4680 800-241-3333	Outdoors	136
The Ritz-Carlton, Key Biscayne www.ritzcarlton.com	455 Grand Bay Dr. (Crandon Blvd.) $$$$ Colonial design, beachfront spa.	KB	305-365-4500 800-241-3333	Outdoors	137
The Ritz-Carlton, South Beach www.ritzcarlton.com	One Lincoln Rd. (Collins Ave.) $$$$ Dazzling Deco renovation.	SB	786-276-4000 800-241-3333	Hot & Cool	*71*, 78

* Area Key Code: AI=Airport; BH=Bal Harbour; CG=Coconut Grove; DD=Design District; DO=Doral; DM=Downtown Miami; ES=East Side Miami; FI=Fisher Island; GA=Coral Gables; HA=Little Haiti; KB=Key Biscayne; LH=Little Havana; MB=Mid-Beach; ML=Miami Lakes; NB=North Bay Village; NM=North Miami Beach; SB=South Beach

** Note regarding page numbers: *Italic* = itinerary listing; Roman = description in theme chapter listing.

Hotels (cont.)

NAME WEBSITE	ADDRESS (CROSS STREET) PRICE DESCRIPTION	AREA	PHONE 800 NUMBER	EXPERIENCE PERFECT	PAGE PAGE
Sagamore Hotel www.sagamorehotel.com	1671 Collins Ave. (17th St.) $$$ Stark, sleek Art Deco hotel.	SB	305-535-8088 877-242-6673	Arty Party	107
The Shore Club www.shoreclub.com	1901 Collins Ave. (19th St.) $$$$ Uber-trendy, hot Nobu, hip Skybar.	SB	305-695-3100 800-606-6090	Hot & Cool	78
Sonesta Beach Resort Key Biscayne www.sonesta.com	350 Ocean Dr. (Crandon Blvd.) $$ Casual beachfront resort, spa.	KB	305-361-2021 800-766-3782	Outdoors	138
The Tides www.thetideshotel.com	1220 Ocean Dr. (12th St.) $$$$ Coolly elegant Art Deco hotel.	SB	305-604-5070 866-438-4337	Hot & Cool	79
TownHouse Hotel www.townhousehotel.com	150 20th St. (Collins Ave.) $$ Groovy, affordable hipster hangout.	SB	305-534-3800 877-534-3800	Arty Party	108

Restaurants

NAME	ADDRESS (CROSS STREET) PRICE DESCRIPTION	AREA	PHONE	EXPERIENCE PERFECT	PAGE PAGE
11th Street Diner	1065 Washington Ave. (11th St.) $ 1946 stainless steel diner, funky décor, comfort food.	SB	305-534-6373	Hot & Cool Late-Night Eats	73, 80 48
1200 Restaurant & Courtyard	1200 Anastasia Ave. (Granada Blvd.) $$$ Spectacular Sunday brunch in a romantic setting.	GA	305-445-1926	Outdoors Sunday Brunches	134, 139 61
1220 at The Tides (The Tides)	1220 Ocean Dr. (12th St.) $$$ Elegant fine dining on terrace, lobby of The Tides hotel.	SB	305-604-5070	Hot & Cool	80
A La Folie Cafe Français	519 Espanola Way (Euclid Ave.) $ Delightful sidewalk cafe, crepes, French bistro fare.	SB	305-538-4484	Arty Party	103, 109
Ago (The Shore Club)	1901 Collins Ave. (19th St.) $$$ Robert De Niro—owned Italian eatery, outdoor tables.	SB	305 695 3226	Hot & Cool	72, 80
Aria (The Ritz-Carlton, Key Biscayne)	455 Grand Bay Dr. (Crandon Blvd.) $$$$ Mediterranean cuisine, elegant indoor/outdoor setting.	KB	305-365-4500	Outdoors	139
Azul (Mandarin Oriental, Miami)	500 Brickell Key Dr. (Brickell Ave.) $$$$ Award-winning signature restaurant.	DM	305-913-8254	Outdoors Fine Dining	134, 139 43
Balans	1022 Lincoln Rd. (Michigan Ave.) $ British cafe, hearty breakfasts, tasty lobster clubs.	SB	305-534-9191	Arty Party	101, 109
Baleen (Grove Isle Hotel and Spa)	Four Grove Isle Dr. (S. Bayshore Dr.) $$$ Romantic waterfront dining, inventive seafood.	CG	305-858-8300	Outdoors Outdoor Dining	134, 140 54
Barton G	1427 West Ave. (14th Terr.) $$$ Outrageous culinary creations, tropical garden.	SB	305-672-8881	Hot & Cool Of-the-Moment Dining	72, 81 53
Bayside Seafood Restaurant	3501 Rickenbacker Causeway $ Waterfront joint, great conch fritters, often live music.	KB	305-361-0808	Outdoors	131, 140
B.E.D.	929 Washington Ave. (10th St.) $$$ Restaurant/lounge with queen-size beds for dining.	SB	305-532-9070	Arty Party Restaurant/Lounges	103, 109 56
Big Fish	55 SW Miami Ave. Rd. (SW 5th St.) $$ Hidden riverfront setting, gorgeous view, Italian food.	DM	305-373-1770	Outdoors Views of Miami	132, 140 66
Big Pink	157 Collins Ave. (2nd St.) $ Hip diner, funky industrial chic setting, comfort food.	SB	305-532-4700	Clásico Late-Night Eats	160, 166 48
Bizcaya (The Ritz-Carlton, Coconut Grove)	3300 SW 27th Ave. (Tigertail Ave.) $$$ Luxurious setting, classic cuisine, lavish brunch.	CG	305-644-4675	Outdoors	141
Bleau View (Fontainebleau Hilton Resort)	4441 Collins Ave. (44th St.) $$$$ Hotel restaurant, extravagant Sunday brunch, seafood.	MB	305-674-4670	Clásico Sunday Brunches	162, 166 61

NAME	ADDRESS (CROSS STREET)	AREA	PHONE	EXPERIENCE	PAGE
	PRICE DESCRIPTION			PERFECT	PAGE
Blue Door (Delano)	1685 Collins Ave. (17th St.)	SB	305-674-6400	Hot & Cool	*73*, 81
	$$$$ Fanciful French cuisine, surreal setting, A-list crowd.			Always-Trendy Tables	36
Boater's Grill	1200 S. Crandon Blvd.	KB	305-361-0080	Outdoors	*132*, 141
	$ Rustic seafood restaurant on beach, stunning view.			Outdoor Dining	54
Bond St. Lounge (TownHouse Hotel)	150 20th St. (Collins Ave.)	SB	305-398-1806	Arty Party	*104*, 110
	$$ Hipster basement lounge, new twists on sushi.			Sushi	63
Cafe Sambal (Mandarin Oriental, Miami)	500 Brickell Key Dr. (Brickell Ave.)	DM	305-913-8251	Outdoors	*132*, 141
	$$$ Casual waterfront cafe, Asian-inspired menu.				
Cafeteria	546 Lincoln Rd. (Pennsylvania Ave.)	SB	305-672-3663	Arty Party	*102*, 110
	$$ Round-the-clock restaurant/lounge.			Late-Night Eats	48
Capital Grille	444 Brickell Ave. (SE 4th St.)	DM	305-374-4500	Clásico	166
	$$$ Downtown steakhouse, high-profile clientele.			Power Lunches	55
Carmen the Restaurant (David William Hotel)	700 Biltmore Way (Segovia Ave.)	GA	305-913-1944	Outdoors	*133*, 142
	$$$ Inventive Puerto Rican/Floribbean food, great wines.				
Casa Tua	1700 James Ave. (17th St.)	SB	305-673-1010	Hot & Cool	*73*, 81
	$$$$ Ultra-hot haute Italian restaurant in restored house.			Of-the-Moment Dining	53
China Grill	404 Washington Ave. (5th St.)	SB	305-534-2121	Arty Party	*104*, 110
	$$$ Always hot, flashy celeb restaurant/bar, Dragon sushi.			Always-Trendy Tables	36
Chispa	225 Altara Ave. (Ponce de Leon Blvd.)	GA	305-648-2600	Clásico	167
	$$ Hispanic cuisine, dramatic décor, buzzing bar.			Tapas Bars	64
Christy's	3101 Ponce de Leon Blvd. (Malaga Ave.)	GA	305-446-1400	Outdoors	*133*, 142
	$$$$ Clubby independent steakhouse, memorable Caesars.			Steakhouses	60
The District Restaurant Lounge	35 NE 40th St. (N. Miami Ave.)	DD	305-576-7242	Arty Party	111
	$$ Indoor/outdoor restaurant/lounge in Design District.				
Dogma Grill	7030 Biscayne Blvd. (NE 70th St.)	ES	305-759-3433	Arty Party	*103*, 111
	$ Hipster gourmet hot-dog hangout.				
Donut Gallery	83 Harbor Dr. (Crandon Blvd.)	KB	305-361-9985	Outdoors	*133*, 142
	$ Tiny breakfast counter, Key Biscayne institution.				
Dulcianna Coffee & Gelato	532 Lincoln Rd. (Pennsylvania Ave.)	SB	305-532-1101	Arty Party	*104*, 111
	$ Argentinean coffee/sweet stop, *dulce de leche* goodies.				
Emeril's Miami Beach (Loews Miami Beach Hotel)	1601 Collins Ave. (16th St.)	SB	305-695-4550	Hot & Cool	*74*, 82
	$$$$ Touristy outpost of Emeril Lagasse, bountiful brunch.				
Escopazzo	1311 Washington Ave. (13th St.)	SB	305-674-9450	Clásico	*159*, 167
	$$$ Opulent institution, OTT cuisine, décor, entertainment.				
A Fish Called Avalon	700 Ocean Dr. (7th St.)	SB	305-532-1727	Hot & Cool	82
	$$ Popular indoor/outdoor seafood restaurant.				
The Forge	432 41st St. (Royal Palm Ave.)	MB	305-538-8533	Clásico	*162*, 167
	$$$$ Opulent institution, OTT cuisine, decor, entertainment.			Always-Trendy Tables	36
The Frieze Ice Cream Factory	1626 Michigan Ave. (Lincoln Rd.)	SB	305-538-2028	Arty Party	*104*, 112
	$ Fabulous housemade ice creams and sorbets.				
Front Porch Cafe (Penguin Hotel)	1418 Ocean Dr. (14th St.)	SB	305-531-8300	Clásico	*159*, 168
	$ Laid-back ocean view cafe, great breakfast.				
Grass Restaurant & Lounge	28 NE 40th St. (N. Miami Ave.)	DD	305-573-3355	Arty Party	*102*, 112
	$$$ Mellow Asian-inspired setting, strict velvet-rope policy.			Outdoor Dining	54
Green Street Cafe	3110 Commodore Plaza (Main Highway)	CG	305-444-0244	Outdoors	*132*, 143
	$ Longtime sidewalk cafe, good weekend brunch.				
IceBox Cafe	1657 Michigan Ave. (Lincoln Rd.)	SB	305-538-8448	Arty Party	*104*, 112
	$ Chic eatery, to-die-for homemade desserts.				

Restaurants (cont.)

NAME	ADDRESS (CROSS STREET) PRICE DESCRIPTION	AREA	PHONE	EXPERIENCE PERFECT	PAGE PAGE
Jerry's Famous Deli	1450 Collins Ave. (Espanola Way) $ Massive deli in old Art Deco ballroom, open 24/7.	SB	305-532-8030	Clásico	*159*, 168
Jimbo's Place	Duck Lake Rd. (Rickenbacker Cwy.) $ Out-of-the-way beer shack, bocce ball tournaments.	KB	305-361-7026	Outdoors Dive Bars	*131*, 143 42
Joe Allen	1787 Purdy Ave. (18th St.) $$ Friendly low-key eatery for movers, shakers.	SB	305-531-7007	Hot & Cool Power Lunches	*72*, 83 55
Joe's Stone Crab Restaurant	11 Washington Ave. (Biscayne St.) $$$$ Legendary stone crab restaurant.	SB	305-673-0365 305-673-4611	Clásico (take away)	*162*, 168
Joia Restaurant Bar/ Upper Lounge	150 Ocean Dr (1st St.) $$$ Chic neighborhood restaurant/lounge.	SB	305-674-8871	Hot & Cool	83
La Carreta	3632 SW 8th St. (36th Ave.) $ Popular chain, classic country style Cuban cuisine.	LH	305-444-7501	Clásico Cuban Food	*160*, 169 40
Le Bouchon du Grove	3430 Main Hwy., (Grand Ave.) $ French sidewalk cafe, terrific tarte Tatin, friendly staff.	CG	305-448-6060	Outdoors	*131*, 143
La Sandwicherie	229 14th St. (Washington St.) $ Juice bar/sandwich counter, popular with clubbers.	SB	305-532-8934	Hot & Cool	*73*, 83
Les Deux Fontaines Lobster Cafe and Bar (Hotel Ocean)	1230 Ocean Dr. (13th St.) $$ Friendly cafe, lobster bar, live jazz and Dixieland.	SB	305-672-7878	Clásico	*160*, 169
Macarena Tavern and Restaurant	1334 Washington Ave. (13th St.) $$ Spanish restaurant/nightclub, salsa, live music.	SB	305-531-3440	Clásico	*159*, 170
Mark's South Beach (Hotel Nash)	1120 Collins Ave. (11th St.) $$$$ Top Florida chef Mark Militello's New World cuisine.	SB	305-604-9050	Hot & Cool	*74*, 84
Metro Kitchen + Bar (Hotel Astor)	956 Washington Ave. (10th St.) $$$ American cuisine, hip clientele, gospel brunch.	SB	305-672-7217	Arty Party Sunday Brunches	*104*, 113 61
Miss Yip Chinese Cafe	1661 Meridian Ave. (Lincoln Rd.) $ Intentionally kitschy-cool Chinese restaurant.	SB	305-534-5488	Arty Party	*101*, 113
Monty's Raw Bar and Outdoors Restaurant	2550 S. Bayshore Dr. (Aviation Ave.) $$ Casual waterfront seafood and raw bar, live reggae.	CG	305-856-3992	Outdoors Waterfront Joints	144 67
Mosaico	1000 S. Miami Ave. (SW 10th St.) $$ Adventurous cuisine from Spain, seductive terrace.	DM	305-371-3473	Clásico	170
Mundo (Village of Merrick Park)	325 San Lorenzo Ave. (Ponce de Leon Blvd.) $$$ New World cuisine tapas from Norman Van Aken.	GA	305-442-6787	Hot & Cool Tapas Bars	*72*, 84 64
Nemo	100 Collins Ave. (1st St.) $$$ Convivial indoor/outdoor space, creative cuisine.	SB	305-532-4550	Hot & Cool	*74*, 84
News Cafe	800 Ocean Dr. (8th St.) $ See-and-be-seen institution for breakfast, lunch.	SB	305-538-6397	Hot & Cool	*72*, 85
Nobu (The Shore Club)	1901 Collins Ave. (19th St.) $$$$ Superchef Nobu Matsuhisa's sushi restaurant.	SB	305-695-3232	Hot & Cool Sushi	*72*, 85 63
Norman's	21 Almeria Ave. (SW 37th Ave.) $$$$ Norman Van Aken's signature fine-dining restaurant.	GA	305-446-6767	Clásico Fine Dining	*161*, 170 43
Novecento Miami	1080 Alton Rd. (11th St.) $$ Argentinean/Mediterranean bistro fare.	SB	305-531-0900	Clásico	*162*, 171
OLA Restaurant	5061 Biscayne Blvd. (NE 50th St.) $$$ Latin-American cuisine, memorable mojitos.	ES	305-758-9195	Clásico Mojitos	*161*, 171 52
Ortanique on the Mile	278 Miracle Mile, (Ponce de Leon Blvd.) $$$ Tropical/Caribbean dishes in sunny setting, lively bar.	GA	305-446-7710	Clásico Mojitos	*161*, 171 52
The Palm (Village of Merrick Park)	4425 Ponce de Leon Blvd. (San Lorenzo Ave.) $$$$ New York chain steakhouse.	GA	786-552-7256	Outdoors Power Lunches	*133*, 144 55

NAME	ADDRESS (CROSS STREET) PRICE DESCRIPTION	AREA	PHONE	EXPERIENCE PERFECT	PAGE PAGE
Palme d'Or (The Biltmore Hotel)	1200 Anastasia Ave. (Granada Blvd.) $$$$ Biltmore Hotel's signature restaurant.	GA	305-913-3201	Outdoors Fine Dining	134, 144 43
Paninoteca European Eatery	809 Lincoln Rd. (Meridian Ave.) $ European sidewalk cafe, panini, pizza, pasta.	SB	305-538-0058	Arty Party	102, 113
Pascal's Restaurant and Bar	2611 Ponce de Leon Blvd. (Valencia Ave.) $$$ Light French cuisine, charming ambience.	GA	305-444-2024	Outdoors	145
Pearl Restaurant & Lounge (Nikki Beach Club)	One Ocean Dr. (1st St.) $$$$ Beachfront restaurant/lounge, champagne bar.	SB	305-538-1111	Hot & Cool Restaurant/Lounges	74, 86 56
Pelican Cafe	826 Ocean Dr. (8th St.) $ Hot breakfast spot at quirky Pelican Hotel.	SB	305-673-3373	Clásico	161, 172
Piola	1625 Alton Rd. (Lincoln Rd.) $ Wood-burning oven pizzas, hip European crowd.	SB	305-674-1660	Clásico	172
Pizza Rustica	863 Washington Ave. (8th St.) $ Popular takeout stand for post-clubbers, $4 pizza slices.	SB	305-674-8244	Hot & Cool	72, 86
Prime 112 (The Browns Hotel)	112 Ocean Dr. (1st St.) $$$$ Hot, trendy new steakhouse in historic Browns Hotel.	SB	305-532-8112	Hot & Cool Steakhouses	73, 86 60
Puerto Sagua	700 Collins Ave. (7th St.) $ Longtime Cuban diner, authentic food.	SB	305-673-1115	Arty Party	102, 114
Purple Dolphin (Sonesta Beach Resort Key Biscayne)	350 Ocean Dr. (Crandon Blvd.) $$ Casual oceanview restaurant, seafood cuisine.	KB	305-361-2021	Outdoors	133, 145
The Raleigh Coffee Shop	1775 Collins Ave. (18th St.) $ Fabulous restored Art Deco breakfast counter.	SB	305-534-6300	Arty Party	114
Restaurant St. Michel (Hotel Place St. Michel)	162 Alcazar Ave. (Ponce de Leon Blvd.) $$$ Romantic ivy-covered restaurant, antiques.	GA	305-444-1666	Outdoors Romantic Dining	145 57
The River Oyster Bar	650 S. Miami Ave. (SE 6th St.) $$ Oyster bar, seafood, after-work watering hole.	DM	305-530-1915	Clásico	172
Roger's Restaurant and Bar	1601 79th St. Cwy. $ Casual waterfront dining, tiki bar, fresh ahi tuna.	NB	305-866-7111	Outdoors	134, 146
Rumi	330 Lincoln Rd. (Collins Ave.) $$$ Modern supper club, lounge after dinner.	SB	305-672-4353	Arty Party Restaurant/Lounges	103, 114 56
Rusty Pelican	3201 Rickenbacker Cwy. $$ Fabulous skyline, bay views, outdoor terrace.	KB	305-361-3818	Outdoors Views of Miami	133, 146 66
Sage on Fifth	425 Washington Ave. (5th St.) $$$ Casual neighborhood eatery, eclectic cuisine.	SB	305-672-3737	Arty Party	115
Sandbar Grill	455 Grand Bay Dr. (Crandon Blvd.) $$ Relaxed al fresco waterfront seafood/grill.	KB	305-365-4500	Outdoors	146
Scotty's Landing	3381 Pan American Dr. (S. Bayshore Dr.) $ Waterfront beer/wine joint, good seafood, dog-friendly.	CG	305-854-2626	Outdoors Waterfront Joints	134, 146 67
Segafredo	1040 Lincoln Rd. (Lenox Ave.) $ Trendy European outdoor café, coffee, cocktails.	SB	305-673-0047	Arty Party	101, 115
Smith & Wollensky	One Washington Ave. (1st St.) $$$ Steakhouse, great waterfront view, hot singles scene.	SB	305-673-2800	Outdoors Views of Miami	132, 147 66
Soyka	5556 NE 4th Ct. (Biscayne Blvd.) $$ Industrial chic, trendy crowd, comfort food.	ES	305-759-3117	Arty Party	103, 115
Spris	731 Lincoln Rd. (Meridian Ave.) $ Popular wood-burning pizzeria, people watching.	SB	305-673-2020	Arty Party	101, 115
Sunday's on the Bay	5420 Crandon Blvd. $$ Magnificent bayfront setting, marina views.	KB	305-361-6777	Outdoors Waterfront Joints	131, 147 67

Dinner
ha Carreta p. 40
Scotty's handing p. 176

fun - bar
Fritz + Franz Bierhaus p. 148

Movie
Superman?

Sat. -
TheRaleigh Coffee
Shop
Pg. 114
1775 Collins

Daytime -
Fairchild Tropica Botanic Ga
9:30a - 4:30p p.153

Venetian Pool   pg. 157

Restaurants (cont.)

NAME	ADDRESS (CROSS STREET) PRICE DESCRIPTION	AREA	PHONE	EXPERIENCE PERFECT	PAGE PAGE
SushiSamba Dromo	600 Lincoln Rd. (Pennsylvania Ave.) $$$ Brazilian/Japanese/Peruvian fusion sushi, chic crowd.	SB	305-673-5337	Hot & Cool Sushi	71, 87 63
Talula	210 23rd St. (Collins Ave.) $$ Romantic garden setting, inventive cuisine.	SB	305-672-0778	Hot & Cool	87
Tamara (The National Hotel)	1677 Collins Ave. (17th St.) $$$ Intimate indoor/outdoor space, French fusion.	SB	305-532-2311	Arty Party Romantic Dining	116 57
Tantra Restaurant & Lounge	1445 Pennsylvania Ave. (Espanola Way) $$$$ Sensuous restaurant/lounge with aphrodisiac cuisine.	SB	305-672-4765	Arty Party Romantic Dining	102, 116 57
Tap Tap	819 5th St. (Meridian Ave.) $ Colorful décor, Haitian food, live Caribbean music.	SB	305-672-2898	Clásico	159, 173
Tapas y Tintos	448 Espanola Way (Pennsylvania Ave.) $ Rustic Spanish tapas bar on bohemian Espanola Way.	SB	305-538-8272	Clásico Tapas Bars	159, 173 64
Taverna Opa	36–40 Ocean Dr. (1st St.) $ Greek seafood restaurant, mad dancing on tables.	SB	305-673-6730	Arty Party	102, 116
Touch	910 Lincoln Rd. (Jefferson Ave.) $$$ High energy restaurant/lounge, pole dancers.	SB	305-532-8003	Arty Party	103, 117
Tuscan Steak	433 Washington Ave. (5th St.) $$$ Chic, expensive family-style Italian food.	SB	305-534-2233	Arty Party Steakhouses	104, 117 60
Van Dyke Cafe	846 Lincoln Rd. (Jefferson Ave.) $ Top people-watching cafe on Lincoln Road.	SB	305-534-3600	Hot & Cool	71, 87
Versailles	3555 SW 8th St. (SW 35th Ave.) $ Cuban restaurant, authentic food, garish décor.	LH	305-444-0240	Clásico Cuban Food	160, 173 40
Vita	1906 Collins Ave. (19th St.) $$$$ Hip scenester hangout, stylish Italian cuisine.	SB	305-538-7855	Hot & Cool Of-the-Moment Dining	88 53
Wish (The Hotel)	801 Collins Ave. (8th St.) $$$ Celebs, inventive fusion cuisine, garden.	SB	305-531-2222	Hot & Cool Mojitos	74, 88 52
World Resource Cafe	719 Lincoln Rd. (Meridian Ave.), $$ Indoor/outdoor Thai and sushi.	SB	305-535-8987	Hot & Cool	71, 88
Yuca	501 Lincoln Rd. (Drexel Ave.) $$ Haute Cuban food and entertainment.	SB	305-532-9822	Clásico Cuban Food	162, 174 40

Nightlife

NAME	ADDRESS (CROSS STREET) PRICE DESCRIPTION	AREA	PHONE	EXPERIENCE PERFECT	PAGE PAGE
Amika Loft Lounge & Discotheque	1532 Washington Ave. (15th St.) - New lounge, '60s décor, well-dressed partiers.	SB	305-534-1499	Hot & Cool	74, 89
Automatic Slims	1216 Washington Ave. (13th St.) - Faux gritty bar, sassy female bartenders, bull-riding.	SB	305-695-0795	Hot & Cool Theme Bars	72, 89 65
The Bar	172 Giralda Ave. (Ponce de Leon Blvd.) $ Rockin' bar, live music, imported beers, board games.	GA	305-442-2730	Outdoors	133, 148
Bar at the Marlin	1200 Collins Ave. (12th St.) - Lower-level bar of hip hotel, popular with rockers.	SB	305-604-3595	Arty Party	104, 118
Bar at Sagamore Hotel	1671 Collins Ave. (17th St.) - Dramatic all-white hotel lobby bar.	SB	305-535-8088	Arty Party	103, 118
Bash Club and Lounge	655 Washington Ave. (6th St.) - High-energy dance club, hip Latinos, European crowd.	SB	305-538-2274	Clásico	162, 175

NAME	ADDRESS (CROSS STREET) PRICE DESCRIPTION	AREA	PHONE	EXPERIENCE PERFECT	PAGE PAGE
B.E.D.	929 Washington Ave. (10th St.) $$$ Restaurant/lounge with queen size beds for dining.	SB	305-532-9070	Arty Party Restaurant/Lounges	*103*, 109 56
Blue	222 Espanola Way (Washington Ave.) - Mellow little bar, laid back vibe, deejays.	SB	305-534-1009	Arty Party	*103*, 119
Bongos Cuban Cafe (AmericanAirlines Arena)	601 Biscayne Blvd. (NE. 6th St.) $$ Gloria and Emilio Estefan's sizzling Cuban restaurant.	DM	786-777-2100	Clásico Latin Night Out	*161*, 175 49
Cafeteria	546 Lincoln Rd. (Pennsylvania Ave.) $$ Round-the-clock restaurant/lounge.	SB	305-672-3663	Arty Party	*102*, 110 48
China Grill	404 Washington Ave. (5th St.) $$$ Always hot, flashy celeb restaurant/bar, Dragon sushi.	SB	305-534-2121	Arty Party	*104*, 110 36
Churchill's Pub	5501 NE 2nd Ave. (NE 55th St.) $ Grungy neighborhood bar, live rock, punk, acoustical.	HA	305-757-1807	Arty Party Live Music Venues	119 50
Clevelander	1020 Ocean Dr. (10th St.) - Legendary open-air bar, young, rowdy party crowd.	SB	305-531-3485	Clásico	175
Club Deep	621 Washington Ave. (6th St.) $ Wild club, dance floor atop 2,000-gallon aquarium.	SB	305-532-1509	Clásico	*159*, 176
crobar	1445 Washington Ave. (Espanola Way) $$ Hugely popular dance club with superstar deejays.	SB	305-672-8084	Hot & Cool Dance Clubs	*72*, 89 41
DiLido Beach Club (The Ritz-Carlton, South Beach)	One Lincoln Rd. (Collins Ave.) - Poolside/beachfront party central.	SB	786-276-4000	Hot & Cool Sunday Parties	*74*, 90 62
The District Restaurant Lounge	35 NE 40th St. (N. Miami Ave.) $$ Indoor/outdoor restaurant/lounge in Design District.	DD	305-576-7242	Arty Party	111
D'Lounge (The National Hotel)	1677 Collins Ave. (17th St.) - Stylish vintage bar and lounge, cabaret.	SB	305-532-2311	Arty Party Classic Hotel Bars	*103*, 120 39
Fallabella Bar (The Albion)	1650 James Ave. (Lincoln Rd.) - Smart hotel lobby bar catering to fashionistas.	SB	305-913-1000	Arty Party	*103*, 120
Felt Billiards Club	1242 Washington Ave. (12th St.) $ Friendly neighborhood billiards hall.	SB	305-531-2114	Arty Party	*102*, 120
Flute Champagne Lounge	500 S. Pointe Dr. (Collins Ave.) - Miami edition of Manhattan champagne bar, caviar, jazz.	SB	305-674-8680	Hot & Cool	*74*, 90
Fritz & Franz Bierhaus	60 Merrick Way (Aragon Ave.) $ Bavarian-themed restaurant and sports bar.	GA	305-774-1883	Outdoors	*133*, 148
The Globe Cafe and Bar	377 Alhambra Circle (LeJeune Rd.) $ Popular after-work, happy hour singles hangout.	GA	305-445-3555	Outdoors Meet Markets	*133*, 148 51
Gordon Biersch Brewery Restaurant	1201 Brickell Ave. (SE 12th St.) - Restaurant/brewery, mobbed after-work singles scene.	DM	786-425-1130	Outdoors Meet Markets	*132*, 148 51
Grass Restaurant & Lounge	28 NE 40th St. (N. Miami Ave.) $$$ Asian-inspired setting, strict velvet-rope policy.	DD	305-573-3355	Arty Party	*102*, 112 54
Houston's	201 Miracle Mile, (Ponce de Leon Blvd.) - Wildly popular after-work bar scene.	GA	305-529-0141	Outdoors Meet Markets	*133*, 149 51
Hoy Como Ayer	2212 SW 8th St. (SW 22nd Ave.) $ Smoky nightclub, Cuban musicians, local color.	LH	305-541-2631	Clásico Latin Night Out	*161*, 176 49
Jade	1766 Bay Rd. (18th St.) $ Chic upscale Asian-themed bar, gay, straight.	SB	305-695-0000	Arty Party Gay Bars	*102*, 121 44
Jazid	1342 Washington Ave. (13th St.) $ Smoky nightclub with live jazz every night.	SB	305-673-9372	Arty Party Live Music Venues	*102*, 121 50
Jimmy'Z	432 41st St. (Royal Palm Ave.) $$$ See-and-be-seen hot spot for celebs, socialites.	MB	305-538-8533	Clásico	*162*, 176

Nightlife (cont.)

NAME	ADDRESS (CROSS STREET) PRICE DESCRIPTION	AREA	PHONE	EXPERIENCE PERFECT	PAGE PAGE
JohnMartin's Restaurant and Irish Pub	253 Miracle Mile (Ponce de Leon Blvd.) - Classic Irish pub, live entertainment on weekends.	GA	305-445-3777	Outdoors	*133*, 149
Laundry Bar	721 N. Lincoln Lane (Meridian Ave.) - Fun mostly gay laundromat-themed bar.	SB	305-531-7700	Arty Party Theme Bars	*101*, 121 65
Macarena Tavern and Restaurant	1334 Washington Ave. (13th St.) $$ Spanish restaurant/nightclub, salsa, live music.	SB	305-531-3440	Clásico	*159*, 170
Mac's Club Deuce	222 14th St. (Collins Ave.) $ Longtime dive bar, bikers, drag queens, socialites.	SB	305-531-6200	Arty Party Dive Bars	*103*, 121 42
Mango's Tropical Cafe	900 Ocean Dr. (9th St.) - Steamy Latin-Caribbean club, costumed dancers.	SB	305-673-4422	Clásico	*159*, 177
Mansion	1235 Washington Ave. (12th St.) $$ Mega-club for celebs and trendsters.	SB	786-229-7857	Hot & Cool Dance Clubs	*74*, 90 41
M-Bar (Mandarin Oriental, Miami)	500 Brickell Key Dr. (Brickell Ave.) - Chic hotel bar, skyline view, 250 martinis.	DM	305-913-8288	Outdoors Classic Hotel Bars	134, 149 39
Metro Kitchen + Bar (Hotel Astor)	956 Washington Ave. (10th St.) $$$ American cuisine, hip clientele, gospel brunch.	SB	305-672-7217	Arty Party	*104*, 113 61
Miami Jai-Alai	3500 NW 37th Ave. (NW 34th St.) $ Fast-moving Basque pari-mutuel fronton.	AI	305-633-6400	Clásico	*160*, 177
Mr. Moe's	3131 Commodore Plaza, (Main Hwy.) $ Rowdy sports bar, karaoke, late-night food.	CG	305-442-1114	Outdoors	*132*, 150
Mynt Lounge	1921 Collins Ave. (19th St.) $$ Ultra-hip VIP hangout, toughest velvet rope in town.	SB	786-276-6132	Hot & Cool See-and-Be-Seen	*73*, 91 58
Nikki Beach Club	One Ocean Dr. (1st St.) $ Beachfront beautiful-people hangout with tepees.	SB	305-538-1111	Hot & Cool Sunday Parties	*74*, 91 62
Onda Lounge	1248 Washington Ave. (12th St.) $ New nightspot lounge, New York vibe, hot deejays.	SB	305-674-4464	Hot & Cool	*72*, 91
Opium Garden	136 Collins Ave. (1st St.) $$ Asian-inspired open-air see-and-be-seen club.	SB	305-531-5535	Hot & Cool Dance Clubs	*73*, 92 41
Orchid Lounge (Mayfair House)	3000 Florida Ave. (Virginia St.) - Stylish Art Nouveau–style champagne bar.	CG	305-441-0000	Outdoors	150
Oxygen Lounge (Streets of Mayfair)	2911 Grand Ave. (Virginia St.) $ South Beach-style nightclub lounge, sushi bar.	CG	305-476-0202	Outdoors	*132*, 150
Pawn Shop Lounge	1222 NE 2nd Ave. (12th St.) $ Former pawn shop turned nightclub.	DM	305-373-3511	Arty Party	*104*, 122
Pearl Restaurant & Lounge (Nikki Beach Club)	1 Ocean Dr. (1st St.) $$$$ Beachfront restaurant/lounge, champagne bar.	SB	305-538-1111	Hot & Cool Restaurant/Lounges	*74*, 86 56
Playwright Irish Pub & Restaurant	1265 Washington Ave. (13th St.) - Irish Pub food, decor, televised European soccer.	SB	305-534-0667	Arty Party Theme Bars	*104*, 122 65
Privé	136 Collins Ave. (1st St.) $$ Celeb haunt, VIP club-within-a-club at Opium Garden.	SB	305-531-5535	Hot & Cool See-and-Be-Seen	*73*, 92 58
RokBar	1905 Collins Ave. (19th St.) - Rocker Tommy Lee's '80s rock and punk club.	SB	305-538-7171	Hot & Cool	*73*, 92
Rooftop Lounge (TownHouse Hotel)	150 20th St. (Collins Ave.) $ Cool lounge with waterbeds, glow-in-the-dark tower.	SB	305-534-3800	Arty Party	*102*, 123
Rose Bar (Delano)	1685 Collins Ave. (17th St.) - Exceedingly hip Delano lobby bar.	SB	305-672-2000	Hot & Cool Classic Hotel Bars	*73*, 93 39
Rumi	330 Lincoln Rd. (Collins Ave.) $$$ Modern supper club that turns into lounge after dinner.	SB	305-672-4353	Arty Party Restaurant/Lounges	*103*, 114 56

| NAME | ADDRESS (CROSS STREET) | AREA | PHONE | EXPERIENCE | PAGE |
	PRICE DESCRIPTION			PERFECT	PAGE
Score	727 Lincoln Rd. (Meridian Ave.)	SB	305-535-1111	Hot & Cool	71, 93
	- Popular gay nightclub with three bars, karaoke.			Gay Bars	44
Señor Frog's	616 Collins Ave. (6th St.)	SB	305-673-5262	Clásico	162, 177
	$ Frenetic Mexican restaurant/nightspot, weekly parties.				
Skybar (The Shore Club)	1901 Collins Ave. (19th St.)	SB	305-695-3100	Hot & Cool	72, 93
	- Highly trendy, attitudinous nightclub, boldface names.			See-and-Be-Seen	58
Space	34 NE 11th St. (NE 1st Ave.)	DM	305-375-0001	Arty Party	104, 123
	$ Huge warehouse dance complex.				
Spire Bar & Lounge (The Hotel)	801 Collins Ave. (8th St.)	SB	305-531-2222	Hot & Cool	73, 93
	- Rooftop lounge atop The Hotel, electronic cocktails.				
State	320 Lincoln Rd. (Washington Ave.)	SB	786-621-5215	Hot & Cool	94
	$$ Upscale lounge/nightclub known for special events.				
Sunday Soiree at the Raleigh (The Raleigh)	1775 Collins Ave. (18th St.)	SB	305-534-6300	Arty Party	104, 123
	$ Hip Sunday afternoon pool party scene.			Sunday Parties	62
Tantra Restaurant & Lounge	1445 Pennsylvania Ave. (Espanola Way)	SB	305-672-4765	Arty Party	102, 116
	$$$$ Sensuous restaurant/lounge with aphrodisiac cuisine.				57
Taverna Opa	36–40 Ocean Dr. (1st St.)	SB	305-673-6730	Arty Party	102, 116
	$ Greek seafood restaurant, mad dancing on tables.				
Tobacco Road	626 S. Miami Ave. (SW 7th St.)	DM	305-374-1198	Outdoors	132, 150
	$ Funky longtime dive bar, live rock, blues, jazz.			Dive Bars	42
Touch	910 Lincoln Rd. (Jefferson Ave.)	SB	305-532-8003	Arty Party	103, 117
	$$$ High-energy restaurant/lounge, pole dancers.				
Tropical Cigars	740 Lincoln Rd. (Meridian Ave.)	SB	305-673-3194	Clásico	162, 178
	$ Sidewalk cigar cafe with mojitos, live Latin music.				
Tropigala (Fontainebleau Hilton Resort)	4441 Collins Ave. (44th St.)	MB	305-672-7469	Clásico	178
	$$$$ Gaudy supper club, showgirls, Latin performers.			Latin Night Out	49
Twist	1057 Washington Ave. (10th St.)	SB	305-538-9478	Hot & Cool	73, 94
	- Huge gay club with seven bars.			Gay Bars	44
Upstairs at the Van Dyke Cafe	846 Lincoln Rd. (Jefferson Ave.)	SB	305-534-3600	Arty Party	124
	$ Live jazz, intimate club vibe.			Live Music Venues	50
Zee Lounge (The National Hotel)	1677 Collins Ave. (17th St.)	SB	305-532-2311	Arty Party	104, 124
	- Casual ultra chill poolside lounge.				

Attractions

| NAME | ADDRESS (CROSS STREET) | AREA | PHONE | EXPERIENCE | PAGE |
	PRICE DESCRIPTION			PERFECT	PAGE
ArtCenter/South Florida	800 Lincoln Rd. (Meridian Ave.)	SB	305-674-8278	Arty Party	101, 125
	- Artists' studios and exhibition galleries open to the public.				
Barnacle Historic State Park	3485 Main Hwy., (Commodore Plaza)	CG	305-442-6866	Outdoors	134, 151
	$ Pioneer house on scenic bayfront land.				
Bass Museum of Art	2121 Park Ave. (Collins Ave.)	SB	305-673-7530	Hot & Cool	71, 96
	$ Huge art collection, updated Art Deco building.			Art Spaces	37
Bill Baggs Cape Florida State Park	1200 S. Crandon Blvd.	KB	305-361-5811	Outdoors	132, 151
	$ Pristine beach, lighthouse, rustic seafood restaurant.			Beaches	38
Britto Central	818 Lincoln Rd. (Meridian Ave.)	SB	305-531-8821	Arty Party	101, 125
	- Headquarters of Brazilian pop artist Romero Britto.				

Attractions (cont.)

NAME	ADDRESS (CROSS STREET) PRICE DESCRIPTION	AREA	PHONE	EXPERIENCE PERFECT	PAGE PAGE
Downtown Coconut Grove	Main Hwy. and Grand Ave. - Historic bohemian village, boutiques, galleries, cafes.	CG		Outdoors	*134*, 152
Coral Gables	LeJeune Rd. and Miracle Mile - A lush suburb with numerous architectural landmarks.	GA		Outdoors	*131*, 151
Design District	NE 40th St. and 2 Ave. - Hip design community, galleries, interior design, cafes.	DD		Arty Party	*103*, 126
Fairchild Tropical Botanic Garden	10901 Old Cutler Rd. $ Lush 83-acre subtropical botanic garden, tram tours.	GA	305-667-1651	Outdoors	*131*, 153
Haulover Beach Park	10800 Collins Ave. (Collins Ave.) $ Full-service dive charter boat.	MB	305-944-3040	Outdoors Beaches	*134*, 154 38
Historical Museum of Southern Florida	101 W. Flagler St. (NW 1st Ave.) $ Exhibits on South Florida multicultural diversity.	DM	305-375-1492	Clásico	*160*, 181
Holocaust Memorial	1933–1945 Meridian Ave. (Dade Blvd.) - Monument to Jewish victims of the Nazis.	SB	305-538-1663	Arty Party	*104*, 127
The Kampong	4013 Douglas Rd. (El Prado Blvd.) $ National Tropical Botanical Garden, tours by appt.	CG	305-445-8076	Outdoors	*134*, 154
Little Havana	SW 8th St (12th and 17th Avenues) - Hispanic neighborhood with cafes, cultural sights.	LH		Clásico	*160*, 181
Lowe Art Museum (University of Miami)	1301 Stanford Dr. $ A wide-ranging art museum.	GA	305-284-3536	Arty Party	*103*, 127
Lummus Park Beach	Ocean Dr. (5th–15th streets) - South Beach's popular public beach.	SB	305-673-7714	Clásico Beaches	*159*, 182 38
Margulies Collection	591 NW 27th St. (NW 5th Ave.) - Extensive collection of contemporary and vintage art.	DM	305-576-1051	Arty Party	*102*, 128
Miami Art Central	5960 57th Ave. (SW 60th St.. - Miami's newest venue for visual and performing arts.	GA	305-455-3333	Arty Party	*104*, 128
Miami Art Museum	101 W. Flagler St. (NW 1st Ave.) $ International art reflecting cultural traditions.	DM	305-375-3000	Clásico	*160*, 182
Miami Beach Botanical Garden	2000 Convention Center Dr. (19th St.) - Oasis of palms, trees near Convention Center.	SB	305-673-7256	Arty Party	*104*, 128
Miami Seaquarium	4400 Rickenbacker Cwy. $$$ Marine attraction, killer whale, dolphin interaction.	KB	305-361-5705	Clásico	*162*, 183
Museum of Contemporary Art—MoCA	770 NE 125th St. (NE 8th Ave.) $ Innovative exhibitions from contemporary artists.	NM	305-893-6211	Arty Party Art Spaces	*102*, 128 37
Oleta River State Park	3400 NE 163rd St. (NE 34th Ave.) $ Large park, kayaking, canoeing, mountain biking.	NM	305-919-1846	Outdoors	*134*, 155
Parrot Jungle Island	1111 Parrot Jungle Trail, (MacArthur Cwy.) $$ Longtime attraction, with parrots and reptiles.	DM	305-258-6453	Clásico	*162*, 183
Rubell Collection	95 NW 29th St. (NW 1st Ave.) $ Extraordinary private contemporary art collection.	DM	305-573-6090	Arty Party Art Spaces	*102*, 129 37
Venetian Pool	2701 De Soto Blvd. (Toledo St.) $ Historic grotto pool in suburban Coral Gables.	GA	305-460-5356	Outdoors	*131*, 157
Vizcaya Museum and Gardens	3251 S. Miami Ave. (32nd Rd.) $ Lush bayfront digs and garden.	CG	305-250-9133	Clásico	*162*, 183
The Wolfsonian—FIU	1001 Washington Ave. (10th St.) $ Unusual collection of modern art, design objects.	SB	305-531-1001	Arty Party	*101*, 129

Golf and Tennis

NAME	ADDRESS (CROSS STREET)	AREA	PHONE	EXPERIENCE	PAGE
	PRICE DESCRIPTION			PERFECT	PAGE
Crandon Park Golf Course	6700 Crandon Blvd.	KB	305-361-9129	Outdoors	*132*, 152
	$$$$ Scenic championship 18-hole golf course.			Golf Courses	45
Don Shula's Golf Club	7601 Miami Lakes Dr. (NW 77th Ave.)	ML	305-820-8088	Arty Party	*102*, 126
	$$$$ 72-par championship course in NW county.				
Doral Golf Resort & Spa	4400 NW 87th Ave. (NW 44th St.)	DO	305-592-2000	Clásico	*162*, 180
	$$$$ Five 18-hole championship golf courses.			Golf Courses	45
Miami Beach Golf Club	2301 Alton Rd. (W. 23rd St.)	SB	305-532-3350	Hot & Cool	*72*, 98
	$$$$ Newly redone 18-hole, par-72 course.			Golf Courses	45
Tennis Center at Crandon Park	7300 Crandon Blvd.	KB	305-365-2300	Outdoors	*132*, 156
	$ Clay, grass, hard courts; site of NASDAQ-100.				

Spas and Fitness

NAME	ADDRESS (CROSS STREET)	AREA	PHONE	EXPERIENCE	PAGE
	PRICE DESCRIPTION			PERFECT	PAGE
Agua (Delano)	Delano, 1685 Collins Ave. (17th St.)	SB	305-672-2000	Hot & Cool	*73*, 95
	$$$$ Rooftop bathhouse, solarium, health bar.				
Brownes & Co./ Some Like It Hot	841 Lincoln Rd. (Jefferson Ave.)	SB	305-538-7544	Hot & Cool	*71*, 96
	– Apothecary, beauty emporium, and spa.				
Crunch	1259 Washington Ave. (12th St.)	SB	305-674-8222	Hot & Cool	*72*, 97
	$$ Huge gym, top-notch equipment, variety of classes.				
The Ritz-Carlton Spa, South Beach	One Lincoln Rd. (Collins Ave.)	SB	786-276-4090	Hot & Cool	*73*, 98
	$$$$ Glam French spa, chic specialized treatments.			Spas	59
The Spa at Mandarin Oriental	500 Brickell Key Dr. (Brickell Ave.)	DM	305-913-8288	Outdoors	*133*, 156
	$$$$ Exotic treatments in spa, special spa suites.			Spas	59
The Spa at Ritz-Carlton, Key Biscayne	455 Grand Bay Dr. (Crandon Blvd.)	KB	305-365-4500	Outdoors	*133*, 156
	$$$$ Beachfront hotel spa, Florida botanical treatments.			Spas	59

Services and Shops

NAME	ADDRESS (CROSS STREET)	AREA	PHONE	EXPERIENCE	PAGE
	PRICE DESCRIPTION			PERFECT	PAGE
Art Deco Welcome Center	1001 Ocean Dr. (10th St.)	SB	305-531-3484	Clásico	*159*, 179
	$ Beachfront center with Deco tours, souvenirs.			Guided Tours	46
Bal Harbour Shops	9700 Collins Ave. (96th St.)	BH	305-866-0311	Hot & Cool	*72*, 95
	– Legendary designer mall for fashionistas, socialites.				
Base	939 Lincoln Rd. (Jefferson Ave.)	SB	305-531-6470	Hot & Cool	*71*, 95
	– Retail shop/lounge.				
Beach Scooter Rental	1341 Washington Ave. (13th St.)	SB	305-538-7878	Arty Party	*104*, 125
	$$$ Scooter and bicycle rentals.				
Books & Books	933 Lincoln Rd. (Jefferson Ave.)	SB	305-532-3222	Hot & Cool	*71*, 96
	– Outstanding collection of books/periodicals.				
Collins & Washington Avenues	Collins & Washington Avenues	SB		Clásico	*159*, 179
	– Trendy boutiques, music stores, clubs, restaurants.				
Deep Sea Sport Fishing Boat *Therapy IV*	Haulover Dock, 10800 Collins Ave.	MB	305-945-1578	Outdoors	*134*, 152
	$$$$ Half-day fishing tours aboard 58-foot fishing yacht.				

Services and Shops (cont.)

NAME	ADDRESS (CROSS STREET) PRICE DESCRIPTION	AREA	PHONE	EXPERIENCE PERFECT	PAGE PAGE
Dog Bar	723 N. Lincoln Lane (Euclid Ave.) - Amusing shop filled with pet trinkets.	SB	305-532-5654	Hot & Cool	*71*, 97
Dr. Paul George's Tours	 $$ Historian-led cultural tours in South Florida.	DM	305-375-1621	Clásico Guided Tours	*161*, 179 46
El Club	425 Grand Bay Dr. (Crandon Blvd.) $$ Watersport rentals: wave runners, sailboats, kayaks.	KB	305-361-9191	Outdoors Watersports	*131*, 153 68
El Credito Cigar Factory	1106 SW 8th St. (SW 11th Ave.) - Working cigar factory, tours and cigar sales.	LH	305-858-4162	Clásico	*160*, 180
Espanola Way	Collins to Washington (btwn. 14th &15th Sts.) SB - Historic Bohemian stretch with galleries, shops.			Arty Party	*104*, 126
H2O Scuba	160 Sunny Isles Blvd. (Collins Ave.) $$$$ Full-service dive facility rentals, instruction, charters.	MB	305-956-3483	Outdoors	*134*, 153
Hector's Jetskis	 $$$$ South Beach guided tours on jetskis	SB	305-318-9268	Hot & Cool Guided Tours	*74*, 97 46
Lincoln Road Mall	Lincoln Rd. (Alton Rd. & Washington Ave.) SB - Sidewalk cafes, galleries, shops, people-watching.			Arty Party	*101*, 127
Little Havana To Go	1442 SW 8th St. (SW 14th Ave.) - Cuban souvenirs, dominoes, CDs, cigars, guayaberas.	LH	305-857-9720	Clásico	*161*, 182
Mangrove Cycles	260 Crandon Blvd. (East Dr.) $ Bike rental store, detailed trail info.	KB	305-361-5555	Outdoors	*132*, 154
Miami Catamarans	Rickenbacker Cwy. $$$$ Instruction, rentals of Hobie Cats, trifoilers.	KB	305-345-4104	Outdoors Watersports	*131*, 154 68
Sailboards Miami	Rickenbacker Cwy. $$$$ Windsurfing, kiteboarding rental and instruction.	KB	305-361-7245	Outdoors Watersports	*131*, 155 68
Segway Excursion Center (Sonesta Beach Resort Key Biscayne)	350 Ocean Dr. (Crandon Blvd.) $$$$ Segway training/rental center, tours.	KB	305-365-4087	Outdoors	*133*, 155
Ultralight Adventures	3401 Rickenbacker Cwy. $$$$ Ultralight tours, flight instruction.	KB	305-361-3909	Outdoors	*131*, 157
Village of Merrick Park	358 San Lorenzo Ave. (Ponce de Leon Blvd.) GA - High-fashion open-air shopping center.		305-529-0200	Hot & Cool	*72*, 99

Notes

The Fun Seeker's Miami Black Book
By Neighborhood

Airport (AI)
Nightlife
Miami Jai-Alai

Bal Harbour (BH)
Services
Bal Harbour Shops

Coconut Grove (CG)
Hotels
Grove Isle Hotel and Spa
The Ritz-Carlton,
  Coconut Grove

Restaurants
Baleen
Bizcaya
Green Street Cafe
Le Bouchon du Grove
Monty's Raw Bar and
  Outdoors Restaurant
Scotty's Landing

Nightlife
Mr. Moe's
Orchid Lounge
Oxygen Lounge

Attractions
Barnacle Historic
  State Park
Downtown Coconut Grove
The Kampong
Vizcaya Museum
  and Gardens

Coral Gables (GA)
Hotels
The Biltmore Hotel

Restaurants
1200 Restaurant
  & Courtyard
Carmen the Restaurant
Chispa
Christy's
Mundo
Norman's

Ortanique on the Mile
The Palm
Palme d'Or
Pascal's Restaurant
  and Bar
Restaurant St. Michel

Nightlife
The Bar
Fritz & Franz Bierhaus
The Globe Cafe and Bar
Houston's
JohnMartin's Restaurant
  and Irish Pub

Attractions
Fairchild Tropical
  Botanic Garden
Lowe Art Museum
Miami Art Central
Venetian Pool

Services
Village of Merrick Park

Design District (DD)
Restaurants
The District
  Restaurant Lounge
Grass Restaurant
  & Lounge

Nightlife
The District
  Restaurant Lounge
Grass Restaurant
  & Lounge

Doral (DO)
Golf
Doral Golf Resort & Spa

Downtown Miami (DM)
Hotels
Four Seasons Hotel Miami
Mandarin Oriental, Miami

Restaurants
Azul

Big Fish
Cafe Sambal
Capital Grille
Mosaico
The River Oyster Bar

Nightlife
Bongos Cuban Cafe
Gordon Biersch Brewery
  Restaurant
M-Bar
Pawn Shop Lounge
Space
Tobacco Road

Attractions
Historical Museum of
  Southern Florida
Margulies Collection
Miami Art Museum
Parrot Jungle Island
Rubell Collection

Spas
The Spa at Mandarin
  Oriental

Services
Dr. Paul George's Tours

East Side Miami (ES)
Restaurants
Dogma Grill
OLA Restaurant
Soyka

Fisher Island (FI)
Hotels
Fisher Island Club

Key Biscayne (KB)
Hotels
The Ritz-Carlton,
  Key Biscayne
Sonesta Beach Resort
  Key Biscayne

The Fun Seeker's Miami Black Book
By Neighborhood (cont.)

Restaurants
Aria
Bayside Seafood
 Restaurant
Boater's Grill
Donut Gallery
Jimbo's Place
Purple Dolphin
Rusty Pelican
Sandbar Grill
Sunday's on the Bay

Attractions
Bill Baggs Cape Florida
 State Park
Miami Seaquarium

Golf/Tennis
Crandon Park Golf Course
Tennis Center at
 Crandon Park

Spas
The Spa at Ritz-Carlton,
 Key Biscayne

Services
El Club
Mangrove Cycles
Miami Catamarans
Sailboards Miami
Segway Excursion Center
Ultralight Adventures

Little Haiti (HA)

Nightlife
Churchill's Pub

Little Havana (LH)

Restaurants
La Carreta
Versailles

Nightlife
Hoy Como Ayer

Services
El Credito Cigar Factory
Little Havana To Go

Miami Lakes (ML)

Golf
Don Shula's Golf Club

Mid-Beach (MB)

Hotels
Fontainebleau
 Hilton Resort

Restaurants
Bleau View
The Forge

Nightlife
Jimmy'Z
Tropigala

Attractions
Haulover Beach Park

Services
Deep Sea Sport Fishing
 Boat *Therapy IV*
H2O Scuba

North Bay Village (NB)

Restaurants
Roger's Restaurant
 and Bar

North Miami Beach (NM)

Attractions
Museum of Contemporary
 Art—MoCA
Oleta River State Park

South Beach (SB)

Hotels
The Albion
Delano
The Hotel
Hotel Astor
Hotel Impala
Hotel Nash
Hotel Ocean

Hotel Victor
Lido Spa Hotel/
 The Standard
The Marlin
The National Hotel
The Raleigh
The Ritz-Carlton,
 South Beach
Sagamore Hotel
The Shore Club
The Tides
TownHouse Hotel

Restaurants
11th Street Diner
1220 at The Tides
A La Folie Cafe Français
Ago
Balans
Barton G
D.C.D.
Big Pink
Blue Door
Bond St. Lounge
Cafeteria
Casa Tua
China Grill
Dulcianna Coffee & Gelato
Emeril's Miami Beach
Escopazzo
A Fish Called Avalon
The Frieze Ice
 Cream Factory
Front Porch Cafe
IceBox Cafe
Jerry's Famous Deli
Joe Allen
Joe's Stone
 Crab Restaurant
Joia Restaurant Bar/
 Upper Lounge
La Sandwicherie
Les Deux Fontaines
 Lobster Cafe and Bar
Macarena Tavern
 and Restaurant

Mark's South Beach
Metro Kitchen + Bar
Miss Yip Chinese Cafe
Nemo
News Cafe
Nobu
Novecento Miami
Paninoteca
   European Eatery
Pearl Restaurant
   & Lounge
Pelican Cafe
Piola
Pizza Rustica
Prime 112
Puerto Sagua
The Raleigh Coffee Shop
Rumi
Sage on Fifth
Segafredo
Smith & Wollensky
Spris
SushiSamba Dromo
Talula
Tamara
Tantra Restaurant
   & Lounge
Tap Tap
Tapas y Tintos
Taverna Opa
Touch
Tuscan Steak
Van Dyke Cafe
Vita
Wish
World Resource Cafe
Yuca

Nightlife

Amika Loft Lounge
   & Discotheque
Automatic Slims
Bar at the Marlin
Bar at Sagamore Hotel
Bash Club and Lounge

B.E.D.
Blue
Cafeteria
China Grill
Clevelander
Club Deep
crobar
DiLido Beach Club
D'Lounge
Fallabella Bar
Felt Billiards Club
Flute Champagne Lounge
Jade
Jazid
Laundry Bar
Macarena Tavern
   and Restaurant
Mac's Club Deuce
Mango's Tropical Cafe
Mansion
Metro Kitchen + Bar
Mynt Lounge
Nikki Beach Club
Onda Lounge
Opium Garden
Pearl Restaurant
   & Lounge
Playwright Irish Pub
   & Restaurant
Privé
RokBar
Rooftop Lounge
Rose Bar
Rumi
Score
Señor Frog's
Skybar
Spire Bar & Lounge
State
Sunday Soiree at
   the Raleigh
Tantra Restaurant
   & Lounge
Taverna Opa
Touch

Tropical Cigars
Twist
Upstairs at the
   Van Dyke Cafe
Zee Lounge

Attractions

ArtCenter/South Florida
Bass Museum of Art
Britto Central
Holocaust Memorial
Lummus Park Beach
Miami Beach Botanical
   Garden
The Wolfsonian—FIU

Golf

Miami Beach Golf Club

Spas

Agua
Brownes & Co./Some Like
   It Hot
Crunch
The Ritz-Carlton Spa,
   South Beach

Services

Art Deco Welcome Center
Base
Beach Scooter Rental
Books & Books
Collins & Washington
   Avenues
Dog Bar
Espanola Way
Hector's Jetskis
Lincoln Road Mall

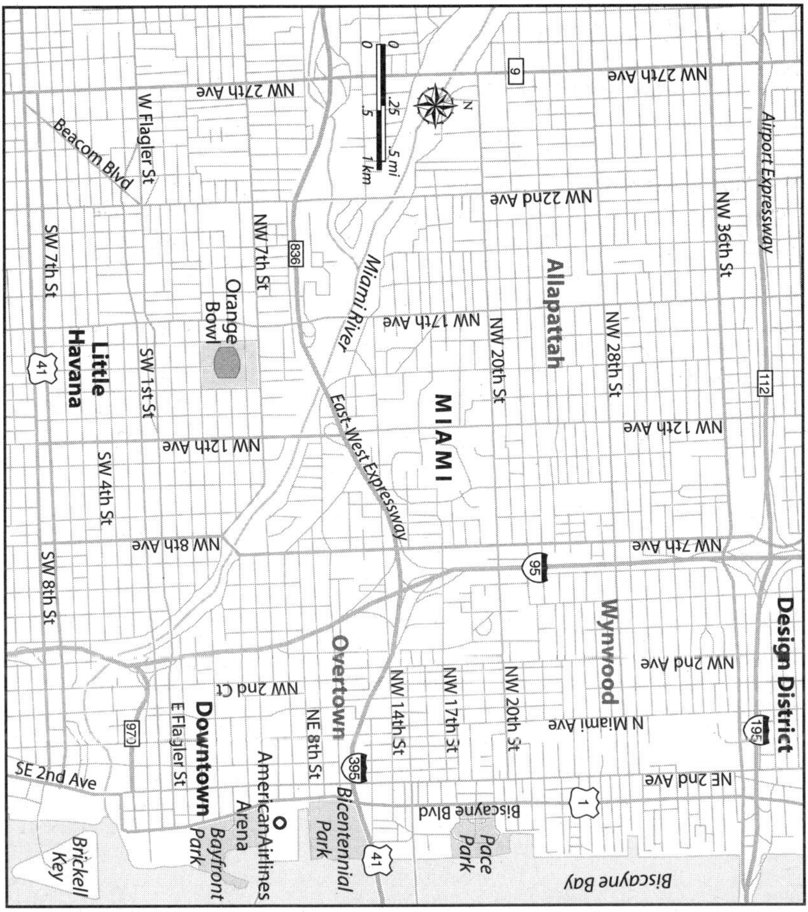

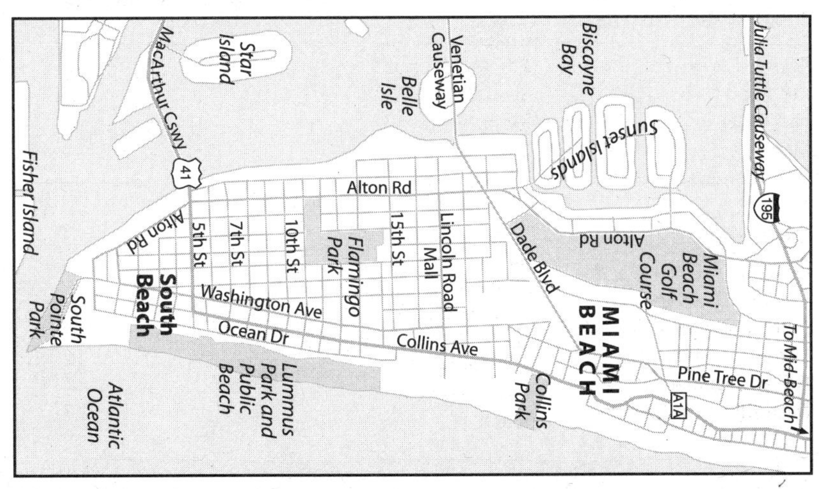
N
0
0 .25 .5 mi
0 .5 1 km
9
27
Airport Expressway
NW 27th Ave
NW 22nd Ave
NW 36th St
112
W Flagler St
Beacom Blvd
SW 7th St
NW 27th Ave
NW 7th St
836
Miami River
NW 17th Ave
NW 20th St
NW 28th St
Allapattah
NW 12th Ave
Orange Bowl
Little Havana
41
SW 1st St
SW 4th St
MIAMI
East-West Expressway
NW 12th Ave
NW 8th Ave
NW 7th Ave
95
Wynwood
NW 2nd Ave
SW 8th St
Overtown
NW 2nd Ct
Downtown
E Flagler St
97
SE 2nd Ave
Brickell Key
AmericanAirlines Arena
Bayfront Park
NE 8th St
Bicentennial Park
395
41
NW 14th St
NW 17th St
NW 20th St
N Miami Ave
Design District
195
NE 2nd Ave
1
Biscayne Blvd
Pace Park
Biscayne Bay
Fisher Island
MacArthur Cswy
41
Star Island
Alton Rd
South Pointe Park
South Beach
Alton Rd
5th St
7th St
10th St
Washington Ave
Ocean Dr
Atlantic Ocean
Lummus Park and Public Beach
Flamingo Park
15th St
Belle Isle
Venetian Causeway
Lincoln Road Mall
Collins Ave
Dade Blvd
Biscayne Bay
Sunset Islands
Alton Rd
Miami Beach Golf Course
MIAMI BEACH
Collins Park
Pine Tree Dr
A1A
Julia Tuttle Causeway
195
To Mid-Beach

What makes *The Fun Seeker's Miami* the *ultimate* guide to one of the world's hottest cities?

We put you in the right place at the right time at all the best restaurants, nightlife, attractions, and hotels with our attention to detail, insights, and easy-to-use format.

Hit the Ground Running
From how to get around to what to wear, find all the **logistical information** you need to plan a successful vacation. (p. 15)

The Perfect Miami
With detailed descriptions and insider tips, select from the **best of the best** in 33 categories—such as Best Sunday Parties, Best Art Spaces, Best Latin Night Out—to create your own fabulous vacation. (p. 35)

The Miami Experience
Choose the experience (Hot & Cool, Arty Party, Outdoors, or Clásico) that suits you best with four unique theme-based **three-day itineraries** followed by descriptions of all related venues. (p. 69)

Leaving Miami
When you need a break from the city, head out to one of these **day trips** or **overnight** destinations. (p. 185)

The Miami Calendar
For even more fun, time your vacation around a selection of the best **world-class events** and local festivals. (p. 199)

The Miami Black Book
Quickly find all important information, including phone numbers, addresses, and brief descriptions, in the most **complete and accurate list** of what is cool, hip, funky, classic, and chic. (p. 207)

MAPS

Greater Miami — View the entire city. (p. 14)

Miami Region — Pinpoint each *Leaving Miami* destination (p. 184)

Miami Area — Zoom in on key streets in frequented areas. (p. 223)

Our Philosophy: Time Is Precious. Have Fun!